A Century of Sonnets

Plate 4.　　　　　　　　　　　　　　　　　　Sonnet 4.

Arbould del.　　　　　　　　　　　　　　　　Milton sculp.

A Century of Sonnets

The Romantic-Era Revival

1750–1850

EDITED BY

Paula R. Feldman

Daniel Robinson

New York   Oxford

OXFORD UNIVERSITY PRESS

1999

Oxford University Press

Oxford   New York

Athens   Auckland   Bangkok   Bogotá   Buenos Aires
Calcutta   Cape Town   Chennai   Dar es Salaam
Delhi   Florence   Hong Kong   Istanbul   Karachi
Kuala Lumpur   Madrid   Melbourne   Mexico City
Mumbai   Nairobi   Paris   São Paulo   Singapore
Taipei   Tokyo   Toronto   Warsaw

and associated companies in
Berlin   Ibadan

Copyright © 1999 by Oxford University Press

Published by Oxford University Press, Inc.
198 Madison Avenue, New York, New York 10016

Oxford is a registered trademark of Oxford University Press

Library of Congress Cataloging-in-Publication Data
A century of sonnets: the romantic-era revival,
1750–1850/edited by Paula R. Feldman and Daniel Robinson.
p.   cm.   Includes index.
ISBN 0-19-511561-9
1. Sonnets, English.
2. English poetry—18th century.
3. English poetry—19th century.
4. Romanticism—Great Britain.
I. Feldman, Paula R.
II. Robinson, Daniel, 1969–   .
PR1195.S5C46   1998   820.9—dc21   97-51208

Frontispiece: *Queen of the Silver Bow,* 1789.
Illustration to Charlotte Smith's sonnet "To the Moon"
from *Elegiac Sonnets, and Other Poems.* Copperplate
engraving by Milton after Corbauld.

1 3 5 7 9 8 6 4 2

Printed in the United States of America
on acid-free paper

Contents

Acknowledgments

T he editors gratefully acknowledge those whose advice has helped us shape this book, who have given us encouragement and offered valuable suggestions for revision, including Dan Albergotti, Stephen C. Behrendt, Matthew Bruccoli, Maura E. Burnett, Catherine Burroughs, Frederick Burwick, Susan Chang, Stuart Curran, Glenn Dibert-Himes, Elizabeth Fay, Catherine Fenner, Marilyn Gaull, Nicholas Jones, Gary Kelly, Jack Kolb, Don Le Pan, Harriet Kramer Linkin, Charles Mahoney, Jerome J. McGann, James McKusick, Helen Mules, Joel Myerson, Robert Newman, Eric W. Nye, Brennan O'Donnell, David Owens, William Richey, Daniel Riess, Talia Rogers, Jan van Rosevelt, John Serembus, C. S. Tucker, Wendy Warren, and Susan Wolfson. We also wish to thank the staffs in the Interlibrary Loan Department and the Special Collections Department at Thomas Cooper Library, University of South Carolina; Alderman Library, University of Virginia; Wilson Library, University of North Carolina at Chapel Hill; and the British Library, London. The University of South Carolina English Department and the Widener University Humanities Division provided clerical support.

A Century of Sonnets

Introduction

The sonnet was one of the leading poetic forms of the Romantic period, and many of the best-known poems of the period are sonnets, including Percy Bysshe Shelley's "Ozymandias," John Keats's "On First Looking into Chapman's Homer," and William Wordsworth's "Composed upon Westminster Bridge." Most of the sonnets in this book appeared between 1789 and 1837, the traditional dates associated with British Romanticism. But, in order to place the Romantic-era sonnet within its broad and rich literary context, this selection spans the one hundred years from 1750 to 1850 and documents the sonnet revival from its beginning in the hands of Thomas Edwards and Charlotte Smith to its culmination in the work of Elizabeth Barrett Browning and Dante Gabriel Rossetti. This is a century of impressive and sustained achievement in one of the most challenging and enduring lyric forms in the English language.

The sonnet was a maturing form, growing into its majority as a staple of English poetry between 1750 and 1850, and the poets who practiced it then seem to have felt an obligation to make it something more than it had been. They drew on the strength of its tradition in full confidence that it would endure. The sonnet became, during this period, something uniquely suited for a new age of poetry, full of innovation, while not wholly divorcing itself from its origins in the Renaissance poetry of Italy and England. Indeed, this golden age of the sonnet is largely responsible for the qualities and eccentricities now commonly associated with the form. The sonnet was pervasive, appearing not only in individual books of poetry but also in periodicals, anthologies, annuals, gift books, and even novels. At the height of the sonnet's popularity it seemed that nearly everyone wrote them—women and men, the rich and the poor, rural and urban poets, established professional writers and those struggling to make a name for themselves. Their subject matter is diverse—disappointed love, radical politics, the natural world, friendship, art and aesthetics, historical and political figures, religion and spirituality, birth and death, and parents and children, among other topics. These sonnets range in tone from pathos to bathos, from private to public, from desperate to comic. They are sometimes descriptive and meditative, sometimes fantastic and imaginative, sometimes sentimental and poignant, and sometimes whimsical and playful. But they always seem to turn upon the intensity of feeling, the clarity of perception, and the harmony of language.

For the second time in the history of English literature, the sonnet became a poetic staple and a means for poets to assert themselves as proficient in the art of lyric poetry. The story of the Romantic-era sonnet revival begins hundreds of years earlier in the aftermath of the English Renaissance when sonnets originally proliferated. The sonnet developed in Italy in the thirteenth century. Dante practiced it in *La vita nuova;* Petrarch, however, perfected it in the fourteenth century, and the sonnet has been associated with him ever since. Petrarch's sonnets established a mode for both style and substance in the English-language sonnet, echoes of which are audible in the sonnets of today. Petrarch's *Canzoniere,* or "Songbook," which consists of many different kinds of lyric poems—chief among them sonnets—is the primary text that established the sonnet tradition. The standard Petrarchan subject is erotic love, highly intellectualized and symbolized, of a male lover for an unattainable and idealized woman. Petrarch's love for Laura (in Italian also *l'aura*—the light, or the air) transcends earthly passion and contains oxymoronic speech (his love for her is "bittersweet," giving him both joy and despair); his sonnets express the hopelessness of his ever consummating his erotic desire. This conflicting passion develops psychologically and resolves itself spiritually but takes shape through figurative language, elaborate comparisons or conceits, hyperbole, the sonnet form itself, and other literary devices. Petrarch also embeds in Laura's name a pun on "laurel," the emblem of Apollo, the god of poetry, and *l'oro,* Italian for "gold."

The Petrarchan sonnet (often called the Italian sonnet), as it has been passed down to English poets, consists of two main rhetorical and formal parts: the octave, the first eight lines, and the sestet, the last six lines. The first four lines of the octave usually present a proposition; the next four lines either restate, qualify, or contrast with them. These eight lines are held together by the standard enveloping rhyme scheme of the octave—*abbaabba.* The sestet, or final six lines of the sonnet, begins with what is called the volta, a turn in thought from problem to resolution. The first three lines, or tercet, begin the resolution, and the final tercet provides the conclusion. According to tradition, the sestet has no prescribed rhyme scheme but usually follows some variation of *cdecde* or a more demanding rhyme pattern such as *cdccdc.* The rhyme scheme for a proper Italian sonnet permits no more than five rhymes. In English, the most common meter for poets to use is iambic pentameter. While the form of the Italian sonnet frequently remains intact, in practice English poets often violate the rhetorical development of the sonnet. Dante Gabriel Rossetti's well-known sonnet "Silent Noon" from his cycle *The*

House of Life, which he began writing in the late 1840s, is a fairly faithful adoption of Petrarchan form and development:

> Your hands lie open in the long fresh grass—
>   The finger-points look through like rosy blooms:
>   Your eyes smile peace. The pasture gleams and glooms
> 'Neath billowing skies that scatter and amass.
> All round our nest, far as the eye can pass,
>   Are golden kingcup-fields with silver edge
>   Where the cow-parsley skirts the hawthorn-hedge.
> 'Tis visible silence, still as the hour-glass.
>
> Deep in the sun-searched growths the dragonfly
> Hangs like a blue thread loosened from the sky:
>   So this winged hour is dropped to us from above.
> Oh! clasp we to our hearts, for deathless dower,
> This close-companioned inarticulate hour
>   When twofold silence was the song of love.

The sonnet's octave establishes the situation and mood: two lovers recline together in a peaceful natural scene in which the loved object reflects the natural peace in her gaze. The first quatrain is self-contained, end-stopped at the fourth line, but the rhyme continues into the second quatrain, where the speaker directs his view outward to find peace in the world around them. The sonnet turns upon a singular description of the dragonfly that suggests, in the first tercet of the sestet, that the peace, fragile and delicate, comes from heaven. The sonnet concludes in the final tercet that the lovers must cherish this time when their silence sang "the song of love." The theme is simple but elegantly developed through the Italian sonnet's encoded rhetorical thrust.

Many of the sonnets included in this book follow Petrarch's form, although there is much variation in terms of subject and theme. Among many others, Keats's famous "On First Looking into Chapman's Homer," Mary Robinson's *Sappho and Phaon,* and Elizabeth Barrett Browning's *Sonnets from the Portuguese* are useful examples of how Romantic-era poets adopted Petrarch's form while altering standard Petrarchan content. Significantly, the sonnet revival coincides with a renewed interest in Petrarch's poetry and a rage for translating his sonnets into English.

Thomas Wyatt introduced the sonnet form to English poets in the sixteenth century with his fairly rough translations and imitations of Petrarch's sonnets. Many English poets found the demand for rhyme too difficult to manage in English and sought a form better suited to the multiplicity of sounds in English. Henry Howard, Earl of Surrey, traditionally has been credited with the sixteenth-century invention of the English sonnet, though it is now often called the Shakespearean sonnet because of Shakespeare's own innovations. This new sonnet form altered the rhetorical pattern of the Italian sonnet, with its octave, volta, and sestet, by dividing the sonnet into three four-line segments, or quatrains, and a couplet. Many English sonnets, however, have a stronger division between the second and third quatrains to suggest a turn. Moreover, the English sonnet rhymes *abab cdcd efef gg,* permitting a greater number of rhymes than the Italian sonnet, and is better suited to the relative difficulty of rhyming in English as compared to Italian. Michael Drayton's fine sonnet "Since There's No Help" (1619) illustrates the English sonnet's formal variations on the Italian, even as it makes fun of the patient resignation of the Petrarchan erotic sonnet:

> Since there's no help, come, let us kiss and part,—
> Nay, I have done, you get no more from me;
> And I am glad, yea glad with all my heart,
> That thus so cleanly I myself can free;
> Shake hands for ever, cancel all our vows,
> And when we meet at any time again,
> Be it not seen in either of our brows
> That we one jot of former love retain.
> Now at the last gasp of Love's latest breath,
> When his pulse failing, Passion speechless lies,
> When Faith is kneeling by his bed of death,
> And Innocence is closing up his eyes,—
> > Now if thou would'st, when all have given him over,
> > From death to life thou might'st him yet recover.

The sonnet is typical of the way in which the English structure provides more freedom for the poet, particularly, in this case, as it permits Drayton to defy Petrarchan expectations with good humor and a new sense of fun.

Like any negotiation with form, sonnet writing is also a way to place the poet within a specific literary tradition. The sonnet became, during the English Renaissance, an experiment by which poets could prove their virtuosity and technical skill as well as their earnestness. Not to be outdone by the Italian poets, Edmund Spenser developed his own sonnet form for his sequence, the *Amoretti,* that matched the difficulty of the Italian sonnet by linking the quatrains through an intricate rhyme pattern (*ababbcbccdcdee*); but, because of its idiosyncratic form, the Spenserian sonnet seldom was adopted by subsequent poets. Sir Philip Sidney's *Astrophel and Stella,* the first sustained sonnet sequence in English, was inspired by the sonnet explosion of the 1590s. In it, Sidney playfully explores the problems and limitations of Petrarchan attitudes towards love, women, and sex, appropriating Petrarch's tradition and revising it for a new era of sonnet writing. Shakespeare, in addition to his own sequence of 154 sonnets, made sonnets an important part of the stage business in early plays such as *Love's Labour's Lost* and *Romeo and Juliet*—most notably the "Pilgrim" sonnet spoken by Romeo and Juliet during their first meeting. In the seventeenth century, John Donne and John Milton broadened the scope of the sonnet in terms of its subject matter by abandoning characteristic erotic themes in favor of devotional and political, though at times intensely personal, ones. Donne's *Holy Sonnets* radically revised the Petrarchan tradition by using the erotic idiom of the sonnet to express religious devotion. The introduction of the sonnet to English literature during the Renaissance provided impetus and momentum for the form. Fittingly, Milton would add the finishing touches to the Renaissance sonnet in English, but he would also, in many ways, initiate an entirely new movement within the sonnet's long tradition. The titanic shade of Milton looms over the Romantic-era sonnet: his influence substantially shaped the sonnets of those who would follow him.

The sonnet fell into disfavor and disuse shortly after Milton's practice, although it can hardly be said to have slept for a century, as some early twentieth-century commentators suggest.[1] Milton's introduction of new subject matter marked the end of the Renaissance sonnet tradition as practiced by such descendants of Petrarchanism as Wyatt, Sidney, Spenser, and Shakespeare. Unlike those of earlier sonneteers, Milton's sonnets do not develop erotic themes and are not strictly religious, as are Donne's *Holy Sonnets.* Instead, they frequently deal with political subjects, such as the sonnets "To the Lord General Cromwell" and "On the Late Massacre in Piedmont," or they are quite personal, such as the sonnet on his blindness, "When I Consider How My Light is Spent." Milton also favored the Italian sonnet over the English form developed by Shakespeare; writing five sonnets in Italian and adopting the model for the others in English, he defied the metrical and rhetorical divisions of Petrarch, following the example of Italian poet Giovanni Della Casa. Milton not only favored enjambment between lines (the running on of the sense and grammar of one line to the next), but he also generally straddled the octave and the sestet (ran them together) to avoid dividing the sense of the poem. His famous sonnet "When I Consider How My Light is Spent," published in 1673, illustrates his technical mastery of the form:

> When I consider how my light is spent
>   Ere half my days, in this dark world and wide,
>   And that one talent which is death to hide
>   Lodged with me useless, though my soul more bent
> To serve therewith my Maker, and present
>   My true account, lest he returning chide;
>   "Doth God exact day-labor, light denied?"
>   I fondly ask; but Patience to prevent
> That murmur, soon replies, "God doth not need
>   Either man's work or his own gifts; who best
>   Bear his mild yoke, they serve him best. His state
> Is kingly. Thousands at his bidding speed
>   And post o'er land and ocean without rest:
>   They also serve who only stand and wait."

This sonnet nicely illustrates Milton's enjambment, not only between lines but between quatrains and between the octave and the sestet; the turn, or volta, comes after the second foot of line 8, instead of at the beginning of line 9. These enjambments create a strong sense of "unity," a quality of Milton's sonnets that William Wordsworth later admired. In a letter to Alexander Dyce, Wordsworth praises Milton for dropping the rhetorical division of the Italian sonnet, creating what Wordsworth refers to as the "intense Unity" of "the image of an orbicular body,—a sphere—or a dew drop."[2] But while Wordsworth justifies, on one hand, the structural importance of the sonnet as a symbol for its content, on the other, he casts aspersions on the prevailing English and Italian forms that neatly divide the sonnet into movable parts. Of course, Wordsworth himself preferred the Miltonic variation on the Italian sonnet for its unity over the so-called "illegitimate" English forms, including the Shakespearean, which popular sonnet-writers such as Charlotte Smith and William Lisle Bowles used almost exclusively.

For eighteenth- and nineteenth-century readers especially, Milton rescued the sonnet from courtly sonneteers and preserved the tradition for them: as Walter Savage Landor writes in *The Last Fruit off an Old Tree* (1853),

> He caught the sonnet from the dainty hand
> Of Love, who cried to lose it; and he gave
> The notes to Glory.[3]

Though Milton wrote few sonnets—only twenty-four survive—he was the last major poet, prior to the sonnet's eighteenth-century revival, to contribute to the project begun by Surrey of adapting the original Italian form to a mode specifically English in style. He gave to the individual lines of the sonnet a stateliness much like that of his blank verse, at times adopting the authoritative prophetic voice of his epic poetry. In his subject matter, if not wholly in technical manner, Milton obliterated all vestiges of Petrarchanism from the English sonnet, paving the way for an English sonnet phenomenon free of the burden of the Italian erotic tradition. He demonstrated a potential in the sonnet for exploring private and public themes.

Despite the implications of Milton's innovations on English sonnet practice, the sonnet seemed hackneyed to early eighteenth-century readers hungry for satire, reason, and clarity rather than for the eroticism, emotion, and conceit of Renaissance sonnets. Alexander Pope satirizes the sonnet in part two of his *Essay on Criticism*: "What woful stuff this madrigal would be / In some starv'd hackney sonneteer, or me!"[4] Likewise, Samuel Johnson disparaged the sonnet in *A Dictionary of the English Language* as "not very suitable to the English language" and went on to define "sonneteer" as a term of contempt for a "small poet."[5] In response to Hannah More's wonder that the author of *Paradise Lost* could write "such poor sonnets," Johnson quipped, "Milton, Madam, was a genius that could cut a Colossus from a rock; but could not carve heads upon cherry-stones."[6] That More would think Milton's sonnets mediocre further indicates the disfavor into which the whole genre had fallen. Later in the century, critics praised George Stevens for omitting the sonnets from his 1793 edition of Shakespeare. In *Literary Hours* (1798), for example, Nathan Drake writes that Shakespeare's sonnets are "buried beneath a load of obscurity and quaintness."[7] It was not until the nineteenth century that taste would change and the English sonnet, previously considered "illegitimate," would be canonized as the Shakespearean sonnet.

Despite the pronouncements of many eighteenth-, nineteenth-, and twentieth-century literary authorities on the death of the sonnet, this literary form, in fact, lived and breathed and even spawned in the eighteenth century. "The sonnet in the eighteenth century," wrote John Fuller in 1972, "lives under the shadow of Milton if it can be said to live at all."[8] For the first few decades of that century, the sonnet may have had an underground existence but it clearly came to life in the 1740s. Although many of these sonnets, as R. D. Havens points out, were not published until the early nineteenth century, Thomas Edwards' sonnets published in 1748 mark him as "the real father of the eighteenth-century sonnet, 'the only begetter' whom his contemporaries knew as such."[9] The most notable of his sonnets prefaces his *Canons of Criticism,* addressing William Warburton as a "tongue-doughty pedant" and continuing his attack on Warburton's infamously absurd notes to Shakespeare's works. Some sonnets, however, have a more general appeal, such as "On a Family-Picture," which begins this collection and which movingly describes Edwards' cosmic abandonment at the loss of his eight brothers and sisters.

Edwards's appearance in 1748 in the first volume of the influential "Dodsley's Miscellany" connects him with Thomas Warton, whose first sonnets appeared in the fourth volume of 1755. Havens regards Warton's sonnets as "among the best the century produced" and notes that these sonnets anticipate Romanticism because they "were the first to turn for their subjects from persons to nature and to places of legendary or historic interest."[10] Warton's "To the River Lodon," for example, is a descriptive meditative poem that anticipates many later Romantic poems in its emphasis on a specific locale and the power of memory acting through poetry in the present. The sonnet is almost a prospectus for Wordsworth's "Tintern Abbey," although it is not as sophisticated in its development and not nearly as optimistic in its implicit faith in nature and memory to restore what is lost. Warton's symbolic use of the river reappears as a major device in Charlotte Smith's sonnets to the river Arun; in William Lisle Bowles's numerous river sonnets, such as those to the Itchin, the Wensbeck, the Tweed, and the Cherwell; in Samuel Taylor Coleridge's "Sonnet to the River Otter"; and in Wordsworth's sequence *The River Duddon.* Seven of Warton's nine sonnets appeared in 1777, and John A. Vance notes that the proliferation of sonnets afterwards coincides with the publication of later editions of Warton's poetry.[11] As poet laureate, Warton exerted influence on Charlotte Smith, John Bampfylde, and particularly William Lisle Bowles, who was a student of his brother, Joseph Warton.

Years before Wordsworth would publicly proclaim his debt to Milton, poets claimed legitimacy by asserting their prowess in deference to Milton's legacy. These new sonneteers, while not always strictly following Milton's style, admired the way in which he rescued the sonnet from courtly son-

neteers and showed how it could be more than what English poets yet had
made it. Reviving the sonnet in Milton's shade, sonnet writers from Edwards
to Anna Seward to Wordsworth, in order to assert their poetic skill and to jus-
tify their own practice, tended to align themselves with the last great English
sonneteer. Critic Nathan Drake, in his popular *Literary Hours* (1798), writes
of the sonnet tradition after Milton:

> After his death, a long chasm intervened in this department of poetry, but
> within the last forty years numerous cultivators of sonnet writing have sprung
> up. Among these, we may mention with peculiar distinction Charlotte Smith
> and Mr. [William Lisle] Bowles.[12]

Just after the middle of the eighteenth century, sonnets became fashion-
able and respectable again in the hands of a new class of poets, many of them
women. But why did these poets choose an essentially outmoded form?
Their choice of the sonnet had a great deal to do with the poetic and philo-
sophical climate of the day and the cult of Sensibility, with its heavy empha-
sis on feeling and mood, and with the need to find a poetic form that was
both demanding and accessible, to convey thoughts and feelings in a more
natural way than poets previously had attempted. It was also a time when
women were becoming successful professional authors and increasingly were
making substantial contributions to literature. In *Poetic Form and British Ro-
manticism,* Stuart Curran notes that the rebirth of the sonnet "coincides with
the rise of a definable woman's literary movement and with the beginnings
of Romanticism." Curran also insists that the sonnet revival of the later eigh-
teenth century is as much a "genuine artistic movement" as that of the six-
teenth century, when the sonnet in English first asserted itself as a major po-
etic form.[13]

As women were practicing and perfecting the novel, some women writers
looked for what might be considered a more legitimate literary form with a
richer heritage in order to advance their careers. They wrote sonnets delib-
erately, with aspirations of joining the ranks of the great writers who had
gone before them. Anna Seward calls this attempt at self-canonization "the
sonnet's claim." In fact, the sonnet revival of the late eighteenth century is the
first period of literary history in which women poets showed that they could
match skills with male poets in an arena earlier closed to them, for previously
women had existed in the sonnet only as love objects to be wooed or ideal-
ized by courtly male sonneteers of the Renaissance in Italy and in England.[14]
These women poets were largely responsible for the sonnet revival of the
1780s and 1790s and established a tradition that important women sonnet
writers would follow well into the nineteenth century.

In 1784, Charlotte Smith was the first eighteenth-century woman poet to
publish a volume of sonnets, *Elegiac Sonnets and Other Essays*; Anna Seward's
Original Sonnets on Various Subjects, not collected and published until 1799,
contains one hundred sonnets, some dated as early as 1773. Seward was the
first woman sonneteer with any substantial impact upon the tradition. She
not only strictly enforced the rules of the legitimate sonnet but praised the

sonnet as a test of poetic skill: in her preface to *Original Sonnets,* she maintained, "the Sonnet is an highly valuable species of Verse; the best vehicle for a single detached thought, an elevated, or a tender sentiment, and for a succinct description." Seward greatly admired Milton's sonnets and chose them as her model for sonnet writing: she praises Milton for the "manly firmness" of his sonnets, and elsewhere she commends their "hardness" and the "strength and majesty" of the sonnets that even the melancholy and contemplative tone, or what she refers to as the "energetic tenderness," of Milton's sonnets cannot and should not soften.[15] Seward's admiration for Milton's sonnets influenced the writing of her own sonnets, if not so much in subject, certainly in style and attitude.

Charlotte Smith, however, deliberately avoided the Italian form. In her preface to the first and second editions of *Elegiac Sonnets* (1784), she herself wrote that the sonnet is "no improper vehicle for a single sentiment" while hinting at the constraints of form. As her title suggests, Smith's series of sonnets combine the formal demands of the sonnet with the elegiac mode of intense grief and mortal lament. Of the ninety-two sonnets published in her posthumous tenth edition of *Elegiac Sonnets* (1811), only two faithfully follow the Petrarchan model.[16] Although many of Smith's sonnets are technically Shakespearean, the majority are irregular in construction. Long before Wordsworth, Smith favored a simpler, more natural language for her poetry, so it is appropriate that she would avoid the highly artificial demands of the Italian sonnet. She opted for a form more specifically English in style, although many of her original sonnet forms have rhyme schemes easily as complex as the Italian or Spenserian sonnets. However, because the sonnet had become known as being better suited to Italian, Smith experimented in order to find a stanza form more adaptable to the English language and more suitable to her own poetic voice. In her preface, she calls the Italian or "legitimate" sonnet "ill calculated for our language." She preferred a more natural, freer English form rather than the elaborate continental sonnet structure. Like Petrarch's, Smith's landscape is pastoral and melancholy; Smith's Muse, however, wanders the English South Downs instead of Vaucluse. And her sorrow is not *dolce amaro* (bittersweet) like Petrarch's, for she sees no glimpses of Laura, Petrarch's living sun, and thus her sonnets are far more bleak than his. The result of her experiments is a simpler, more direct English poem that suited the taste of the day. Keats was indebted to Smith's sonnets, in this regard. His later experiments with the form, for example his sonnet "If By Dull Rhymes Our English Must Be Chained," attempt to devise a new sonnet stanza distinct from the English and the Italian forms.

Smith's success inspired scores of imitators and, inevitably, detractors. Although William Lisle Bowles, a clergyman, made original contributions, many considered him Smith's literary offspring. Bowles published his first sonnets in 1789 as *Fourteen Sonnets written chiefly on Picturesque Spots during a Journey*; and, with extensive additions and revisions, the book went through nine editions by 1805. Bowles's popularity and success was second only to Smith's. In his *Biographia Literaria,* Samuel Taylor Coleridge writes that as a young man he was greatly influenced by Bowles's poetry, which he describes as "so tender and yet so manly, so natural and real, and yet so dignified and harmonious."[17] Bowles's topographical river sonnets, influenced by Thomas Warton and Smith, share with their sonnets the association between landscape and soul. Bowles's sonnet "To the River Itchin" is the most famous of his topographical poems because of Coleridge's deliberate imitation of it in "To the River Otter." In his juxtaposition of youth and nature in the mind of the mature adult, Bowles distinctly echoes both Smith's "To the South Downs," where the River Arun makes its first appearance, and Warton's "Lodon" sonnet. The anonymous first edition of Bowles's *Fourteen Sonnets* immediately struck a responsive chord with admirers of Smith's *Elegiac Sonnets,* and critics were quick to notice the influence of Smith upon the young Wiltshire parson. Reviewers approved of Bowles's simplicity of style, modelled after Smith's, although they easily recognized his derivativeness. With such promising but not wholly exemplary reviews, Bowles responded to charges of imitation in the advertisement to the second edition of 1789:

> It having been said that these Pieces were written in Imitation of the little Poems of Mrs. Smyth[sic], the Author hopes he may be excused adding, that *many* of them were written prior to Mrs. Smyth's Publication. He is conscious of their great Inferiority to those beautiful and elegant Compositions; but, such as they are, they were certainly written from his own Feelings. [See note for sonnets 47–55.]

Bowles's sonnets bear too great a resemblance to Smith's in form, tone, and subject not to make some claim upon her legitimacy as a poet. Even in disavowing imitation, Bowles seems to appreciate the imputation; but his assertion that they were written before 1784 seems almost certainly false, because Bowles made the tours that inspired them in 1788, four years after the first edition of Smith's sonnets. Together, Smith and Bowles set the tone for the Romantic sonnet and its emphasis on feeling; their influence is evident in the sonnets of subsequent poets such as Samuel Taylor Coleridge, Charles Lloyd, Susan Evance, Martha Hanson, and John Keats.

When poets such as Smith and Bowles began popularizing a new English sonnet, their emphasis on feeling within a primarily English structure incurred the inevitable conservative backlash against innovation; the early eighteenth-century distaste for Petrarchan technique, paradoxically, metamorphosed into reverence for it later in the century. Most literary critics of the day considered the English variation on the Italian model, or Shakespearean sonnet, as practiced by these sonneteers, to be "illegitimate." The critical and aesthetic bias against the English sonnet derives from the difficulty—due to a fewer number of similar word-endings—of creating the same intertwining rhyme scheme in English that exists in the Italian sonnet; so those English authors who can manage the rhymes, most authorities believed, showed a stronger verbal aptitude and a greater command of English vocabulary than those who practiced the English sonnet. Only the Petrarchan or Miltonic was legitimate, therefore, because it seemed the more difficult form. William

Beckford, for instance, parodies Smith's brand of sonnet and its perceived ease of composition in his "Elegiac Sonnet to a Mopstick." Though plenty of mediocre sonnets appeared during this period (often in tribute to other poets such as Smith or Bowles), the popular craze for the "elegiac" sonnet indicates that, for the first time in literary history, the sonnet became accessible to masses of readers of all classes, all ages, and both sexes.

Although this conservative backlash was partly a reaction to the "feminine" sensibility of these sonnets, two important eighteenth-century women poets, Anna Seward and Mary Robinson, rejected the popular manifestations of the sonnet in favor of the legitimate Petrarchan or Miltonic forms. In her letters, Seward castigates Smith for her deviations from prescribed form. In 1796, Mary Robinson published one of the few sonnet sequences of the eighteenth century, *Sappho and Phaon: In a Series of Legitimate Sonnets*. A highly original and innovative poet, Robinson set out to prove her poetic skill in 44 sonnets strictly adhering to Petrarchan form. She writes in her preface,

> With this idea, I have ventured to compose the following collection; not presuming to offer them as imitations of *Petrarch,* but as specimens of that species of sonnet writing, so seldom attempted in the English language; though adopted by that sublime Bard, whose Muse produced the grand epic of *Paradise Lost . . .*[18]

Seward, Robinson, and, later, Elizabeth Barrett Browning would insist upon the established conventions of sonnet writing, as if following the sonnet's strict rules would more strongly assert their own legitimacy as poets. Robinson claims that she has written "legitimate" sonnets and thus belongs to the Petrarchan tradition; her preface further asserts her authority through associating herself with Sappho, the preeminent woman poet. Browning's *Sonnets from the Portuguese* also follow the Italian form. Both sequences subvert the erotic tradition of the Petrarchan form by presenting a woman poet as the passionate lover, while the man appears as the beloved, the passive and silent object of desire. In this way, both Robinson and Barrett Browning follow, probably unconsciously, the example of seventeenth-century poet Lady Mary Wroth and anticipate the frank eroticism of Edna St. Vincent Millay or Elinor Wylie in their sonnets of the 1920s and 1930s. These two early sequences are strikingly different in tone, but the less familiar *Sappho and Phaon* is the most immediate—and the most relevant—precursor to the *Sonnets from the Portuguese.*

Robinson and Barrett Browning both assimilate the Renaissance tradition, but they do so quite self-consciously as *women* poets. In both sequences the woman is the lover—in Robinson's case, as an intensely passionate sexual being—rather than as an unattainable and passive ideal. The *Sonnets from the Portuguese,* recording the stages of Elizabeth Barrett's love for Robert Browning but disguised as a translation, are more tender than the sonnets in *Sappho and Phaon* but are no less revolutionary, particularly because they established a standard for subsequent sonnets of the nineteenth century. Other women poets such as Mary Bryan and Elizabeth Cobbold directly address erotic themes in their sonnets. The history of the sonnet revival reveals many excellent sonnets by other women poets such as Helen Maria Williams, Ann Radcliffe, Mary F. Johnson, Felicia Hemans, and Frances Ann Kemble, to name only a few. These poets gave the sonnet many of the qualities we associate with it today, and some, particularly Mary Tighe, achieve a nearly unsurpassed excellence in the form.

The sonnet is a much more pervasive Romantic form than many would suspect: all of the canonized poets, with the exception of Blake, wrote and published sonnets. But it was Wordsworth, beginning in 1787 with his sonnet to Helen Maria Williams, who had the most curious relationship with the sonnet—obsessive, prodigious, at times masterful, but at other times apologetic. In the preface to the second edition of *Lyrical Ballads* (1800), the poem Wordsworth singles out as representative of the stilted and elaborate poetic diction of his predecessors is not a poem by Alexander Pope, who would seem to be the most obvious target, but Thomas Gray's only sonnet, "On the Death of Mr. Richard West." Wordsworth objects to the way in which this sonnet obscures its honest emotion through poetic artifice, although he admits that there are at least a few lines that express "natural and human" emotion. He selects only five of the fourteen lines as being valuable for approximating the language of prose. His attention to these particular lines is significant because, in addition to their naturalness, they, more than the other, more artificial lines, establish this sonnet within the tradition of Sensibility; for example, the sonnet turns upon Gray's lament, "My lonely anguish melts no heart but mine; / And in my breast the imperfect joys expire."

Written during the early 1740s but published posthumously in 1775, Gray's sonnet, despite its imperfections, anticipates the cult of Sensibility that would manifest itself in the sonnets of Charlotte Smith and William Lisle Bowles, the two most popular practitioners of the sonnet, in the 1780s and 1790s. Smith's innovations included gradually moving away from artificial poetic diction adopted by Gray; and by borrowing from the popular ballad tradition and elsewhere, she gave the sonnet a new voice to express human feeling. In the 1800 preface to *Lyrical Ballads,* Wordsworth writes that "poetry sheds no tears 'such as the Angels weep,' but natural and human tears; she can boast of no celestial ichor that distinguishes her vital juices from those of prose; the same human blood circulates through the veins of both." The aesthetic of Sensibility, emotional and natural, resounds throughout Wordsworth's preface, and he disparages the degree to which Gray's sonnet fails to capture honest emotion in natural language, as Smith and others had already done. But Wordsworth neglects to mention his debt to his more immediate predecessors such as Smith, opting instead to attack a writer such as Gray who anticipates Wordsworth's aesthetic in a few lines of natural diction but nonetheless fails to achieve it overall.

Wordsworth's obsession with the sonnet may seem incongruous with his role as the promoter of a more natural kind of poetry. But Wordsworth holds nothing against the artificiality of poetic form: he does not attack Gray's sonnet, for example, because it is a sonnet. He seeks instead a purification of poetic language, while maintaining traditional verse forms. Early in his career, Samuel Taylor Coleridge also wrote sonnets, although without the same compulsive fascination as Wordsworth. His sequence *Sonnets on Eminent Characters,* published in the *Morning Chronicle* in 1794–95, marked an important return in the sonnet to a Miltonic sense of public responsibility. Coleridge also collected sonnets from various poets for a pamphlet in 1796 and published the following year, under the pseudonym Nehemiah Higgenbottom, the parody "Sonnets, Attempted in the Manner of 'Contemporary Writers.'" Coleridge quickly pointed out the form's inappropriateness to capture what Wordsworth called "the real language of men in a state of vivid sensation." "Now," Coleridge wrote in his introduction to his pamphlet *Sonnets from Various Authors* (1796), "if there be one species of composition more difficult and artificial than another, it is an English Sonnet on the Italian Model." Coleridge points out the contradictory nature of being both the academic sonneteer and the spontaneous Romantic. While even the most passionate erotic sonnet of the Elizabethans was hardly spontaneous, the sonnet, with its poetic demands and necessarily reflective qualities, does seem an appropriate vehicle for "emotion recollected in tranquility" or meditation. Coleridge admired Smith's and Bowles's sonnets for precisely this reason, for their meditative qualities: as he writes in the introduction to *Sonnets from Various Authors,* "those Sonnets appear to me the most exquisite, in which moral Sentiments, Affections, or Feelings, are deduced from, and associated with, the scenery of Nature"; and he admired the form for providing "a sweet and indissoluble union between the intellectual and the material world."[19]

Wordsworth's later pronouncements on his debt to Milton make the true influences on his sonnets somewhat confusing. Wordsworth knew Smith and her poetry. As early as 1789, when he was an undergraduate at Cambridge, Wordsworth obtained a copy of the fifth edition of Smith's *Elegiac Sonnets,* in which he made some notes, added his name to a list of late subscribers, and copied by hand early versions of two sonnets that would not appear until the sixth edition.[20] Wordsworth also recommended in a letter to his friend Alexander Dyce that he include in his *Specimens of British Poetesses* more sonnets by Smith and Anna Seward, as well as sonnets by Williams, whose works he also owned.[21] Dorothy Wordsworth documents in her journal of 24 December 1802 that her brother was again reading Smith's sonnets.[22] Significantly, 1802 marks the beginning of Wordsworth's career as a serious sonneteer, for it was during this year that he wrote some of his most famous sonnets, such as "1801," "It Is a Beauteous Evening, Calm and Free," "Nuns Fret Not at their Convent's Narrow Room," and "The World is Too Much With Us." In May of 1802, inspired in part by Dorothy Wordsworth's reading Milton's sonnets to him, he began writing in the form that would dominate his literary career for more than four and a half decades.[23] He returned to his copy of Smith's sonnets shortly after he seriously took up the form.

Wordsworth seems to have viewed sonnet writing as procrastinatory activity, diverting him from more ambitious projects such as the *Recluse.* As he wrote to Walter Savage Landor, "... I have filled up many a moment in writing Sonnets, which, if I had never fallen into the practice, might easily have been better employed."[24] Although Wordsworth frequently apologized for working in a form he once considered "egregiously absurd," he nonetheless wrote well over 500 sonnets and made the most substantial contribution to the sonnet tradition after Milton and Smith. For the hundreds of sonnets he wrote, Wordsworth never publicly acknowledged any debt to Charlotte Smith, William Lisle Bowles, and other sonnet writers of the eighteenth century. Instead, he claimed Milton as his precursor in order to distance himself from a practice that he believed had become hackneyed by the end of the century. Wordsworth's sonnets do bear a stronger resemblance to Milton's sonnets than to Smith's, particularly in their formal qualities. Moreover, his anxiety over Milton's influence, as far as most twentieth-century representations of the sonnet tradition are concerned, very nearly obliterated the importance of those more contemporary sonnets, the stylistic and thematic resonances of which had become ubiquitous by the 1780s and 1790s. Wordsworth's adoption of Miltonic sonnet practices seems in many ways to be a deliberate erasure of the sonnet of Sensibility: Wordsworth appears to be taking the baton directly from Milton because he never explicitly claimed a place for himself in the more immediate sonnet tradition.

Only in his 1820 sonnet sequence, *The River Duddon,* does Wordsworth seem to be balancing his debts between Milton and the sonnet tradition of the late eighteenth century. *The River Duddon* is one of Wordsworth's last truly fine compositions, but, curiously, it remains one of the most obscure works of his later years. In this work, Wordsworth adopts one of the most common symbols in the eighteenth century sonnet, the river, a prevalent symbol of the flow of human life in sonnets by Thomas Warton, Anna Seward, Smith, Bowles, and many others. But the river also represents the sonnet tradition, of which Wordsworth himself is a part. The sequence concludes with the assurance "Still glides the Stream, and shall forever glide"— an assertion of the permanence of the sonnet tradition.

Wordsworth freely admits that he borrowed the concept for *The River Duddon* from Coleridge's idea for a poem to be entitled "The Brook." In the postscript to the first edition of *The River Duddon,* Wordsworth discusses the constraints of the sonnet form, justifying his borrowing of Coleridge's idea on the grounds that Coleridge may feel free to go ahead with his own poem due to "the restriction which the frame of the Sonnet" has imposed upon him, "narrowing unavoidably the range of thought, and precluding, though not without its advantages, many graces to which a freer movement of verse would naturally have led." The image of the narrow room is one Wordsworth frequently associates with the sonnet, and he shows that he is comfortable within its bounds. One of the things that so appealed to him about Milton's sonnets was what he described as the "energetic and varied flow of sound crowding into narrow room" with "the combined effect of rhyme and blank verse."[25] In "Nuns Fret Not at Their Convent's Narrow Room," Wordsworth asserts that he can move about freely within the confines of the sonnet:

In sundry moods, 'twas pastime to be bound
Within the Sonnet's scanty plot of ground:
Pleased if some souls (for such there needs must be)
Who have felt the weight of too much liberty,
Should find short solace there, as I have found.

It is precisely in this narrow room where Wordsworth distinguishes him-
self from his immediate predecessors. In "Scorn not the Sonnet," published
after *The River Duddon* in 1827, Wordsworth does not defend the sonnet so
much as he includes himself among the distinguished writers whose names
he so blatantly drops, beginning with Shakespeare, Petrarch, Tasso, Camöens,
Dante, Spenser, Milton, and, implicitly, ending with himself. However, in *The
River Duddon*, Wordsworth not only broadens his canvas beyond the narrow
room to accommodate the vast expanse of the Duddon but he also quietly
notes the tributary influence of his immediate predecessors as he follows the
river—and the tradition of the sonnet—from its source to infinity.

The sonnet tradition did not end with Wordsworth, the poet who figures
most prominently in this collection, or with Elizabeth Barrett Browning, the
poet who concludes it. The first half of the nineteenth century saw sonnets
by such accomplished poets as Mary Tighe, John Keats, Percy Bysshe Shelley,
Felicia Hemans, and Charles Tennyson Turner. Keats's sonnets, in particular,
demonstrate the lyrical power that a poet could compress within a small
space. Keats comes into his own as a poet with the sonnet, and it is significant
that a poem such as "On First Looking into Chapman's Homer" celebrates
discovery and expansion. Even Alfred Tennyson wrote sonnets early in his ca-
reer, although he would go on to other forms later. Dante Gabriel Rossetti's
short sequence *Sonnets for Pictures,* published in the Pre-Raphaelite magazine
The Germ, marks an important stage of evolution for the sonnet in its
ekphrastic delight in visual representation and the stasis in which the sonnets
hold their subjects, like pictures themselves. Browning's *Sonnets from the Por-
tuguese* provides a fitting close to this book not only because the sequence
carries the erotic elements of the sonnet to a higher spiritual plane but also
because, after Shakespeare's, it is the most popular and enduring sonnet se-
quence in English.

In the latter half of the nineteenth century, the sonnet would continue to
develop with the publication of such important sonnet sequences as George
Meredith's *Modern Love* (1862), Dante Gabriel Rossetti's *House of Life* (1870,
1881), and Christina Rossetti's *Monna Innominata* (1881), all of which radi-
cally revise the erotic tradition associated with the form. The sonnets of Ger-
ard Manley Hopkins, E. A. Robinson, and Thomas Hardy carry the tradition
into the twentieth century with new philosophical concerns, with new
touches of despair and cosmic irony, and with new metrical innovations. As
Jennifer Ann Wagner notes in *A Moment's Monument: Revisionary Poetics and
the Nineteenth-Century English Sonnet* (1995), elements of the Wordsworthian
sonnet tradition persist in the sonnets of Robert Frost. In the 1920s, poets
such as Edna St. Vincent Millay and Elinor Wylie reassert the role of women

in the sonnet tradition. Millay's sonnets, in particular the sequences *Sonnets from an Ungrafted Tree* and *Fatal Interview,* pick up where Barrett Browning leaves off, further revising the woman lover's stance in the amorous and erotic negotiation. Despite not being particularly well suited for modernist experimentation, the sonnet has persisted in the poetry of e.e. cummings, John Crowe Ransom, Allen Tate, and John Berryman, among others. The sonnet remains an important part of any good poet's training. Even a contemporary poet such as James Dickey, who is not known for sonnets, made the sonnet an integral part of the teaching of poetry composition because he believed poets should learn the received forms of the craft. This is what the poets included in this collection knew as they set out to become poets and to improve their skills by meeting the demands of the form. Reading these sonnets now helps us to understand the cultural climate that produced them and the other poetic works that form their context. In the pages that follow, we offer this century of sonnets in the hope that today's readers, like those of the past, will find much to ponder, to discuss, and to enjoy.

—DANIEL ROBINSON
AND PAULA R. FELDMAN

Notes

1. For example, R. F. Brewer's 1928 book *The Art of Versification and the Technicalities of Poetry* asserts that "After Milton's time the sonnet was scarcely cultivated at all by our poets for upwards of a hundred years, till . . . Wordsworth revived its flickering flame, and caused it to break forth again with a new beauty and sweetness peculiarly his own" ([Edinburgh: John Grant, 1928], p. 211).

2. *The Letters of William and Dorothy Wordsworth: The Later Years,* ed. Ernest de Selincourt. Vol. 2 (Oxford: Clarendon, 1939), p. 653.

3. Walter Savage Landor. *The Last Fruit off an Old Tree* (London: Edward Moxon, 1853), p. 473.

4. Alexander Pope. *Poetical Works,* ed. Herbert Davis (Oxford: Oxford University Press, 1978), p. 76, lines 418–9.

5. Samuel Johnson. *A Dictionary of the English Language* (London: W. Strahan, 1755).

6. James Boswell. *Life of Johnson,* ed. George Birkbeck Hill, Vol. 4 (Oxford: Clarendon, 1971), p. 305.

7. Nathan Drake. *Literary Hours: Or Sketches Critical, Narrative, and Poetical,* Vol. 1., 3rd. ed. (London: T. Cadell, 1804), p. 108.

8. John Fuller. *The Sonnet* (London: Methuen, 1972), p. 9.

9. R. D. Havens. *The Influence of Milton on English Poetry,* 1922 (New York: Russell & Russell, 1961), p. 492. Havens's book still contains the most authoritative and comprehensive study of the eighteenth-century sonnet published to date.

10. Havens, pp. 495–7.

11. John A. Vance. *Joseph and Thomas Warton* (Boston: Twayne, 1983), p. 50.

12. Drake, p. 113.

13. Stuart Curran. *Poetic Form and British Romanticism* (New York: Oxford University Press, 1986), pp. 30–1.

14. For a more detailed discussion of the ways in which poets claimed legitimacy through writing sonnets and of the revival of the sonnet, see Daniel Robinson, "Reviv-

ing the Sonnet: Women Romantic Poets and the Sonnet Claim," *European Romantic Review* 6.1 (1995): 98–127.

15. *Letters of Anna Seward: Written Between the Years 1784 and 1807,* ed. A. Constable, 6 vols. (Edinburgh: George Ramsay & Co., 1811) Vol. 1, p. 201; Vol. 2, p. 258; Vol. 2, p. 303.

16. In Smith's complete series, these are sonnet 32, "To Melancholy," and sonnet 34, "To a Friend." See notes for poems 10–30.

17. Samuel Taylor Coleridge. *Biographia Literaria,* eds. James Engell and W. Jackson Bate (Princeton, NJ: Princeton University Press, 1983), Vol. 1, p. 17.

18. See the Appendix of this book for Robinson's complete preface.

19. Coleridge's pamphlet *Sonnets from Various Authors* was printed privately in 1796.

20. Bishop C. Hunt, Jr. "Wordsworth and Charlotte Smith." *The Wordsworth Circle* 1 (1970), p. 85, p. 101.

21. *Later Years,* Vol. 1, pp. 478–79.

22. *Journals of Dorothy Wordsworth,* ed. Ernest de Selincourt.Vol. 1 (London: Macmillan, 1952), p. 186.

23. Ibid, p. 149.

24. *Later Years,* Vol. 1, pp. 70-1.

25. *The Early Letters of William and Dorothy Wordsworth (1787–1805),* ed. Ernest de Selincourt (Oxford: Oxford University Press, 1935), p. 312.

Suggested Further Reading

T he following is a select list of secondary materials recommended for those interested in reading more about the sonnets included in this book.

Bhattacharyya, Arunodoy. *The Sonnet and the Major English Romantic Poets.* Calcutta: Firma KLM Private Limited, 1976.

Cooper, Howard. "William Lisle Bowles: A Wiltshire Parson and his Place in Literary History." *The Hatcher Review* 3 (1989): 316–22.

Curran, Stuart. *Poetic Form and British Romanticism.* New York: Oxford University Press, 1986.

Feldman, Paula R. *British Women Poets of the Romantic Era: An Anthology.* Baltimore: The Johns Hopkins University Press, 1997.

Going, William T. *Scanty Plot of Ground: Studies in the Victorian Sonnet.* Paris: Mouton, 1976.

Hall, Spencer. "Scorn Not the Sonnet." *Approaches to Teaching Wordsworth's Poetry.* Ed. Spencer Hall with Jonathan Ramsey. New York: Modern Language Association, 1986. 70–4.

Harvey, G. M. "The Design of Wordsworth's Sonnets." *Ariel: A Review of International English Literature* 6 (1975): 78–90.

Havens, Raymond Dexter. *The Influence of Milton on English Poetry,* 1922; New York: Russell & Russell, 1961.

Hunt, Bishop C., Jr. "Wordsworth and Charlotte Smith." *The Wordsworth Circle* 1 (1970): 85–103.

Johnson, Lee M. *Wordsworth and the Sonnet.* Copenhagen: Rosenkilde and Bagger, 1973.

Jost, François. "Anatomy of an Ode: Shelley and the Sonnet Tradition." *Comparative Literature* 34 (1982): 223–46.

Kennedy, Deborah. "Thorns and Roses: The Sonnets of Charlotte Smith." *Women's Writing* 2.1 (1995): 43–53.

Kerrigan, John. "Wordsworth and the Sonnet: Building, Dwelling, Thinking." *Essays in Criticism* 35 (1985): 45–75.

Mazzaro, Jerome. "Tapping God's Other Book: Wordsworth at Sonnets." *Studies in Romanticism* 33 (1994): 337–54.

McGann, Jerome J. "Mary Robinson and the Myth of Sappho." *Modern Language Quarterly* 56.1 (1995): 55–76.

Mermin, Dorothy. "The Female Poet and the Embarrassed Reader: Elizabeth Barrett Browning's *Sonnets from the Portuguese.*" *ELH* 248 (1988): 351–67.

Ponder, Melinda M. "Echoing Poetry with History: Wordsworth's Duddon Sonnets and Their Notes." *Genre* 21 (1988): 157–78.

Robinson, Daniel. "Reviving the Sonnet: Women Romantic Poets and the Sonnet Claim." *European Romantic Review* 6 (1995): 98–127.

Stanton, Judith Phillips. "Charlotte Smith's 'Literary Business': Income, Patronage, and Indigence." *The Age of Johnson: A Scholarly Annual I.* Ed. Paul J. Korshin. New York: AMS Press, 1987. 375–401.

Wagner, Jennifer Ann. *A Moment's Monument: Revisionary Poetics and the Nineteenth-Century English Sonnet.* Madison, WI, and Teaneck, NJ: Fairleigh Dickinson University Press; London: Associated University Presses, 1996.

Wolfson, Susan J. *Formal Charges: The Shaping of Poetry in British Romanticism.* Stanford, CA: Stanford University Press, 1997.

Zillman, Lawrence John. *John Keats and the Sonnet Tradition: A Critical and Comparative Study.* Los Angeles: Lymanhouse, 1939.

Editorial Principles

We have selected a variety of sonnets that, we hope, provide for the scholarly reader a sense of the form's development during this period and that appeal to the general reader. Our guiding principle for reprinting the texts is (1) to represent the ways in which these sonnets were read from 1750 to 1850 and (2) to make the sonnets as accessible as possible for the greatest number of readers. Therefore, our copy texts are always drawn from sources published within this time frame. For the most part, we have preferred the earliest published versions of the sonnets or, in some cases, the earliest accessible version, unless there is a compelling reason to use a different version, such as in cases of significant authorial revision. When we have used later editions, we have provided the date of first publication, if known. Except in cases where the poet died prior to publication, we have attempted to use versions of sonnets that the poet would have seen and approved. The notes at the back of the book indicate the source for the text of each sonnet.

The sonnets are organized by author and are arranged chronologically according to the date of their earliest significant publication of sonnets. Thus, we represent the authors in the order in which they made contributions to the sonnet tradition, while maintaining the cohesion of the poets' work. This method avoids the confusion that would result from representing the poets by their dates of birth: for example, Anna Seward and William Wordsworth were born before Charlotte Smith and Samuel Taylor Coleridge; however, Smith and Coleridge made more substantial contributions to the sonnet tradition before Seward and Wordsworth did. The order of the poets within this book, then, reflects the chronology of significant contributions to the sonnet tradition.

To avoid repetition, we usually have eliminated the word "Sonnet" at the beginning of any title in which it may appear. Spelling and capitalization are

modernized as are elisions such as "deriv'd," except when the elision is nec-
essay to preserve the meter of a sonnet—for example in the case of elisions
such as "o'er" or "whisp'ring." We have eliminated small capitals for proper
nouns and for the first words of each sonnet but in most other cases we have
changed small capitals to italics when the text calls for special emphasis. We
have retained all original italics but have eliminated capital letters except for
proper names and poetic personifications. Such accidental features of the
sonnets do not affect greatly the reader's appreciation of the poems and were
often the decision of printers. We have preserved, however, the original punc-
tuation (Elizabeth Barrett Browning's idiosyncratic ellipses, for example), ex-
cept in the few cases where it creates substantial obstacles for reading and
comprehension. Explanatory notes appear with textual sources at the back
of the book.

—DANIEL ROBINSON
AND PAULA R. FELDMAN

Thomas Edwards

(1699–1757)

Thomas Edwards's more-than-fifty sonnets were instrumental in reviving the sonnet form. After retiring from the legal profession he pursued a literary career. A serious classical scholar and friend of novelist Samuel Richardson (1689–1761), Edwards was best known for his public attack on William Warburton's (1698–1779) 1747 edition of Shakespeare's plays, calling it sloppy and pedantic. Warburton responded by attacking Edwards in the notes to his edition of Pope's *Dunciad*. In 1750, Edwards retorted with the sonnet beginning "Tongue-doughty pedant" and a mock dedication to his enlarged edition of *The Canons of Criticism*.

1. On a Family-Picture

When pensive on that portraiture I gaze,
  Where my four brothers round about me stand,
  And four fair sisters smile with graces bland,
The goodly monument of happier days;

And think how soon insatiate Death, who preys
  On all, has cropped the rest with ruthless hand;
  While only I survive of all that band,
Which one chaste bed did to my father raise;

It seems that like a column left alone,
  The tottering remnant of some splendid fane,
   'Scaped from the fury of the barbarous Gaul,
And wasting Time, which has the rest o'erthrown;
  Amidst our house's ruins I remain
   Single, unpropped, and nodding to my fall.

(1748)

2. 'Tongue-doughty pedant'

Tongue-doughty pedant; whose ambitious mind
  Prompts thee beyond thy native pitch to soar;
  And, imped with borrowed plumes of index-lore,
Range through the vast of science unconfined!

Not for thy wing was such a flight designed:
  Know thy own strength, and wise attempt no more;
  But lowly skim round error's winding shore,
In quest of paradox from sense refined.

Much hast thou written—more than will be read;
  Then cease from Shakespeare thy unhallowed rage;

Nor by a fond o'er-weening pride misled,
Hope fame by injuring the sacred dead:
   Know, who would comment well his godlike page,
Critic, must have a heart as well as head.

(1750)

Thomas Gray
(1716–71)

Thomas Gray and Richard West became friends at Eton College in 1734 and wrote to each other for eight years, until West's premature death in 1742. Gray composed this tribute, "On the Death of Mr. Richard West," his only sonnet, in 1742; it was published posthumously in 1775 with a group of poems attached to a memoir of Gray by William Mason. William Wordsworth features Gray's sonnet in his critique of poetic diction in the 1800 preface to *Lyrical Ballads*. Gray worked in a variety of poetic forms, most notably the ode, but is best remembered for his *Elegy Written in a Country Churchyard* (1751).

3. On the Death of Mr. Richard West

In vain to me the smiling mornings shine,
And redd'ning Phoebus lifts his golden fire:
The birds in vain their amorous descant join;
Or cheerful fields resume their green attire:
These ears, alas! for other notes repine,
A different object do these eyes require.
My lonely anguish melts no heart but mine;
And in my breast the imperfect joys expire.
Yet morning smiles the busy race to cheer,
And new-born pleasure brings to happier men:
The fields to all their wonted tribute bear:
To warm their little loves the birds complain:
I fruitless mourn to him, that cannot hear,
And weep the more, because I weep in vain.

(1775)

Thomas Warton
(1728–90)

Thomas Warton followed in the footsteps of his father, Thomas Warton the elder (c. 1688–1745), not only as a poet but also as a professor of poetry at Oxford University. Warton established a model for eighteenth-century sonnet writing that would influence Charlotte Smith, William Lisle Bowles, and William Wordsworth. He wrote the first substantial literary history, *The History of English Poetry* (1774–81), and became poet laureate in 1785, the year in which he also produced an edition of Milton's poetry.

4. 'While summer-suns o'er the gay prospect played'

While summer-suns o'er the gay prospect played,
Through Surrey's verdant scenes, where Epsom spreads
Mid intermingling elms her flowery meads,
And Hascombe's hill, in towering groves arrayed,
Reared its romantic steep, with mind serene,
I journeyed blithe. Full pensive I returned;
For now my breast with hopeless passion burned,
Wet with hoar mists appeared the gaudy scene,
Which late in careless indolence I passed;
And autumn all around those hues had cast
Where past delight my recent grief might trace.
Sad change, that Nature a congenial gloom
Should wear, when most, my cheerless mood to chase,
I wished her green attire, and wonted bloom!

(1777)

5. To the River Lodon

Ah! what a weary race my feet have run,
Since first I trod thy banks with alders crowned,
And thought my way was all through fairy ground,
Beneath thy azure sky, and golden sun:
Where first my Muse to lisp her notes begun!
While pensive Memory traces back the round,
Which fills the varied interval between;
Much pleasure, more of sorrow, marks the scene.
Sweet native stream! those skies and suns so pure
No more return, to cheer my evening road!
Yet still one joy remains, that not obscure,
Nor useless, all my vacant days have flowed,
From youth's gay dawn to manhood's prime mature;
Nor with the Muse's laurel unbestowed.

(1777)

John Codrington Bampfylde
(1754–96)

John Codrington Bampfylde's Sixteen Sonnets (1778) were dedicated to the niece of the prominent painter Sir Joshua Reynolds. Reynolds's disapprobation of the match prompted Bampfylde, in a rage, to break Reynolds's windows, landing Bampfylde in Newgate Prison. Bampfylde spent most of the rest of his life in a private lunatic asylum. Though Bampfylde wrote little else during his life, Robert Southey considered his sonnets "some of the most original in our language."

6. 'As when, to one who long hath watched'

As when, to one who long hath watched, the morn
   Advancing, slow forewarns the approach of day,
   (What time the young and flowery-kirtled May
   Decks the green hedge and dewy grass unshorn
With cowslips pale, and many a whitening thorn;
   And now the sun comes forth with level ray,)
   Gilding the high-wood top and mountain gray;
   And as he climbs, the meadows' gins adorn:
The rivers glisten to the dancing beam,
   The awakened birds begin their amorous strain,
   And hill and vale with joy and fragrance teem;
Such is the sight of thee; thy wished return
   To eyes, like mine, that long have waked to mourn,
   That long have watched for light, and wept in vain.

(1778)

7. Written at a Farm

Around my porch and lowly casement spread;
   The myrtle never-sear, and gadding vine,
   With fragrant sweet-briar love to intertwine;
   And in my garden's box-encircled bed,
The pansy pied, and musk-rose white and red,
   The pink and tulip, and honeyed woodbine,
   Fling odors round; the flaunting eglantine
   Decks my trim fence, 'neath which, by silence led,
The wren hath wisely placed her mossy cell;
   And, far from noise, in courtly land so rife,
   Nestles her young to rest, and warbles well.
Here in this safe retreat and peaceful glen
   I pass my sober moments, far from men;
   Nor wishing death too soon, nor asking life.

(1778)

8. On a Frightful Dream

This morn ere yet had rung the matin peal,
   The cursed Merlin, with his potent spell,
   Aggrieved me sore, and from his wizard cell,
   (First fixing on mine eyes a magic seal)
Millions of ghosts and shadowy shapes let steal;
   Who, swarming round my couch, with horrid yell,
   Chattered and mocked, as though from deepest Hell
   They had escaped.—I oft, with fervent zeal,
Essayed, and prayer, to mar the enchanter's power.
   In vain; for thicker still the crew came on,

And now had weighed me down, but that the day
Appeared, and Phoebus, from his eastern tower,
  With new-tricked beam, like truth immortal, shone,
And chased the visionary forms away.

(1778)

9. On Christmas

With footstep slow, in furry pall yclad,
  His brows enwreathed with holly never-sear,
  Old Christmas comes, to close the waned year;
  And ay the shepherd's heart to make right glad;
Who, when his teeming flocks are homeward had,
  To blazing hearth repairs, and nut-brown beer,
  And views, well-pleased, the ruddy prattlers dear
  Hug the gray mongrel; meanwhile maid and lad
Squabble for roasted crabs.—Thee, Sire, we hail,
  Whether thine aged limbs thou dost enshroud,
  In vest of snowy white, and hoary veil,
Or wrap'st thy visage in a sable cloud;
  Thee we proclaim with mirth and cheer, nor fail
  To greet thee well with many a carol loud.

(1778)

Charlotte Smith
(1749–1806)

During the last two decades of the eighteenth century, Charlotte Smith was England's preeminent sonneteer. The first edition of her *Elegiac Sonnets* in 1784 galvanized interest in the sonnet and became one of the most well-respected and popular books of the century. John Thelwall, Samuel Taylor Coleridge, Sir Walter Scott, and Leigh Hunt were among the contemporary writers who celebrated Smith's poetic achievements. She was also a best-selling novelist. The hardships of Smith's personal life find expression in the intense melancholy of her sonnets. She continued to expand *Elegiac Sonnets* for most of the rest of her career, producing nine editions by 1800. Her blank-verse tour de force, *Beachy Head,* appeared posthumously in 1807.

10. 'The partial Muse has from my earliest hours'

The partial Muse has from my earliest hours
  Smiled on the rugged path I'm doomed to tread,
And still with sportive hand has snatched wild flowers,
  To weave fantastic garlands for my head:
But far, far happier is the lot of those
  Who never learned her dear delusive art;

Which, while it decks the head with many a rose,
　　Reserves the thorn to fester in the heart.
For still she bids soft pity's melting eye
　　Stream o'er the ills she knows not to remove,
Points every pang, and deepens every sigh
　　Of mourning friendship, or unhappy love.
Ah! then, how dear the Muse's favors cost,
If those paint sorrow best—who feel it most!

(1784)

11. Written at the Close of Spring

The garlands fade that Spring so lately wove,
　　Each simple flower which she had nursed in dew,
Anemonies, that spangled every grove,
　　The primrose wan, and hare-bell mildly blue.
No more shall violets linger in the dell,
　　Or purple orchis variegate the plain,
Till Spring again shall call forth every bell,
　　And dress with humid hands her wreaths again.—
Ah! poor Humanity! so frail, so fair,
　　Are the fond visions of thy early day,
Till tyrant Passion, and corrosive Care,
　　Bid all thy fairy colors fade away!
Another May new buds and flowers shall bring;
Ah! why has happiness——no second Spring?

(1784)

12. To a Nightingale

Poor melancholy bird—that all night long
　　Tell'st to the moon thy tale of tender woe;
　　From what sad cause can such sweet sorrow flow,
And whence this mournful melody of song?

Thy poet's musing fancy would translate
　　What mean the sounds that swell thy little breast,
　　When still at dewy eve thou leavest thy nest,
Thus to the listening night to sing thy fate?

Pale sorrow's victims wert thou once among,
　　Though now released in woodlands wild to rove?
　　Say—hast thou felt from friends some cruel wrong,
Or died'st thou—martyr of disastrous love?
Ah! songstress sad! that such my lot might be,
To sigh, and sing at liberty—like thee!

(1784)

13. To the Moon

Queen of the silver bow!—by thy pale beam,
  Alone and pensive, I delight to stray,
And watch thy shadow trembling in the stream,
  Or mark the floating clouds that cross thy way.
And while I gaze, thy mild and placid light
  Sheds a soft calm upon my troubled breast;
And oft I think—fair planet of the night,
  That in thy orb the wretched may have rest:
The sufferers of the earth perhaps may go,
  Released by death—to thy benignant sphere;
And the sad children of Despair and Woe
  Forget, in thee, their cup of sorrow here.
Oh! that I soon may reach thy world serene,
Poor wearied pilgrim—in this toiling scene!

(1784)

14. To the South Downs

Ah! hills beloved!—where once a happy child,
  Your beechen shades, "your turf, your flowers among,"
I wove your blue-bells into garlands wild,
  And woke your echoes with my artless song.
Ah! hills beloved!—your turf, your flowers remain;
  But can they peace to this sad breast restore;
For one poor moment soothe the sense of pain,
  And teach a breaking heart to throb no more?
And you, Aruna!—in the vale below,
  As to the sea your limpid waves you bear,
Can you one kind Lethean cup bestow,
  To drink a long oblivion to my care?
Ah, no!—when all, e'en Hope's last ray is gone,
There's no oblivion—but in death alone!

(1784)

15. To Sleep

Come, balmy Sleep! tired Nature's soft resort!
  On these sad temples all thy poppies shed;
And bid gay dreams, from Morpheus' airy court,
  Float in light vision round my aching head!
Secure of all thy blessings, partial power!
  On his hard bed the peasant throws him down;
And the poor sea-boy, in the rudest hour,
  Enjoys thee more than he who wears a crown.
Clasped in her faithful shepherd's guardian arms,
  Well may the village-girl sweet slumbers prove;

And they, O gentle Sleep! still taste thy charms,
  Who wake to labor, liberty, and love.
But still thy opiate aid dost thou deny
To calm the anxious breast; to close the streaming eye.

(1784)

16. *Supposed to be Written by Werter*

Go, cruel tyrant of the human breast!
  To other hearts thy burning arrows bear;
Go where fond Hope, and fair Illusion rest;
  Ah! why should Love inhabit with Despair!
Like the poor maniac I linger here,
  Still haunt the scene where all my treasure lies;
Still seek for flowers where only thorns appear,
  "And drink delicious poison from her eyes!"
Towards the deep gulf that opens on my sight
  I hurry forward, Passion's helpless slave!
And scorning Reason's mild and sober light,
  Pursue the path that leads me to the grave!
So round the flame the giddy insect flies,
And courts the fatal fire by which it dies.

(1784)

17. *By the Same. To Solitude*

O Solitude! to thy sequestered vale
  I come to hide my sorrow and my tears,
And to thy echoes tell the mournful tale
  Which scarce I trust to pitying Friendship's ears!
Amidst thy wild-woods, and untrodden glades,
  No sounds but those of melancholy move;
And the low winds that die among thy shades,
  Seem like soft Pity's sighs for hopeless love!
And sure some story of despair and pain,
  In yon deep copse thy murmuring doves relate;
And, hark, methinks in that long plaintive strain,
  Thine own sweet songstress weeps my wayward fate!
Ah, Nymph! that fate assist me to endure,
And bear awhile—what Death alone can cure!

(1784)

18. *By the Same*

Make there my tomb, beneath the lime-tree's shade,
  Where grass and flowers in wild luxuriance wave;
Let no memorial mark where I am laid,
  Or point to common eyes the lover's grave!

But oft at twilight morn, or closing day,
   The faithful friend with faltering step shall glide,
Tributes of fond regret by stealth to pay,
   And sigh o'er the unhappy suicide!
And sometimes, when the sun with parting rays
   Gilds the long grass that hides my silent bed,
The tears shall tremble in my Charlotte's eyes;
   Dear, precious drops!—they shall embalm the dead!
Yes—Charlotte o'er the mournful spot shall weep,
Where her poor Werter—and his sorrows sleep!

                      (1784)

19. From Petrarch

Loose to the wind her golden tresses streamed,
   Forming bright waves with amorous Zephyr's sighs;
   And though averted now, her charming eyes
Then with warm love, and melting pity beamed.
Was I deceived?—Ah! surely, nymph divine!
   That fine suffusion on thy cheek was love;
   What wonder then those beauteous tints should move,
Should fire this heart, this tender heart of mine!
Thy soft melodious voice, thy air, thy shape,
   Were of a goddess—not a mortal maid;
   Yet though thy charms, thy heavenly charms should fade,
My heart, my tender heart could not escape;
   Nor cure for me in time or change be found:
   The shaft extracted does not cure the wound!

                      (1784)

20. 'Blest is yon shepherd, on the turf reclined'

Blest is yon shepherd, on the turf reclined,
   Who on the varied clouds which float above
Lies idly gazing—while his vacant mind
   Pours out some tale antique of rural love!
   Ah! *he* has never felt the pangs that move
The indignant spirit, when with selfish pride,
   Friends, on whose faith the trusting heart relied,
   Unkindly shun the imploring eye of woe!
The ills they ought to soothe, with taunts deride,
   And laugh at tears themselves have forced to flow.
Nor *his* rude bosom those fine feelings melt,
   Children of Sentiment and Knowledge born,
Through whom each shaft with cruel force is felt,
   Empoisoned by deceit—or barbed with scorn.

                      (1784)

21. Written on the Sea Shore.—October, 1784

On some rude fragment of the rocky shore,
　　Where on the fractured cliff the billows break,
　　Musing, my solitary seat I take,
And listen to the deep and solemn roar.

O'er the dark waves the winds tempestuous howl;
　　The screaming sea-bird quits the troubled sea:
　　But the wild gloomy scene has charms for me,
And suits the mournful temper of my soul.

Already shipwrecked by the storms of fate,
　　Like the poor mariner, methinks, I stand,
　　Cast on a rock; who sees the distant land
From whence no succor comes—or comes too late.
Faint and more faint are heard his feeble cries,
'Till in the rising tide the exhausted sufferer dies.

(1786)

22. To the River Arun

On thy wild banks, by frequent torrents worn,
　　No glittering fanes, or marble domes appear,
Yet shall the mournful Muse thy course adorn,
　　And still to her thy rustic waves be dear.
For with the infant Otway, lingering here,
　　Of early woes she bade her votary dream,
While thy low murmurs soothed his pensive ear,
　　And still the poet—consecrates the stream.
Beneath the oak and birch that fringe thy side,
　　The first-born violets of the year shall spring;
And in thy hazels, bending o'er the tide,
　　The earliest nightingale delight to sing:
While kindred spirits, pitying, shall relate
Thy Otway's sorrows, and lament his fate!

(1786)

23. To Melancholy. Written on the Banks of the Arun, October 1785

When latest Autumn spreads her evening veil,
　　And the gray mists from these dim waves arise,
　　I love to listen to the hollow sighs,
Through the half-leafless wood that breathes the gale:
For at such hours the shadowy phantom pale,
　　Oft seems to fleet before the poet's eyes;
　　Strange sounds are heard, and mournful melodies,
As of night-wanderers, who their woes bewail!

Here, by his native stream, at such an hour,
  Pity's own Otway I methinks could meet,
    And hear his deep sighs swell the saddened wind!
O Melancholy!—such thy magic power,
  That to the soul these dreams are often sweet,
  And soothe the pensive visionary mind!

(1786)

24. To the Naiad of the Arun

Go, rural Naiad! wind thy stream along
  Through woods and wilds: then seek the ocean caves
Where sea-nymphs meet their coral rocks among,
  To boast the various honors of their waves!
'Tis but a little, o'er thy shallow tide,
  That toiling trade her burdened vessel leads;
But laurels grow luxuriant on thy side,
  And letters live along thy classic meads.
Lo! where 'mid British bards thy natives shine!
  And now another poet helps to raise
Thy glory high—the poet of the Mine!
  Whose brilliant talents are his smallest praise:
And who, to all that genius can impart,
Adds the cool head, and the unblemished heart!

(1786)

25. 'Should the lone wanderer, fainting on his way'

Should the lone wanderer, fainting on his way,
  Rest for a moment of the sultry hours,
And though his path through thorns and roughness lay,
  Pluck the wild rose, woodbine's gadding flowers,
Weaving gay wreaths beneath some sheltering tree,
  The sense of sorrow he awhile may lose;
So have I sought thy flowers, fair Poesy!
  So charmed my way with Friendship and the Muse.
But darker now grows life's unhappy day,
  Dark with new clouds of evil yet to come,
Her pencil sickening Fancy throws away,
  And weary Hope reclines upon the tomb;
And points my wishes to that tranquil shore,
Where the pale specter Care pursues no more.

(1786)

26. To Night

I love thee, mournful, sober-suited Night!
  When the faint moon, yet lingering in her wane,

And veiled in clouds, with pale uncertain light
  Hangs o'er the waters of the restless main.
In deep depression sunk, the enfeebled mind
  Will to the deaf cold elements complain,
  And tell the embosomed grief, however vain,
To sullen surges and the viewless wind.
Though no repose on thy dark breast I find,
  I still enjoy thee—cheerless as thou art;
  For in thy quiet gloom the exhausted heart
Is calm, though wretched; hopeless, yet resigned.
While to the winds and waves its sorrows given,
May reach—though lost on earth—the ear of Heaven!

                           (1788)

27. Written in the Churchyard at Middleton in Sussex

Pressed by the Moon, mute arbitress of tides,
  While the loud equinox its power combines,
  The sea no more its swelling surge confines,
But o'er the shrinking land sublimely rides.
The wild blast, rising from the western cave,
  Drives the huge billows from their heaving bed;
  Tears from their grassy tombs the village dead,
And breaks the silent sabbath of the grave!
With shells and sea-weed mingled, on the shore
  Lo! their bones whiten in the frequent wave;
  But vain to them the winds and waters rave;
They hear the warring elements no more:
While I am doomed—by life's long storm oppressed,
To gaze with envy on their gloomy rest.

                           (1789)

28. The Captive Escaped in the Wilds of America. Addressed to the Hon. Mrs. O'Neill

If, by his torturing, savage foes untraced,
  The breathless captive gain some trackless glade,
Yet hears the war-whoop howl along the waste,
  And dreads the reptile-monsters of the shade;
The giant reeds that murmur round the flood,
  Seem to conceal some hideous form beneath;
And every hollow blast that shakes the wood,
  Speaks to his trembling heart of woe and death.
With horror fraught, and desolate dismay,
  On such a wanderer falls the starless night;
But if, far streaming, a propitious ray
  Leads to some amicable fort his sight,

He hails the beam benign that guides his way,
  As I, my Harriet, bless thy friendship's cheering light.

                                                        (1792)

29. To Dependence

Dependence! heavy, heavy are thy chains,
  And happier they who from the dangerous sea,
Or the dark mine, procure with ceaseless pains
  An hard-earned pittance—than who trust to thee!
More blest the hind, who from his bed of flock
  Starts—when the birds of morn their summons give,
And wakened by the lark—"the shepherd's clock,"
  Lives but to labor—laboring but to live.
More noble than the sycophant, whose art
  Must heap with tawdry flowers thy hated shrine;
I envy not the meed thou canst impart
  To crown *his* service—while, though pride combine
With fraud to crush me—my unfettered heart
  Still to the Mountain Nymph may offer mine.

                                                        (1792)

30. Written in September 1791, During a Remarkable Thunder Storm, in which the Moon Was Perfectly Clear, while the Tempest Gathered in Various Directions Near the Earth

What awful pageants crowd the evening sky!
  The low horizon gathering vapors shroud;
  Sudden, from many a deep-embattled cloud
Terrific thunders burst, and lightnings fly—
While in serenest azure, beaming high,
  Night's regent, of her calm pavilion proud,
Gilds the dark shadows that beneath her lie,
  Unvexed by all their conflicts fierce and loud.
—So, in unsullied dignity elate,
  A spirit conscious of superior worth,
In placid elevation firmly great,
  Scorns the vain cares that give contention birth;
And blessed with peace above the shocks of fate,
  Smiles at the tumult of the troubled earth.

                                                        (1792)

31. On Being Cautioned Against Walking on an Headland Overlooking the Sea, Because It Was Frequented by a Lunatic

Is there a solitary wretch who hies
  To the tall cliff, with starting pace or slow,

And, measuring, views with wild and hollow eyes
   Its distance from the waves that chide below;
Who, as the sea-born gale with frequent sighs
   Chills his cold bed upon the mountain turf,
With hoarse, half-uttered lamentation, lies
   Murmuring responses to the dashing surf?
In moody sadness, on the giddy brink,
   I see him more with envy than with fear;
He has no *nice felicities* that shrink
   From giant horrors; wildly wandering here,
He seems (uncursed with reason) not to know
The depth or the duration of his woe.

                                            (1797)

32. 'Where the wild woods and pathless forests frown'

Where the wild woods and pathless forests frown,
   The darkling pilgrim seeks his unknown way,
Till on the grass he throws him weary down,
   To wait in broken sleep the dawn of day:
Through boughs just waving in the silent air,
   With pale capricious light the summer moon
Chequers his humid couch; while Fancy there,
   That loves to wanton in the night's deep noon,
Calls from the mossy roots and fountain edge
   Fair visionary nymphs that haunt the shade,
Or Naiads rising from the whispering sedge;
   And, 'mid the beauteous group, his dear loved maid
Seems beckoning him with smiles to join the train:
Then, starting from his dream, he feels his woes again!

                                            (1797)

33. The Sea View

The upland shepherd, as reclined he lies
   On the soft turf that clothes the mountain brow,
Marks the bright sea-line mingling with the skies;
   Or from his course celestial, sinking slow,
   The summer-sun in purple radiance low,
Blaze on the western waters; the wide scene
   Magnificent, and tranquil, seems to spread
Even o'er the rustic's breast a joy serene,
   When, like dark plague-spots by the demons shed,
Charged deep with death, upon the waves, far seen,
   Move the war-freighted ships; and fierce and red,
   Flash their destructive fires—The mangled dead
And dying victims then pollute the flood.
Ah! thus man spoils Heaven's glorious works with blood!

                                            (1797)

34. Written Near a Port on a Dark Evening

Huge vapors brood above the clifted shore,
  Night on the ocean settles, dark and mute,
Save where is heard the repercussive roar
  Of drowsy billows, on the rugged foot
Of rocks remote; or still more distant tone
  Of seamen in the anchored bark that tell
The watch relieved; or one deep voice alone
  Singing the hour, and bidding "Strike the bell."
All is black shadow, but the lucid line
  Marked by the light surf on the level sand,
Or where afar the ship-lights faintly shine
  Like wandering fairy fires, that oft on land
Mislead the pilgrim—such the dubious ray
That wavering reason lends, in life's long darkling way.

                                                    (1800)

35. Written at Bignor Park in Sussex, in August, 1799

Low murmurs creep along the woody vale,
  The tremulous aspens shudder in the breeze,
Slow o'er the downs the leaden vapors sail,
  While I, beneath these old paternal trees,
Mark the dark shadows of the threatened storm,
  As gathering clouds o'erveil the morning sun;
They pass!—But oh! ye visions bright and warm
  With which even here my sanguine youth begun,
Ye are obscured for ever!—And too late
  The poor slave shakes the unworthy bonds away
  Which crushed her!—Lo! the radiant star of day
Lights up this lovely scene anew—My fate
  Nor hope nor joy illumines—Nor for me
  Return those rosy hours which here I used to see!

                                                    (1800)

Samuel Egerton Brydges
(1762–1837)

Samuel Egerton Brydges is remembered chiefly for his valuable work as an antiquarian, printer, and bibliographer. He also wrote poetry, fiction, and an idiosyncratic autobiography. Brydges was knighted in 1807 and made a baronet in 1814.

36. On Dreams

O gentle Sleep, come, wave thine opiate wing,
  And with thy dewy fingers close mine eyes!

Then shall freed Fancy from her cell arise,
     And elves, and fairies dance in airy ring
Before her sight, and melting visions bring
     Of virgin love, pure faith, and lonely sighs;
     While on the passing gale soft music dies,
     And hands unseen awake the aerial string.
Ye dreams, to me than waking bliss more dear;
     Love-breathing forms, before my view displayed;
     And fairy songs, that charm my ravished ear;
Let blackening cares my day with darkness shade,
     In smiling patience every wrong I'll bear,
     While ye relume me with your nightly aid!

                                                                      (1785)

37. 'No more by cold philosophy confined'

No more by cold philosophy confined;
     By fearful models now no more depressed;
     I give full range to my erratic mind,
     And with wild visions soothe my beating breast!
Hail, thou loved season, when the hollow wind
     Strips the torn forest of its golden vest;
     Shrieks in the echoing domes, and frights the hind,
     Who sees sad spirits through his broken rest!
But while the rain descends, and while the storm
     Bursts in loud eddies through the sobbing grove,
     Spirits before my view of heavenly form,
And scenes of wondrous beauty seem to rove!
     Sweet Inspiration's voice my Fancy hears;
     And verse immortal seems to meet my ears!

                                                                      (1807)

William Hayley
(1745–1820)

William Hayley was one of the most prolific men of letters of his day (as biographer, translator, editor, and playwright). After Thomas Warton's death, he was offered but declined the poet laureateship. Robert Southey said of him, "Everything about that man is good except his poetry." Wealth and social position allowed Hayley to serve as patron to Charlotte Smith and William Blake.

38. To Mrs. Hayley, On her Voyage to America. 1784

Thou vexed Atlantic, who hast lately seen
     Britain's vain thunder on her offspring hurled,
And the blind parent, in her frantic spleen,

Pouring weak vengeance on a filial world!
  Thou, whose rough billows in loud fury curled,
Have roared indignant under many a keel;
  And while contention all her sails unfurled,
Have groaned the weight of ill-starred war to feel;
  Now let thy placid waters gaily bear
A freight far differing from blood-thirsty steel;
  See Hayley now to cross thy flood prepare,
  A female merchant, fraught with friendly zeal!
Give her kind gales, ye spirits of the air,
Kind as her heart, and as her purpose fair!

(1785)

Mary Hays
(1760–1843)

The pioneering feminist Mary Hays was the friend of William Godwin, Mary Wollstonecraft, and Joseph Priestley. Hays's writing was unconventional and progressive. Her radical novels, *Memoirs of Emma Courtney* (1796) and *The Victim of Prejudice* (1799), revise the conventions of eighteenth-century fiction while condemning the ways in which a patriarchal culture exploits and victimizes women. Hays was also the author of *Letters and Essays, Moral and Miscellaneous* (1793) and *An Appeal to the Men of Great Britain in Behalf of Women* (1798). Her six-volume *Female Biography* (1803) is an important feminist chronicle of the achievements of women throughout history.

39. 'Ah! let not hope fallacious, airy, wild'

Ah! let not hope fallacious, airy, wild,
  Illusive rays amid the tempest blend!
No more my soul with varied feelings rend,
  Soft sensibility—refinement's child!

May apathy her wand oblivious spread
  Steeped in lethean waves, with poppies twined,
And gently bending o'er my languid head,
  To long repose beguile a wayward mind.

While keen reflection throbs in every vein,
  Thy aid oblivion, vainly I implore!
This heart shall tremble with the sense of pain,
  Till death's cold hand a lasting peace restore.

Ah! say can reason's feebler power control,
The finer movements of the feeling soul?

(1785)

Helen Maria Williams
(1761?–1827)

In the 1790s, the Paris salon of Helen Maria Williams was the meeting place of many writers and intellectuals. Her *Letters from France,* published between 1790 and 1815, were important and widely read accounts of Revolutionary and post-Revolutionary events. Some of her sonnets first appeared in her novel *Julia* (1790) and in her translation of Bernardin St. Pierre's *Paul et Virginie* (1795). William Wordsworth could recite from memory her sonnet "To Hope," and his earliest published poem was entitled "Sonnet, on Seeing Miss Helen Maria Williams Weep at a Tale of Distress" (1787).

40. To Twilight

Meek Twilight! soften the declining day,
   And bring the hour my pensive spirit loves;
When, o'er the mountain slow descends the ray
   That gives to silence the deserted groves.
Ah, let the happy court the morning still,
   When, in her blooming loveliness arrayed,
She bids fresh beauty light the vale, or hill,
   And rapture warble in the vocal shade.
Sweet is the odor of the morning's flower,
   And rich in melody her accents rise;
Yet dearer to my soul the shadowy hour,
   At which her blossoms close, her music dies—
For then, while languid nature droops her head,
She wakes the tear 'tis luxury to shed.

(1786)

41. To Hope

Oh, ever skilled to wear the form we love!
To bid the shapes of fear and grief depart,
Come, gentle Hope! with one gay smile remove
The lasting sadness of an aching heart.
Thy voice, benign enchantress! let me hear;
Say that for me some pleasures yet shall bloom!
That fancy's radiance, friendship's precious tear,
Shall soften, or shall chase, misfortune's gloom.—
But come not glowing in the dazzling ray
Which once with dear illusions charmed my eye!
Oh strew no more, sweet flatterer! on my way
The flowers I fondly thought too bright to die.
Visions less fair will soothe my pensive breast,
That asks not happiness, but longs for rest!

(1790)

42. To the Moon

The glitt'ring colors of the day are fled;
Come, melancholy orb! that dwell'st with night,
Come! and o'er earth thy wandering luster shed,
Thy deepest shadow, and thy softest light;
To me congenial is the gloomy grove,
When with faint light the sloping uplands shine;
That gloom, those pensive rays alike I love,
Whose sadness seems in sympathy with mine!
But most for this, pale orb! thy beams are dear,
For this, benignant orb! I hail thee most:
That while I pour the unavailing tear,
And mourn that hope to me in youth is lost,
Thy light can visionary thoughts impart,
And lead the Muse to soothe a suffering heart.

(1790)

43. To the Strawberry

The strawberry blooms upon its lowly bed,
Plant of my native soil!—the lime may fling
More potent fragrance on the zephyr's wing;
The milky cocoa richer juices shed;
The white guava lovelier blossoms spread—
But not like thee to fond remembrance bring
The vanished hours of life's enchanting spring,
Short calendar of joys for ever fled!—
Thou bidst the scenes of childhood rise to view,
The wild-wood path which fancy loves to trace;
Where veiled in leaves, thy fruit of rosy hue
Lurked on its pliant stem with modest grace—
But ah! when thought would later years renew,
Alas, successive sorrows crowd the space!

(1795)

44. To the Curlew

Soothed by the murmurs on the sea-beat shore,
His dun-gray plumage floating to the gale,
The Curlew blends his melancholy wail,
With those hoarse sounds the rushing waters pour—
Like thee, congenial bird! my steps explore
The bleak lone sea-beach, or the rocky dale,
And shun the orange bower, the myrtle vale,
Whose gay luxuriance suits my soul no more.
I love the ocean's broad expanse, when dressed
In limpid clearness, or when tempests blow;

When the smooth currents on its placid breast
Flow calm as my past moments used to flow;
Or, when its troubled waves refuse to rest,
And seem the symbol of my present woe.

(1795)

45. To the Torrid Zone

Pathway of light! o'er thy empurpled zone,
With lavish charms perennial summer strays;
Soft 'midst thy spicy groves the zephyr plays,
While far around the rich perfumes are thrown;
The amadavid-bird for thee alone,
Spreads his gay plumes that catch thy vivid rays;
For thee the gems with liquid luster blaze,
And nature's various wealth is all thy own.
But ah! not thine is twilight's doubtful gloom,
Those mild gradations, mingling day with night;
Here, instant darkness shrouds thy genial bloom,
Nor leaves my pensive soul that lingering light,
When musing memory would each trace resume
Of fading pleasures in successive flight.

(1795)

46. To the White Bird of the Tropic

Bird of the Tropic! thou, who lov'st to stray,
Where thy long pinions sweep the sultry line,
Or mark'st the bounds which torrid beams confine
By thy averted course, that shuns the ray
Oblique, enamored of sublimer day—
Oft' on yon cliff thy folded plumes recline,
And drop those snowy feathers Indians twine,
To crown the warrior's brow with honors gay—
O'er trackless oceans what impels thy wing?
Does no soft instinct in thy soul prevail?
No sweet affection to thy bosom cling,
And bid thee oft thy absent nest bewail?—
Yet thou again to that dear spot can'st spring—
But I my long-lost home no more shall hail!

(1795)

William Lisle Bowles
(1762–1850)

William Lisle Bowles was a clergyman whose literary pursuits kept him in the public eye for much of his life. The success of his *Fourteen Sonnets* (1789) encouraged him to expand this series of topographical sonnets. Reviewers initially compared Bowles's sonnets with Charlotte Smith's, sometimes accusing him of imitating her. Samuel Taylor Coleridge praised both Smith and Bowles for reviving the sonnet and, in his *Biographia Literaria,* remarks upon the enormous influence Bowles's sensibility and technique had on him as a young man. Censurious remarks in Bowles's 1806 edition of Alexander Pope's poetry provoked an angry attack by Lord Byron.

47. To a Friend

Bereave me not of these delightful dreams,
    Which charmed my youth; or mid her gay career
    Of hope, or when the faintly-paining tear
Sat sad on memory's cheek—though loftier themes
Await the awakened mind, to the high prize
    Of wisdom, hardly earned with toil and pain,
    Aspiring patient; yet on life's wide plain
Cast friendless, where unheard some sufferer cries
Hourly, and oft our road is lone and long,
    'Twere not a crime, should we awhile delay,
    Amid the sunny field, and happier they
Who, as they wander, woo the charm of song,
    To cheer their path—till they forget to weep,
    And the tired sense is hushed, and sinks to sleep.

                                        (1789)

48. 'Languid, and sad, and slow'

Languid, and sad, and slow from day to day,
    I journey on, yet pensive turn to view
    (Where the rich landscape gleams with softer hue)
The streams, and vales, and hills, that steal away.
So fares it with the children of the earth:
    For when life's goodly prospect opens round,
    Their spirits beat to tread that fairy ground,
Where every vale sounds to the pipe of mirth.
But them, vain hope, and easy youth beguiles,
    And soon a longing look, like me, they cast
    Back o'er the pleasing prospect of the past:
Yet fancy points where still far onward smiles
    Some sunny spot, and her fair coloring blends,
    Till cheerless on their path the night descends.

                                        (1789)

49. Written at Tinemouth, Northumberland, after a Tempestuous Voyage

As slow I climb the cliff's ascending side,
    Much musing on the track of terror past,
    When o'er the dark wave rode the howling blast,

Pleased I look back, and view the tranquil tide,
  That laves the pebbled shore; and now the beam
Of evening smiles on the gray battlement,
And yon forsaken tower that time has rent:—
  The lifted oar far off with silver gleam
Is touched, and the hushed billows seem to sleep!
  Soothed by the scene, even thus on sorrow's breast
  A kindred stillness steals, and bids her rest;
Whilst sad airs stilly sigh along the deep,
  Like melodies which mourn upon the lyre,
  Waked by the breeze, and as they mourn, expire.

                                                      (1789)

50. Written at Bamborough Castle

Ye holy towers that shade the wave-worn steep,
  Long may ye rear your aged brows sublime,
  Though, hurrying silent by, relentless Time
Assail you, and the winter whirlwind's sweep!
  For far from blazing grandeur's crowded halls,
Here charity hath fixed her chosen seat,
Oft listening tearful when the wild winds beat,
  With hollow bodings round your ancient walls;
And pity, at the dark and stormy hour
  Of midnight, when the moon is hid on high,
Keeps her lone watch upon the topmost tower,
  And turns her ear to each expiring cry;
Blest if her aid some fainting wretch might save,
And snatch him cold and speechless from the wave.

                                                      (1789)

51. To the River Wensbeck

As slowly wanders thy sequestered stream,
  Wensbeck! the mossy-scattered rocks among,
  In fancy's ear still making plaintive song
To the dark woods above, that waving seem
To bend o'er some enchanted spot, removed
  From life's vain scenes; I listen to the wind,
  And think I hear meek sorrow's plaint, reclined
O'er the forsaken tomb of one she loved!—
Fair scenes, ye lend a pleasure, long unknown,
  To him who passes weary on his way—
  The farewell tear, which now he turns to pay,
Shall thank you,—and whene'er of pleasures flown
  His heart some long-lost image would renew,
  Delightful haunts! he will remember you.

                                                      (1789)

52. To the River Tweed

O Tweed! a stranger, that with wandering feet
   O'er hill and dale has journeyed many a mile,
   (If so his weary thoughts he might beguile)
Delighted turns thy beauteous scenes to greet.
   The waving branches that romantic bend
O'er thy tall banks, a soothing charm bestow;
The murmurs of thy wandering wave below
   Seem to his ear the pity of a friend.
Delightful stream! though now along thy shore,
   When spring returns in all her wonted pride,
The shepherd's distant pipe is heard no more,
   Yet here with pensive peace could I abide,
Far from the stormy world's tumultuous roar,
   To muse upon thy banks at eventide.

                                (1789)

53. To the River Itchin, Near Winton

Itchin, when I behold thy banks again,
   Thy crumbling margin, and thy silver breast,
   On which the self-same tints still seem to rest,
Why feels my heart the shivering sense of pain?
   Is it—that many a summer's day has past
Since, in life's morn, I caroled on thy side?
Is it—that oft, since then, my heart has sighed,
   As youth, and hope's delusive gleams, flew fast?
Is it—that those, who circled on thy shore,
Companions of my youth, now meet no more?
   Whate'er the cause, upon thy banks I bend
Sorrowing, yet feel such solace at my heart,
   As at the meeting of some long-lost friend,
From whom, in happier hours, we wept to part.

                                (1789)

54. On Dover Cliffs. July 20, 1787

On these white cliffs, that calm above the flood
   Uplift their shadowing heads, and, at their feet,
   Scarce hear the surge that has for ages beat,
Sure many a lonely wanderer has stood;
   And, whilst the lifted murmur met his ear,
And o'er the distant billows the still eve
   Sailed slow, has thought of all his heart must leave
Tomorrow,—of the friends he loved most dear,—
   Of social scenes, from which he wept to part:—
But if, like me, he knew how fruitless all

The thoughts that would full fain the past recall,
Soon would he quell the risings of his heart,
   And brave the wild winds and unhearing tide,
   The world his country, and his God his guide.

(1789)

55. To the River Cherwell

Cherwell, how pleased along thy willowed edge
   Erewhile I strayed, or when the morn began
   To tinge the distant turret's gleamy fan,
Or evening glimmered o'er the sighing sedge!
And now reposed on thy lorn banks once more,
   I bid the pipe farewell, and that sad lay
   Whose music on my melancholy way
I wooed, amid thy waving willows hoar,
Seeking awhile to rest—till the bright sun
   Of joy returns, as when Heaven's beauteous bow
   Beams on the night-storm's passing wings below:—
Whate'er betide, yet something have I won
   Of solace, that may bear me on serene,
   'Till eve's last hush shall close the silent scene.

(1789)

Thomas Russell
(1762–88)

William Wordsworth admired Thomas Russell's sonnets and recommended some of them to the anthologist Alexander Dyce. Russell, however, did not live long enough to fulfill the promise of his brilliant success in Latin and other language studies at Oxford. His posthumously published *Sonnets and Miscellaneous Poems* (1789) includes among the sonnets translations of Petrarch and Camöens.

56. 'Oxford, since late I left thy peaceful shore'

Oxford, since late I left thy peaceful shore,
   Much I regret thy domes with turrets crowned,
   Thy crested walls with twining ivy bound,
   Thy gothic fanes, dim isles, and cloisters hoar,
And treasured rolls of wisdom's ancient lore;
   Nor less thy varying bells, which hourly sound
   In pensive chime, or ring in lively round,
   Or toll in the slow curfew's solemn roar;
Much too thy moonlight walks, and musings grave
   Mid silent shades of high-embowering trees,
   And much thy sister-streams, whose willows wave

In whispering cadence to the evening breeze;
    But most those friends, whose much-loved converse gave
    Thy gentle charms a tenfold power to please.

                                             (1789)

57. To Valclusa

What though, Valclusa, the fond Bard be fled,
    That wooed his Fair in thy sequestered bowers,
Long loved her living, long bemoaned her dead,
    And hung her visionary shrine with flowers!
What though no more he teach thy shades to mourn
    The hapless chances that to Love belong,
As erst, when drooping o'er her turf forlorn
    He charmed wild Echo with his plaintive song!
Yet still, enamored of the tender tale,
    Pale Passion haunts thy grove's romantic gloom,
Yet still soft music breathes in every gale,
    Still undecayed the fairy-garlands bloom,
Still heavenly incense fills each fragrant vale,
    Still Petrarch's Genius weeps o'er Laura's tomb.

                                             (1789)

58. 'Dear Babe, whose meaning by fond looks expressed'

Dear Babe, whose meaning by fond looks expressed,
    Thy only little eloquence, might move
    The sternest soul to tenderness and love,
    While thus, nor taught by age to fawn, nor dressed
In treachery's mask, not falsehood's glittering vest,
    Thou sweetly smilest, at the pleasing sight,
    Wretch as I am, unwonted to delight,
    A transient gleam of gladness cheers my breast:
Yet soon again bursts forth the unbidden tear,
    And inly bleeds my heart, while I divine
    What chilling blasts may nip thy riper year,
What blackening storms may cloud thy life's decline;
    What for myself I feel, for thee I fear:
Nay! God forbid my woes should e'er be thine!

                                             (1789)

59. To the Spider

Ingenious insect, but of ruthless mould,
    Whose savage craft, as Nature taught, designs
    A mazy web of death, the filmy lines,
    That form thy circling labyrinth, enfold

Each thoughtless fly, that wanders near thy hold,
　　Sad victim of thy guile; nor aught avail
　　His silken wings, nor coat of glossy mail,
　　Nor varying hues of azure, jet, or gold:
Yet, though thus ill the fluttering captive fares,
　　Whom heedless of the fraud thy toils trepan,
　　Thy tyrant-fang, that slays the stranger, spares
The bloody brothers of thy cruel clan;
　　While man against his fellows spreads his snares,
　　Then most delighted, when his prey is man.

(1789)

60. To the Owl

Grave Bird, that sheltered in thy lonely bower,
　　On some tall oak with ivy overspread,
　　Or in some silent barn's deserted shed,
　　Or mid the fragments of some ruined tower,
Still, as of old, at this sad solemn hour,
　　When now the toiling sons of care are fled,
　　And the freed ghost slips from his wormy bed,
　　Complainest loud of man's ungentle power,
That drives thee from the cheerful face of day
　　To tell thy sorrows to the pale-eyed night,
　　Like thee, escaping from the sunny ray,
I woo this gloom, to hide me from the sight
　　Of that fell tribe, whose persecuting sway
　　On me and thee alike is bent to light.

(1789)

Mary Locke
(fl. 1791–1816)

Orphaned at an early age and raised by her uncle, who left her a considerable fortune, Mary Locke contributed poetry to periodicals such as the *Gentleman's Magazine* beginning in 1791. In 1808, she married William Mister, about whom little is known, and, according to Roger Lonsdale, as Mary Mister, published books for children. These include *Mungo, The Little Traveller,* (1811), *Tales from the Mountains* (1811), *Little Anecdotes for Little People* (1814), and *The Adventures of a Doll* (1816).

61. 'I hate the Spring in parti-colored vest'

I hate the Spring in parti-colored vest,
　　What time she breathes upon the opening rose,
When every vale in cheerfulness is dressed,
　　And man with grateful admiration glows.

Still may he glow, and love the sprightly scene,
   Who ne'er has felt the iron hand of Care;
But what avails to me a sky serene,
   Whose mind is torn with Anguish and Despair?
Give me the Winter's desolating reign,
   The gloomy sky in which no star is found;
Howl, ye wild winds, across the desert plain;
   Ye waters roar, ye falling woods resound!
Congenial horrors, hail! I love to see
All Nature mourn, and share my misery.

                                              (1791)

Ann Radcliffe
(1764–1823)

Ann Radcliffe was the best-selling British novelist of the 1790s and the creator of a highly influential school of gothic fiction. *The Mysteries of Udolpho* (1794) was a sensation not only in Britain but on the continent. Radcliffe's experimental poetry interspersed in her fiction helped to delay and give context to the action and keep her readers in suspense. She wrote six novels altogether, all with gutsy heroines subjected to extremes of terror, apparently supernatural events given rational explanations in the end, and villains who are the forerunners of the Byronic hero.

62. To the Visions of Fancy

Dear, wild illusions of creative mind!
   Whose varying hues arise to Fancy's art,
And by her magic force are swift combined
   In forms that please, and scenes that touch the heart:
Oh! whether at her voice ye soft assume
   The pensive grace of sorrow drooping low;
Or rise sublime on terror's lofty plume,
   And shake the soul with wildly thrilling woe;
Or, sweetly bright, your gayer tints ye spread,—
   Bid scenes of pleasure steal upon my view,
Love wave his purple pinions o'er my head,
   And wake the tender thought to passion true;
O! still—ye shadowy forms! attend my lonely hours,
Still chase my real cares with your illusive powers!

                                              (1791)

63. Sun-Rise: A Sonnet

Oft let me wander, at the break of day,
   Through the cool vale o'erhung with waving woods,
Drink the rich fragrance of the budding May,

And catch the murmur of the distant floods;
Or rest on the fresh bank of limpid rill,
　Where sleeps the violet in the dewy shade,
Where opening lilies balmy sweets distill,
　And the wild musk-rose weeps along the glade:
Or climb the eastern cliff, whose airy head
　Hangs rudely o'er the blue and misty main;
Watch the fine hues of morn through ether spread,
　And paint with roseate glow the crystal plain.
Oh! who can speak the rapture of the soul
　When o'er the waves the sun first steals to sight,
And all the world of waters, as they roll,
　And Heaven's vast vault unveils in living light!
So life's young hour to man enchanting smiles,
With sparkling health, and joy, and fancy's fairy wiles!

(1791)

64. Night

O'er the dim breast of ocean's wave
　Night spreads afar her gloomy wings,
　And pensive thought, and silence brings,
Save when the distant waters lave;
　　Or when the mariner's lone voice
　Swells faintly in the passing gale,
　　Or when the screaming sea-gulls poise
　O'er the tall mast and swelling sail,
　　Bounding the gray gleam of the deep,
　Where fancied forms arouse the mind,
　　Dark sweep the shores, on whose rude steep
　Sighs the sad spirit of the wind.
Sweet is its voice upon the air
　At evening's melancholy close,
　When the smooth wave in silence flows!
Sweet, sweet the peace its stealing accents bear!
Blest be thy shades, O Night! and blest the song
Thy low winds breathe the distant shores along!

(1791)

65. 'Now the bat circles on the breeze of eve'

Now the bat circles on the breeze of eve,
That creeps, in shuddering fits, along the wave,
And trembles 'mid the woods, and through the cave
Whose lonely sighs the wanderer deceive;
For oft, when melancholy charms his mind,
He thinks the Spirit of the rock he hears,

Nor listens, but with sweetly-thrilling fears,
To the low, mystic murmurs of the wind!
Now the bat circles; and the twilight-dew
Falls silent round, and, o'er the mountain-cliff,
The gleaming wave and far-discovered skiff,
Spreads the gray veil of soft, harmonious hue.
So falls o'er grief the dew of pity's tear
Dimming her lonely visions of despair.

(1794)

66. Storied Sonnet

The weary traveler, who, all night long,
Has climbed among the Alps' tremendous steeps,
Skirting the pathless precipice, where throng
Wild forms of danger; as he onward creeps
If, chance, his anxious eye at distance sees
The mountain-shepherd's solitary home,
Peeping from forth the moon-illumined trees,
What sudden transports to his bosom come!
But, if between some hideous chasm yawn,
Where the cleft pine a doubtful bridge displays,
In dreadful silence, on the brink, forlorn
He stands, and views in the faint rays
Far, far below, the torrent's rising surge,
And listens to the wild impetuous roar;
Still eyes the depth, still shudders on the verge,
Fears to return, nor dares to venture o'er.
Desperate, at length the tottering plank he tries,
His weak steps slide, he shrieks, he sinks—he dies!

(1794)

67. To the Bat

From haunt of man, from day's obtrusive glare,
Thou shroud'st thee in the ruin's ivied tower,
Or in some shadowy glen's romantic bower,
Where wizard forms their mystic charms prepare,
Where horror lurks, and ever-boding care!
But, at the sweet and silent evening hour,
When closed in sleep is every languid flower,
Thou lov'st to sport upon the twilight air,
Mocking the eye, that would thy course pursue,
In many a wanton-round, elastic, gay,
Thou flitt'st athwart the pensive wanderer's way,
As his lone footsteps print the mountain-dew.

From Indian isles thou com'st, with summer's car,
Twilight thy love—thy guide her beaming star!

(1794)

Anna Maria Jones
(1748–1829)

Anna Maria Jones's literary career began in Calcutta, where she moved with
her husband, the philologist and author Sir William Jones, a pioneer in
comparative linguistics. While in India, she wrote poems and letters and con-
ducted botanical research, recording her discoveries in sketches and water-
colors. Illness forced her return to England shortly after publishing, in
Calcutta, a volume of poems. She edited *The Works of Sir William Jones* (1799)
and gathered materials for John Shore, Lord Teignmouth's memoir of her
husband (1804).

68. *To Echo*

I saw her in the fleeting wind,
   I heard her on the sounding shore;
The fairy nymph of shadowy kind,
   That oft derides the winter's roar:
I heard her lash from rock to rock,
With shrill repeating solemn shock;
I met her in the twilight's shade
As flitting o'er my pensive glade;
O'er yonder tepid lake she flew,
Her mantle gemmed with silver dew;
The bursting note swept through the sky
As the young valleys passed the sigh:
In accents varied as the passions change,
The nymph, wild Echo, sweeps the hallow range.

(1793)

69. *To the Moon*

Thou lovely sorceress of the witching night,
   Whose paly charms through sombre regions glide;
Lured by the softness of thy silver light,
   The Muse pathetic glows with conscious pride.

On the gemmed margin of the lustrous flood,
   Whose ripling waters glide so sweetly by;
Oft have I listening to its murmurs stood,
   Traced thy pure ray, and winged a lonely sigh!

For *Thou*, chaste *Cynthia,* o'er my gentle soul,
   Shed'st the mild beam of contemplation's sway;

Thy fascinating spell with proud control
  Sweeps the full cadence of my trembling lay:
Then gleam, bright orb, from midnight's velvet vest,
And dart thy pearly lustre o'er my pensive breast.

(1793)

Samuel Taylor Coleridge
(1772–1834)

In the years before the landmark volume *Lyrical Ballads* (1798), coauthored
with William Wordsworth, Samuel Taylor Coleridge played a crucial role in
the sonnet revival. In 1796, he published the sequence *Sonnets on Eminent
Characters* and a small pamphlet *Sonnets from Various Authors,* which is the first
edited collection of sonnets from the late eighteenth-century revival. Cole-
ridge is best known for his wildly imaginative and metrically innovative
poems such as "The Rime of the Ancient Mariner," "Christabel," and "Kubla
Khan," as well as his prose works on literary theory and theology. Coleridge
once remarked to fellow sonneteer John Thelwall, "I love Sonnets; but *upon
my honor* I do not love *my* sonnets."

70–80. *Sonnets on Eminent Characters*

70. *No. I. To the Honorable Mr. Erskine*

When British Freedom for an happier land
  Spread her broad wings, that fluttered with affright,
  Erskine! thy voice she heard, and paused her flight—
Sublime of hope, where fearless thou didst stand,

Thy censer glowing with the hallowed flame,
  An hireless Priest before her injured shrine,
  And at her altar pour'dst the stream divine
Of matchless eloquence! Therefore thy name

Her sons shall venerate, and cheer thy breast
  With heaven-breathed blessings; and, when late the doom
  Of Nature bids thee die, beyond the tomb
Thy light shall shine, as sunk beneath the west,

Though the great sun not meets our wistful gaze,
Still glows wide Heaven with his distended blaze!

(1794)

71. *No. II. Burke*

As late I lay in slumber's shadowy vale,
  With wetted cheek and in a mourner's guise,

I saw the sainted form of Freedom rise:
She spake! Not sadder moans the autumnal gale:—

"Great Son of Genius! sweet to me thy name,
    Ere in an evil hour, with altered voice,
    Thou bad'st Oppression's hireling crew rejoice,
Blasting with wizard spell my laurelled fame.

Yet never, Burke! thou drank'st corruption's bowl!
    Thee stormy pity, and the cherished lure
Of pomp, and proud precipitance of soul
    Urged on with wild'ring fires. Ah, Spirit pure!

That error's mist had left thy purged eye—
So might I clasp thee with a mother's joy!"

                                                            (1794)

72. No. III. Priestley

Though king-bred rage, with lawless uproar rude,
    Hath driven our Priestley o'er the ocean swell;
Though Superstition and her wolfish brood
    Bay his mild radiance, impotent and fell;

Calm, in his halls of brightness, he shall dwell:
    For, lo! Religion, at his strong behest,
Disdainful rouses from the Papal spell,
    And flings to earth her tinsel-glittering vest,

Her mitred state, and cumbrous pomp unholy;
    And Justice wakes, to bid the oppressor wail,
That ground the ensnared soul of patient folly;
    And from her dark retreat by wisdom won,
Meek Nature slowly lifts her matron veil,
    To smile with fondness on her gazing son!

                                                            (1794)

73. No. IV. La Fayette

As when far off the warbled strains are heard,
    That soar, on morning's wing, the vales among,
Within his cage the imprisoned matin bird
    Swells the full chorus with a generous song.—

He bathes no pinion in the dewy light;
    No father's joy, no lover's bliss he shares:
Yet still the rising radiance cheers his sight—
    His fellows' freedom soothes the captive's cares!

Thou, Fayette! who didst wake, with startling voice,
  Life's better sun from that long wintry night,
Thus in thy country's triumphs shalt rejoice—
  And mock, with raptures high, the dungeon's might;

For, lo! the morning struggles into day,
And slavery's spectres shriek, and vanish from the ray!

(1794)

74. No. V. Kosciusko

O! what a loud and fearful shriek was there,
  As though a thousand souls one death-groan poured!
  Great Kosciusko, 'neath an hireling's sword,
His country viewed.—Hark! through the listening air,

When pauses the tired Cossack's barbarous yell
  Of triumph, on the chill and midnight gale
Rises with frantic burst, or sadder swell,
  The dirge of murdered Hope: while Freedom pale

Bends in such anguish o'er her destined bier,
  As if from eldest time some spirit meek
Had gathered in a mystic urn each tear
  That ever furrowed a sad patriot's cheek;

And she had drenched the sorrows of the bowl—
E'en till she reeled, intoxicate of soul!

(1794)

75. No. VI. Pitt

Not always should the tear's ambrosial dew,
  Roll its soft anguish down thy furrowed cheek;
  Not always heaven-breathed tones of suppliance meek
Beseem thee, Mercy!—yon dark scowler view,

Who with proud words of dear-loved freedom came,
  More blasting than the mildew from the south—
  And kissed his country with Iscariot mouth
(Staining most foul a godlike father's name)!

Then fixed her on the cross of deep distress,
  And at safe distance marks the thirsty lance
  Pierce her big side! But O! if some strange trance
The eyelids of thy stern-browed sister press,

Seize thou, more terrible, the avenging brand—
And hurl her thunderbolts with fiercer hand!

(1794)

76. No. VII. To the Rev. W. L. Bowles

My heart has thanked thee, Bowles! for those soft strains,
   That, on the still air floating, tremblingly
   Waked in me fancy, love, and sympathy!
For hence, not callous to a brother's pains,

Through youth's gay prime and thornless paths I went;
   And, when the *darker* day of life began,
   And I did roam, a thought-bewildered man!
Thy kindred lays an healing solace lent,

Each lonely pang, with dreamy joys combined,
   And stole from vain regret her scorpion stings;
   While shadowy pleasure, with mysterious wings,
Brooded the wavy and tumultuous mind,

Like that great spirit, who with plastic sweep
Moved on the darkness of the formless deep!

(1794)

77. No. VIII. Mrs. Siddons

As when a child, on some long winter's night,
   Affrighted, clinging to its grandame's knees,
With eager wondering and perturbed delight
   Listens dark tales of fearful strange decrees

Muttered to wretch by necromantic spell
   Of warlock hags, that, at the witching time
   Of murky midnight, ride the air sublime,
Or mingle foul embrace with fiends of Hell—,

Cold horror drinks its blood! Anon the tear
   More gentle starts, to hear the beldame tell
Of pretty babes, that loved each other dear—
   Murdered by cruel uncle's mandate fell:

E'en such the shivering joys thy tones impart;—
E'en so thou, Siddons! meltest my sad heart!

(1794)

78. No. IX. To William Godwin, Author of Political Justice

O! formed t'illume a sunless world forlorn,
　As o'er the chill and dusky brow of night,
In Finland's wintry skies, the mimic morn
　Electric pours a stream of rosy light,

Pleased I have marked Oppression, terror-pale,
　Since, through the windings of her dark machine,
Thy steady eye has shot its glances keen—
　And bade the all-lovely "scenes at distance hail."

Nor will I not thy holy guidance bless,
　And hymn thee, Godwin! with an ardent lay;
　For that thy voice, in passion's stormy day,
When wild I roamed the bleak heath of distress,
　Bade the bright form of Justice meet my way—
And told me, that her name was Happiness.

(1795)

79. No. X. To Robert Southey, of Balliol College, Oxford, Author of the "Retrospect," and Other Poems

Southey! thy melodies steal o'er mine ear,
　Like far off joyance, or the murmuring
　Of wild bees in the sunny showers of spring—
Sounds of such mingled import, as may cheer
The lonely breast—yet rouse a mindful tear:
　Waked by the song doth hope-born fancy fling
　Rich showers of dewy fragrance from her wing,
'Till sickly passion's drooping myrtle's sear
Blossom anew! But, O! more thrilled, I prize
　Thy sadder strains, that bid in mem'ry's dream
The faded forms of past delight arise;
　Then soft, on love's pale cheek, the tearful gleam
Of pleasure smiles—as, faint, yet beauteous lies
　The imaged rainbow on a willowy stream.

(1795)

80. No. XI. To Richard Brinsley Sheridan, Esq.

Was it some Spirit, Sheridan! that breathed
　His *various* influence on thy natal hour?—
　My fancy bodies forth the guardian power

His temples with Hymettian flowrets wreathed;
And sweet his voice, as when, o'er Laura's bier,
  Sad music trembled through Vauclusa's glade;
  Sweet as, at dawn, the love-lorn serenade,
That bears soft dreams to Slumber's listening ear.

Now patriot zeal and indignation high
  Swell the full tones;—and now his eye-beams dance
Meanings of scorn, and wit's quaint revelry!
  While inly writhes, from the soul-probing glance,

The apostate by the brainless rout adored,
As erst that other fiend beneath great Michael's sword.

                                                    (1795)

81. To the Autumnal Moon

Mild splendor of the various-vested night!
Mother of wildly-working visions! hail!
I watch thy gliding, while with wat'ry light
Thy weak eye glimmers through a fleecy veil;
And when thou lovest thy pale orb to shroud
Behind the gathered blackness lost on high;
And when thou dartest from the wind-rent cloud
Thy placid lightning o'er th'awakened sky.
Ah such is Hope! as changeful and as fair!
Now dimly peering on the wistful sight;
Now hid behind the dragon-winged Despair:
But soon emerging in her radiant might
She o'er the sorrow-clouded breast of Care
Sails, like a meteor kindling in its flight.

                                                    (1796)

82. On a Discovery Made Too Late

Thou bleedest, my poor Heart! and thy distress
  Reasoning I ponder with a scornful smile
  And probe thy sore wound sternly, though the while
Swol'n be mine eye and dim with heaviness.
Why didst thou listen to Hope's whisper bland?
  Or, listening, why forget the healing tale,
  When Jealousy with feverish fancies pale
Jarred thy fine fibers with a maniac's hand?
Faint was that Hope, and rayless!—Yet 'twas fair
  And soothed with many a dream the hour of rest:
  Thou should'st have loved it most, when most oppressed,
And nursed it with an agony of care,
Even as a mother her sweet infant heir,
  That wan and sickly droops upon her breast!

83. To the River Otter

Dear native brook! wild streamlet of the west!
  How many various-fated years have past,
  What blissful and what anguished hours, since last
I skimmed the smooth thin stone along thy breast,
  Numbering its light leaps! Yet so deep impressed
  Sink the sweet scenes of childhood, that mine eyes
I never shut amid the sunny blaze,
  But straight with all their tints thy waters rise,
Thy crossing plank, thy margin's willowy maze,
  And bedded sand that veined with various dyes
Gleamed through thy bright transparence to the gaze!
  Visions of childhood! oft have ye beguiled
Lone manhood's cares, yet waking fondest sighs,
  Ah! that once more I were a careless child!

(1797)

84. To a Friend, Who Asked How I Felt, When the Nurse First Presented My Infant to Me

Charles! my slow heart was only sad, when first
I scanned that face of feeble infancy:
For dimly on my thoughtful spirit burst
All I had been, and all my babe might be!
But when I saw it on its mother's arm,
And hanging at her bosom (she the while
Bent o'er its features with a tearful smile)
Then I was thrilled and melted, and most warm
Impressed a father's kiss: and all beguiled
Of dark remembrance, and presageful fear,
I seemed to see an angel's form appear.—
'Twas even thine, beloved woman mild!
So for the mother's sake the child was dear,
And dearer was the mother for the child.

(1797)

85–87. Sonnets, Attempted in the Manner of 'Contemporary Writers'

85. I

Pensive, at eve, on the hard world I mused,
And my poor heart was sad: so at the Moon
I gazed—and sighed, and sighed!—for, ah! how soon
Eve darkens into night. Mine eye perused
With tearful vacancy, the *dampy* grass,
Which wept and glittered in the paly ray:
And I did pause me on my lonely way,

And mused me on those wretched ones, who pass
O'er the black heath of *sorrow*. But, alas!
Most of *myself* I thought: when it befell,
That the sooth *spirit* of the breezy wood
Breathed in mine ear—"All this is very well;
But much of *one* thing is for *no* thing good."
Ah! my poor heart's inexplicable swell!

(1797)

86. II. To Simplicity

O! I do love thee, meek *Simplicity!*
For of thy lays the lulling simpleness
Goes to my heart, and soothes each small distress,
Distress though small, yet haply great to me!
'Tis true, on lady Fortune's gentlest pad
I amble on; yet, though I know not why,
So sad I am!—but should a friend and I
Grow cool and *miff*, O! I am *very* sad!
And then with sonnets and with sympathy
My dreamy bosom's mystic woes I pall;
Now of my false friend plaining plaintively,
Now raving at mankind in general;
But, whether sad or fierce, 'tis simple all,
All very simple, meek *simplicity!*

(1797)

87. III. On a Ruined House in a Romantic Country

And this reft house is that the which he built,
Lamented Jack! And here his malt he piled,
Cautious in vain! These rats that squeak so wild,
Squeak, not unconscious of their father's guilt.
Did ye not see her gleaming through the glade?
Belike, 'twas she, the maiden all forlorn.
What though she milk no cow with crumpled horn,
Yet, *aye,* she haunts the dale where *erst* she strayed:
And, *aye,* beside her stalks her amorous knight!
Still on his thighs their wonted brogues are worn,
And through those brogues, still tattered and betorn,
His hindward charms gleam an unearthly white;
As when through broken clouds at night's high noon
Peeps in fair fragments forth the full-orbed harvest-moon!

(1797)

88. To W. L. Esq. While He Sung a Song to Purcell's Music

While my young cheek retains its healthful hues
And I have many friends who hold me dear;

L———! methinks, I would not often hear
Such melodies as thine, lest I should lose
All memory of the wrongs and sore distress,
  For which my miserable brethren weep!
  But should uncomforted misfortunes steep
My daily bread in tears and bitterness;
And if at Death's dread moment I should lie
  With no beloved face at my bed-side,
To fix the last glance of my closing eye,
  O God! such strains, breathed by my angel guide
Would make me pass the cup of anguish by,
Mix with the blest, nor know that I had died!

(1800)

89. Fancy in Nubibus. Or The Poet in the Clouds

O! it is pleasant, with a heart at ease,
  Just after sunset, or by moonlight skies,
To make the shifting clouds be what you please,
  Or let the easily persuaded eyes
Own each quaint likeness issuing from the mold
  Of a friend's fancy; or with head bent low
And cheek aslant, see rivers flow of gold
  'Twixt crimson banks; and then, a traveler, go
From mount to mount through Cloudland, gorgeous land!
  Or listening to the tide, with closed sight,
Be that blind bard, who on the Chian strand
  By those deep sounds possessed with inward light,
Beheld the *Iliad* and the *Odyssey*
  Rise to the swelling of the voiceful sea.

(1818)

90. Work Without Hope
Lines Composed on a Day in February

All Nature seems at work. Slugs leave their lair—
  The bees are stirring—birds are on the wing—
  And Winter slumbering in the open air,
Wears on his smiling face a dream of Spring!
And I, the while, the sole unbusy thing,
Nor honey make, nor pair, nor build, nor sing.

Yet well I ken the banks where amaranths blow,
Have traced the fount whence streams of nectar flow.
Bloom, O ye amaranths! bloom for whom ye may—
For me ye bloom not! Glide, rich streams, away!
With lips unbrightened, wreathless brow, I stroll:
And would you learn the spells that drowse my soul?

Work without Hope draws nectar in a sieve,
And Hope without an object cannot live.

(1825)

91. The Old Man's Sigh. A Sonnet

Dewdrops are the gems of morning,
But the tears of mournful eve:
Where no hope is, life's a warning
That only serves to make us grave
    In our old age,
Whose bruised wings quarrel with the bars of the still narrowing cage—
That only serves to make us grieve
With oft and tedious taking-leave,
Like a poor nigh-related guest,
Who may not rudely be dismissed;
Yet hath outstayed his welcome while,
And tells the jest without the smile.
O! might life cease! and selfless mind,
Whose total *being* is *act,* alone remain behind!

(1832)

92. Life

As late I journeyed o'er the extensive plain
   Where native Otter sports his scanty stream,
Musing in torpid woe a sister's pain,
   The glorious prospect woke me from the dream;

At every step it widened to my sight,
   Wood, meadow, verdant hill, and dreary steep,
Following in quick succession of delight,
   Till all—at once—did my eye ravished sweep!

May this (I cried) my course through life portray!
New scenes of wisdom may each step display,
   And knowledge open as my days advance!
Till what time death shall pour the undarkened ray,
   My eye shall dart through infinite expanse,
And thought suspended lie in rapture's blissful trance.

(1834)

93. Pantisocracy

No more my visionary soul shall dwell
   On joys that were; no more endure to weigh
   The shame and anguish of the evil day,
Wisely forgetful! O'er the ocean swell
Sublime of hope, I seek the cottaged dell

Where Virtue calm with careless step may stray,
And, dancing to the moonlight roundelay,
The wizard passion wears a holy spell.
Eyes that have ached with anguish! ye shall weep
Tears of doubt-mingled joy, as those who start
From precipices of distempered sleep,
On which the fierce-eyed fiends their revels keep,
And see the rising sun, and feel it dart
New rays of pleasure trembling to the heart.

(1849)

Amelia Opie
(1769–1853)

Amelia Opie (née Alderson) published at least twenty-three books, including
novels, poems, tales, and works for children. Her novel *Adeline Mowbray; or,
The Mother and Daughter* (1804) is loosely based on the lives of Mary Woll-
stonecraft and William Godwin. Her poems include lyrics, odes, and a pow-
erful *Elegy to the Memory of the Late Duke of Bedford*. She was active in the
antislavery campaign, producing works such as *The Negro Boy's Tale, A Poem,
Addressed to Children* (1824) and *The Black Man's Lament; or, How to Make
Sugar* (1826).

94. To Winter

Power of the awful wind, whose hollow blast
Hurls desolation wide, thy sway I hail!
Thou o'er the scene around can'st beauties cast,
Superior far to aught that Summer's gale
Can, in the ripening year, to bloom awake;
To view thy majesty, the cheerful tale,
The dance, the festive song, I, pleased, forsake;
And here, thy power and thy attractions own,
Now the pale regent of thy splendid night
Decks with her yellow rays thy snowy throne;
Richly her beams on Summer's mantle light,
Richly they gild chill Autumn's tawny vest
But, ah! to me they shine more chastely bright,
Spangling the icy robe that wraps thy breast.

(1795)

95. On the Approach of Autumn

Farewell! gay Summer! now the changing wind
    That Autumn brings, commands thee to retreat;
It fades the roses which thy temples bind
    And the green sandals which adorn thy feet.
Now flies with thee the walk at eventide

That favoring hour to bright-eyed Fancy dear,
   When most she loves to seek the mountain side
   And mark the pomp of twilight hast'ning near.
Ah then, what faery forms around her throng!
   On every cloud a magic charm she sees:
Sweet Evening these delights to thee belong,
   But now alas! comes Autumn's chilling breeze
And early night attendant on its sway
Bears in her envious veil, sweet fancy's hour away.

                                                    (1799)

John Thelwall
(1764–1834)

John Thelwall was a radical who sympathized with the democratic principles
of the French Revolution; in the spring of 1794, he was arrested and charged
with high treason for his revolutionary views, along with other leaders of the
London Corresponding Society. He was tried and acquitted after being im-
prisoned in the Tower. The first three of the following sonnets were written
there and appeared in *Poems Written in Close Confinement in the Tower and
Newgate under a Charge of High Treason* (1795). He was a prolific poet, essayist,
pamphleteer, and editor of *The Champion,* a political and literary newspaper.
Thelwall once wrote an essay on the contemporary sonnet that praised Char-
lotte Smith as the best sonneteer in the English language.

96. *To Tyranny*

O Hell-born Tyranny! how blest the land
   Whose watchful citizens with dauntless breast
Oppose thy *first* approach! With aspect bland
   Thou wont, alas! too oft, to lull to rest
   The sterner virtues that should guard the throne
      Of Liberty. Decked with the gaudy zone
Of Pomp, and ushered with lascivious arts
      Of glossing Luxury, thy fraudful smile
Ensnares the dazzled senses, till our hearts
Sink, palsied, in degenerate lethargy.
   Then bursts the swoln destruction forth; and while
      Down the rough tide of Power Oppression drives
      The shipwrecked multitude, no hope survives,
But from the whelming storm of Anarchy.

                                                    (1795)

97. *To Ancestry*

O, that there were, indeed, some hidden charm—
   Some magic power in ancestry!—thy shore,

O Britain! then, renowned in days of yore
For gallant spirits, ne'er should brook the arm
  Of tyrannous oppression;—then no more
  Should thy degenerate progeny adore
The arts of splendid slavery, that now
Unnerve the soul, and of her 'customed vow
  Defraud thy once-loved liberty;—the lore
Of freedom should be reverenced: nor the few,
To ancient fame, and patriot feeling true,
Who dare assert thy rights, deserted mourn—
From each endearing tie of Nature torn,
  And from the dungeon's gloom their country's fall deplore.

(1795)

98. The Vanity of National Grandeur

Ill fares the land to giddy lust of power,
  To pomp, and vain magnificence resigned,
Whose wasteful arts the hard earned fruits devour
  Wrung from the labors of the weary hind,
  And artist's curious hand. The cheated mind
May hail awhile, 'tis true, the splendid hour
  Delusive; but destruction hovers near:
The gaudy vapor fades!—dark tempests lour!
  And fell Oppression's thunder shakes with fear
The enervate soul. So the wayfaring swain,
  Loitering in trackless wilds, intent, admires
  The gaudy clouds tinged with Sol's parting fires,
Till dark'ning mists involve the spacious plain,
And rising tempests wake the prowling train.

(1795)

99. On the Rapid Extension of the Suburbs

Dedicated to Lord Holland.

How far, ye Nymphs and Dryads! must we stray
  Beyond your once-loved haunts, ere we again
May meet you in your freshness? My young day
  Has oft time seen me, in your sylvan train,
  Culling the wild-wood flowers, where now remain
  Nor break nor hedgerow, nor clear bubbling stream
To feed their fragrance, or the fervid ray
  To mitigate; but to the flaunting beam
The domes of tasteless opulence display,
  Shadeless, their glaring fronts; while the pure rill
    That wont to parley, or by noon or night,
    With Phoebus', or with Dian's softer light,

Now through some drain obscene creeps dark and still,
To sweep the waste of luxury away.

(1822)

Mary Julia Young
(fl. 1789–1808)

Mary Julia Young, a relative of the poet Edward Young, lived in London and
supported herself by writing poems, plays, novels, and translations. Her play,
the *Family Party: a Comic Piece, in Two Acts,* appeared anonymously in 1789;
and in 1791, she published a survey of the London stage, *Genius and Fancy;
or, Dramatic Sketches.* Her long narrative poem *Adelaide and Antonine; or, the
Emigrants, A Tale* came out in 1793, followed by *Poems* (1798) and several
novels, including the *East Indian, or Clifford Priory* (1799) and *Donalda, or The
Witches of Glenshiel* (1805). Her memoir of the actress Anna Maria Crouch,
accompanied by a theater history, was published in 1806.

100. To Dreams

Hail, gentle spirits, who with magic wing,
    Chase the dark clouds of sullen night away,
And from her murky cave my freed soul bring,
    To revel in the radiant beams of day.

What are you, say? or earthly, or divine?
    Who thus can cheer the pause of dull repose;
With chemic art the dross of sleep refine,
    And beauteous scenes to *curtained* eyes disclose?

What are you! who subduing time and space,
    To bless these moments can my Love restore?
I hear his voice, behold his form, his face,
    And grateful own your power can give no more.

Hail, gentle spirits! to whose guardian care,
I owe such bliss, yet know not what you are!

(1795)

101. Anxiety

Awakened by the radiant beams of morn,
    My drowsy soul shakes off oblivious sleep;
Hope's gay delusive smiles the day adorn,
    And, charmed awhile, my eyes forget to weep:
But, ah! how transient her enliv'ning power!
Soon disappointment glooms the wished for hour,

That sad and silent glides in tears away;
   Then trembling, chilled with agonizing woe,
   I long, yet dread the fatal cause to know,—
The *cause* that makes my Damon thus delay!
Flutt'ring Anxiety! terrific fears!
   Far from my bosom, halcyon peace, affright,
Till *he* whose every word and look endears,
   That ruffled bosom soothes to *calm delight*.

(1798)

102. Friendship

She came, fair Friendship came, with aspect bland,
   A verdant wreath around her tresses twined,
O'er her cold breast, that scorned love's flaming brand,
   An azure zone the spotless robe confined.

Her modest eyes with tempered radiance shone;
   Her voice was music to attention's ear;
She seemed appointed from the heavenly throne,
   As guardian angel to protect me *here*.

"Arise, ill-fated nymph," she mildly said;
   "Subdue emotions that unnerve thy heart;
Let not perfidious love thy peace invade,
   Or wound thee with a keen impoisoned dart.

Thy soul, from his inglorious bondage free,
And share sublime, celestial bliss with *me*."

(1798)

103. To Time

Rouse thee, old Time, thy folded pinions shake,
   Nor let them useless o'er thy shoulders lie;
Oh! 'tis fond love, impatient, bids thee wake,—
   That bids thee throw each vile encumbrance by.

Thy pond'rous scythe o'er roots of ripened grass,
   With nervous arm let yonder rustic sweep,
And break, in pity *break* thy uncouth glass,
   Through which the heavy sands so slowly creep.

Sluggard, arise! light borne on rapid wing,
   O! glide unwearied through the ambient air!
Haste, swiftly haste, the ecstatic moment bring,
   That gives me all my raptured soul holds dear.

Then, hoary time, while I'm supremely blessed,
Secure beneath thy plumy umbrage *rest*.

(1798)

104. To My Pen

Say, spotless plume, if Damon bade thee go,
And aid this trembling hand to trace my woe?
Ah! if his fond requests are all forgot,
My flowing tears thy every line will blot!
Can *he,* deceitful, act a treacherous part?
Can *he,* remorseless, rend the faithful heart
These oft repeated words have made his *own,*
"Of all mankind, O *love* but *me alone!"*
Famed was his candor, long approved his worth;
I loved, admired, and gloried in the truth;
Then was the *mutual sacred* promise given!
Mine was *sincere,* and registered in *heaven.*
And aid me *still,* fair plume, with pride to own,
Of all mankind *I love* but *him alone.*

(1798)

105. On an Early Spring

Old feeble Winter to gay Spring resigns
The infant year; for whom the rose-buds rend
   Their verdant bands, and in the wreath she twines;
Their blushing charms with her blue violets blend;
   No more a vest of snow the babe confines!
Light o'er his form she throws a robe of green,
Adorned with blossoms, gemmed with dew-drops sheen.
The crimson morn unbars her gates of gold,
   Rousing the torpid songsters of the grove;
And while the russet sprays soft leaves unfold
   The blithesome choir attune their notes to love.
In streams that now no icy fetters hold,
   The fearless nymph her smiling infant laves,
   While sun-beams sparkle on the tissued waves.

(1798)

Charles Lamb
(1775–1834)

Charles Lamb is known today primarily for his *Essays of Elia,* published in the
London Magazine. His early poems appeared in 1796 and 1797 in a volume,
Poems, with those of Samuel Taylor Coleridge, a former schoolmate at
Christ's Hospital. He left school at age fifteen to become a clerk in the ac-
counting department of the East India Company, where he worked for

thirty-five years. In 1796, his sister, Mary Ann (1764–1847), who suffered from schizophrenia, murdered their mother. Lamb, an alcoholic, cared for his sister until his death; they collaborated on the popular *Tales from Shakespeare* (1807), adaptations of the plays into stories for children, and on *Mrs. Leicester's School* (1809), a collection of short stories for children.

106. 'Was it some sweet device of faery land'

Was it some sweet device of faery land
That mocked my steps with many a lonely glade,
And fancied wand'rings with a fair-haired maid?
Have these things been? Or did the wizard wand
Of Merlin wave, impregning vacant air,
And kindle up the vision of a smile
In those blue eyes, that seemed to speak the while
Such tender things, as might enforce Despair
To drop the murd'ring knife, and let go by
His fell resolve? Ah me! the lonely glade
Still courts the footsteps of the fair-haired maid,
Among whose locks the west-winds love to sigh:
But I forlorn do wander, reckless where,
And mid my wand'rings find no Anna there!

(1796)

107. 'We were two pretty babes'

We were two pretty babes, the youngest she,
    The youngest and the loveliest far, I ween,
    And Innocence her name: the time has been,
We two did love each other's company—
    Time was, we two had wept to have been apart!
But when with show of seeming good beguiled
I left the garb and manners of a child,
    And my first love for man's society,
Defiling with the world my virgin heart,
    My loved companion dropped a tear and fled,
And hid in deepest shades her awful head!
    Beloved! who can tell me where thou art,
In what delicious Eden to be found,
That I may seek thee the wide world around!

(1796)

108. 'O! I could laugh to hear the midnight wind'

O! I could laugh to hear the midnight wind
    That rushing on its way with careless sweep
    Scatters the ocean waves—and I could weep,

Even as a child! For now to my rapt mind
On wings of winds comes wild-eyed Fantasy,
  And her dread visions give a rude delight!
  O winged bark! how swift along the night
Passed thy proud keel! Nor shall I let go by
Lightly of that drear hour the memory,
  When wet and chilly on thy deck I stood
  Unbonnetted, and gazed upon the flood,
And almost wished it were no crime to die!
  How reason reeled! What gloomy transports rose!
  Till the rude dashings rocked them to repose.

(1796)

109. *'If from my lips some angry accents fell'*

If from my lips some angry accents fell,
Peevish complaint, or harsh reproof unkind,
'Twas but the error of a sickly mind
And troubled thoughts, clouding the purer well,
And waters clear, of reason; and for me
Let this my verse the poor atonement be—
My verse, which thou to praise wert ever inclined
Too highly, and with a partial eye to see
No blemish. Thou to me didst ever show
Kindest affection, and would oft-times lend
An ear to the desponding love-sick lay,
Weeping my sorrows with me, who repay
But ill the mighty debt of love I owe,
Mary, to thee, my sister, and my friend.

(1797)

110. *The Family Name*

What reason first imposed thee, gentle name,
Name that my father bore, and his sire's sire,
Without reproach? we trace our stream no higher;
And I, a childless man, may end the same.
Perchance some shepherd on Lincolnian plains,
In manners guileless as his own sweet flocks,
Received thee first amid the merry mocks
And arch allusions of his fellow swains.
Perchance from Salem's holier fields returned,
With glory gotten on the heads abhorred
Of faithless Saracens, some martial lord
Took *his* meek title, in whose zeal he burned.
Whate'er the fount whence thy beginnings came,
No deed of mine shall shame thee, gentle name.

(1818)

Mary Robinson
(1758–1800)

Mary Robinson's sonnet sequence, *Sappho and Phaon,* composed of forty-four strictly Petrarchan sonnets, details the passionate but destructive love of a woman poet for a man who abandons her. Combined with its prose preface, the sequence makes a bold claim for the mental preeminence of literary women and identifies Robinson with a woman's poetic tradition represented by Sappho. As an actress, under the tutelage of David Garrick, Robinson attracted the attention of the young Prince of Wales, later George IV; their affair brought her notoriety and made her the subject of national gossip. After the Prince abandoned her, she pursued a career as a professional author, publishing poetry, novels, plays, and essays, including the best-selling novel *Walsingham* (1797), the important volume *Lyrical Tales* (1800), and an autobiography (1801).

111–154. Sappho and Phaon

> Flendus amor meus est; elegeïa flebile carmen;
> Non facit ad lacrymas barbitos ulla meas.
>
> OVID

> Love taught my tears in sadder notes to flow,
> And tuned my heart to elegies of woe.
>
> POPE

111. I. Sonnet Introductory

Favored by Heaven are those, ordained to taste
  The bliss supreme that kindles fancy's fire;
  Whose magic fingers sweep the muses' lyre,
In varying cadence, eloquently chaste!
Well may the mind, with tuneful numbers graced,
  To Fame's immortal attributes aspire,
  Above the treacherous spells of low desire,
That wound the sense, by vulgar joys debased.
  For thou, blest Poesy! with godlike powers
To calm the miseries of man wert given;
  When passion rends, and hopeless love devours,
By memory goaded, and by frenzy driven,
  'Tis thine to guide him 'midst Elysian bowers,
And show his fainting soul,—a glimpse of Heaven.

(1796)

112. II. The Temple of Chastity

High on a rock, coeval with the skies,
  A Temple stands, reared by immortal powers
  To Chastity divine! ambrosial flowers

73

Twining round icicles, in columns rise,
Mingling with pendent gems of orient dyes!
   Piercing the air, a golden crescent towers,
   Veiled by transparent clouds; while smiling hours
Shake from their varying wings—celestial joys!
   The steps of spotless marble, scattered o'er
With deathless roses armed with many a thorn,
   Lead to the altar. On the frozen floor,
Studded with tear-drops petrified by scorn,
   Pale vestals kneel the Goddess to adore,
While Love, his arrows broke, retires forlorn.

                                         (1796)

113. III. *The Bower of Pleasure*

Turn to yon vale beneath, whose tangled shade
   Excludes the blazing torch of noon-day light,
   Where sportive Fawns, and dimpled Loves invite,
The bower of Pleasure opens to the glade:
Lulled by soft flutes, on leaves of violets laid,
   There witching beauty greets the ravished sight,
   More gentle than the arbitress of night
In all her silvery panoply arrayed!
   The birds breathe bliss! light zephyrs kiss the ground,
Stealing the hyacinth's divine perfume;
   While from the pellucid fountains glittering round,
Small tinkling rills bid rival flow'rets bloom!
   Here, laughing Cupids bathe the bosom's wound;
There, tyrant passion finds a glorious tomb!

                                         (1796)

114. IV. *Sappho Discovers her Passion*

Why, when I gaze on Phaon's beauteous eyes,
   Why does each thought in wild disorder stray?
   Why does each fainting faculty decay,
And my chilled breast in throbbing tumults rise?
Mute, on the ground my lyre neglected lies,
   The Muse forgot, and lost the melting lay;
   My down-cast looks, my faltering lips betray,
That stung by hopeless passion,—Sappho dies!
   Now, on a bank of Cypress let me rest;
Come, tuneful maids, ye pupils of my care,
   Come, with your dulcet numbers soothe my breast;
And, as the soft vibrations float on air,
   Let pity waft my spirit to the blessed,
To mock the barbarous triumphs of despair!

                                         (1796)

115. V. Contemns its Power

O! How can Love exulting Reason quell!
  How fades each nobler passion from his gaze!
  E'en Fame, that cherishes the Poet's lays,
That fame, ill-fated Sappho loved so well.
Lost is the wretch, who in his fatal spell
  Wastes the short summer of delicious days,
  And from the tranquil path of wisdom strays,
In passion's thorny wild, forlorn to dwell.
  O ye! who in that sacred temple smile
Where holy Innocence resides enshrined;
  Who fear not sorrow, and who know not guile,
Each thought composed, and every wish resigned;
  Tempt not the path where pleasure's flowery wile
In sweet, but poisonous fetters, holds the mind.

(1796)

116. VI. Describes the Characteristics of Love

Is it to love, to fix the tender gaze,
  To hide the timid blush, and steal away;
  To shun the busy world, and waste the day
In some rude mountain's solitary maze?
Is it to chant *one* name in ceaseless lays,
  To hear no words that other tongues can say,
  To watch the pale moon's melancholy ray,
To chide in fondness, and in folly praise?
  Is it to pour the involuntary sigh,
To dream of bliss, and wake new pangs to prove;
  To talk, in fancy, with the speaking eye,
Then start with jealousy, and wildly rove;
  Is it to loathe the light, and wish to die?
For these I feel,—and feel that they are Love.

(1796)

117. VII. Invokes Reason

Come, Reason, come! each nerve rebellious bind,
  Lull the fierce tempest of my feverish soul;
  Come, with the magic of thy meek control,
And check the wayward wanderings of my mind:
Estranged from thee, no solace can I find,
  O'er my rapt brain, where pensive visions stole,
  Now passion reigns and stormy tumults roll—
So the smooth sea obeys the furious wind!
  In vain philosophy unfolds his store,
O'erwhelmed is every source of pure delight;

Dim is the golden page of wisdom's lore;
All nature fades before my sickening sight:
    For what bright scene can fancy's eye explore,
'Midst dreary labyrinths of mental night?

(1796)

118. VIII. Her Passion Increases

Why, through each aching vein, with lazy pace
    Thus steals the languid fountain of my heart,
    While, from its source, each wild convulsive start
Tears the scorched roses from my burning face?
In vain, O Lesbian Vales! your charms I trace;
    Vain is the poet's theme, the sculptor's art;
    No more the lyre its magic can impart,
Though waked to sound, with more than mortal grace!
    Go, tuneful maids, go bid my Phaon prove
That passion mocks the empty boast of fame;
    Tell him no joys are sweet, but joys of love,
Melting the soul, and thrilling all the frame!
    Oh! may the ecstatic thought in bosom move,
And sighs of rapture, fan the blush of shame!

(1796)

119. IX. Laments the Volatility of Phaon

Ye, who in alleys green and leafy bowers,
    Sport, the rude children of fantastic birth;
    Where frolic nymphs, and shaggy tribes of mirth,
In clamorous revels waste the midnight hours;
Who, linked in flaunting bands of mountain flowers,
    Weave your wild mazes o'er the dewy earth,
    Ere the fierce Lord of Luster rushes forth,
And o'er the world his beamy radiance pours!
    Oft has your clanking cymbal's maddening strain,
Loud ringing through the torch-illumined grove,
    Lured my loved Phaon from the youthful train,
Through rugged dells, o'er craggy rocks to rove;
    Then how can she his vagrant heart detain,
Whose Lyre throbs only to the touch of Love!

(1796)

120. X. Describes Phaon

Dangerous to hear, is that melodious tongue,
    And fatal to the sense those murderous eyes,
    Where in a sapphire sheath, Love's arrow lies,
Himself concealed the crystal haunts among!

Oft o'er that form, enamored have I hung,
　On that smooth cheek to mark the deepening dyes,
　While from that lip the fragrant breath would rise,
That lip, like Cupid's bow with rubies strung!
　Still let me gaze upon that polished brow,
O'er which the golden hair luxuriant plays;
　So, on the modest lily's leaves of snow
The proud sun revels in resplendent rays!
　Warm as his beams this sensate heart shall glow,
Till life's last hour, with Phaon's self decays!

(1796)

121. XI. Rejects the Influence of Reason

O! Reason! vaunted Sovereign of the mind!
　Thou pompous vision with a sounding name!
　Can'st thou, the soul's rebellious passions tame?
Can'st thou in spells the vagrant fancy bind?
Ah, no! capricious as the wavering wind,
　Are sighs of Love that dim thy boasted flame,
　While Folly's torch consumes the wreath of fame,
And Pleasure's hands the sheaves of truth unbind.
　Pressed by the storms of Fate, hope shrinks and dies;
Frenzy darts forth in mightiest ills arrayed;
　Around thy throne destructive tumults rise,
And hell-fraught jealousies, thy rights invade!
　Then, what art thou? O! Idol of the wise!
A visionary theme!—a gorgeous shade!

(1796)

122. XII. Previous to her Interview with Phaon

Now, o'er the tessellated pavement strew
　Fresh saffron, steeped in essence of the rose,
　While down yon agate column gently flows
A glittering streamlet of ambrosial dew!
My Phaon smiles! the rich carnation's hue,
　On his flushed cheek in conscious luster glows,
　While o'er his breast enamored Venus throws
Her starry mantle of celestial blue!
　Breathe soft, ye dulcet flutes, among the trees
Where clustering boughs with golden citron twine;
　While slow vibrations, dying on the breeze,
Shall soothe his soul with harmony divine!
　Then let my form his yielding fancy seize,
And all his fondest wishes, blend with mine.

(1796)

123. XIII. *She Endeavors to Fascinate Him*

Bring, bring to deck my brow, ye Sylvan girls,
    A roseate wreath; nor for my waving hair
    The costly band of studded gems prepare,
Of sparkling crysolite or orient pearls:
Love, o'er my head his canopy unfurls,
    His purple pinions fan the whispering air;
    Mocking the golden sandal, rich and rare,
Beneath my feet the fragrant woodbine curls.
    Bring the thin robe, to fold about my breast,
White as the downy swan; while round my waist
    Let leaves of glossy myrtle bind the vest,
Not idly gay, but elegantly chaste!
    Love scorns the nymph in wanton trappings dressed;
And charms the most concealed, are doubly graced.

                                                        (1796)

124. XIV. *To the Eolian Harp*

Come, soft Eolian harp, while zephyr plays
    Along the meek vibration of thy strings,
    As twilight's hand her modest mantle brings,
Blending with sober gray, the western blaze!
O! prompt my Phaon's dreams with tend'rest lays,
    Ere night o'ershade thee with its humid wings,
    While the lorn Philomel his sorrow sings
In leafy cradle, red with parting rays!
    Slow let thy dulcet tones on ether glide,
So steals the murmur of the amorous dove;
    The mazy legions swarm on every side,
To lulling sounds the sunny people move!
    Let not the wise their little world deride,
The smallest sting can wound the breast of Love.

                                                        (1796)

125. XV. *Phaon Awakes*

Now, round my favored grot let roses rise,
    To strew the bank where Phaon wakes from rest;
    O! happy buds! to kiss his burning breast,
And die, beneath the luster of his eyes!
Now, let the timbrels echo to the skies,
    Now damsels sprinkle cassia on his vest,
    With od'rous wreaths of constant myrtle dressed,
And flowers, deep tinted with the rainbow's dyes!
    From cups of porphyry let nectar flow,
Rich as the perfume of Phoenicia's vine!

Now let his dimpling cheek with rapture glow,
While round his heart love's mystic fetters twine;
And let the Grecian Lyre its aid bestow,
In songs of triumph, to proclaim him mine!

(1796)

126. XVI. Sappho Rejects Hope

Delusive Hope! more transient than the ray
   That leads pale twilight to her dusky bed,
   O'er woodland glen, or breezy mountain's head,
Lingering to catch the parting sigh of day.
Hence with thy visionary charms, away!
   Nor o'er my path the flowers of fancy spread;
   Thy airy dreams on peaceful pillows shed,
And weave for thoughtless brows, a garland gay.
   Farewell low valleys; dizzy cliffs, farewell!
Small vagrant rills that murmur as ye flow:
   Dark bosomed labyrinth and thorny dell;
The task be mine all pleasures to forego;
   To hide, where meditation loves to dwell,
And feed my soul, with luxury of woe!

(1796)

127. XVII. The Tyranny of Love

Love steals unheeded o'er the tranquil mind,
   As summer breezes fan the sleeping main,
   Slow through each fiber creeps the subtle pain,
'Til closely round the yielding bosom twined.
Vain is the hope the magic to unbind,
   The potent mischief riots in the brain,
   Grasps every thought, and burns in every vein,
'Til in the heart the tyrant lives enshrined.
   Oh! victor strong! bending the vanquished frame;
Sweet is the thraldom that thou bid'st us prove!
   And sacred is the tear thy victims claim,
For blest are those whom sighs of sorrow move!
   Then nymphs beware how ye profane my name,
Nor blame my weakness, till like me ye love!

(1796)

128. XVIII. To Phaon

Why art thou changed? O Phaon! tell me why?
   Love flies reproach, when passion feels decay;
   Or, I would paint the raptures of that day,
When, in sweet converse, mingling sigh with sigh,

I marked the graceful languor of thine eye
  As on a shady bank entranced we lay:
    O! Eyes! whose beamy radiance stole away
As stars fade trembling from the burning sky!
  Why art thou changed? dear source of all my woes!
Though dark my bosom's tint, through every vein
  A ruby tide of purest luster flows,
Warmed by thy love, or chilled by thy disdain;
  And yet no bliss this sensate being knows;
Ah! why is rapture so allied to pain?

(1796)

129. XIX. *Suspects his Constancy*

Farewell, ye coral caves, ye pearly sands,
  Ye waving woods that crown yon lofty steep;
    Farewell, ye Nereides of the glittering deep,
Ye mountain tribes, ye fawns, ye sylvan bands:
On the bleak rock your frantic minstrel stands,
  Each task forgot, save that, to sigh and weep;
    In vain the strings her burning fingers sweep,
No more her touch, the Grecian Lyre commands!
  In Circe's cave my faithless Phaon's laid,
Her demons dress his brow with opiate flowers;
  Or, loitering in the brown pomegranate shade,
Beguile with amorous strains the fateful hours;
  While Sappho's lips, to paly ashes fade,
And sorrow's cankering worm her heart devours!

(1796)

130. XX. *To Phaon*

Oh! I could toil for thee o'er burning plains;
  Could smile at poverty's disastrous blow;
    With thee, could wander 'midst a world of snow,
Where one long night o'er frozen Scythia reigns.
Severed from thee, my sickening soul disdains
  The thrilling thought, the blissful dream to know,
  And can'st thou give my days to endless woe,
Requiting sweetest bliss with cureless pains?
  Away, false fear! nor think capricious fate
Would lodge a demon in a form divine!
  Sooner the dove shall seek a tiger mate,
Or the soft snowdrop round the thistle twine;
  Yet, yet, I dread to hope, nor dare to hate,
Too proud to sue! too tender to resign!

(1796)

131. XXI. *Laments her Early Misfortunes*

Why do I live to loathe the cheerful day,
  To shun the smiles of Fame, and mark the hours
  On tardy pinions move, while ceaseless showers
Down my wan cheek in lucid currents stray?
My tresses all unbound, nor gems display,
  Nor scents Arabian! on my path no flowers
  Imbibe the morn's resuscitating powers,
For one blank sorrow, saddens all my way!
  As slow the radiant sun of reason rose,
Through tears my dying parents saw it shine;
  A brother's frailties, swelled the tide of woes,—
And, keener far, maternal griefs were mine!
  Phaon! if soon these weary eyes shall close,
Oh! must that task, that mournful task, be thine?

                                 (1796)

132. XXII. *Phaon Forsakes Her*

Wild is the foaming sea! The surges roar!
  And nimbly dart the livid lightnings round!
  On the rent rock the angry waves rebound;
Ah me! the lessening bark is seen no more!
Along the margin of the trembling shore,
  Loud as the blast my frantic cries shall sound,
  My storm-drenched limbs the flinty fragments wound,
And o'er my bleeding breast the billows pour!
  Phaon! return! ye winds, O! waft the strain
To his swift bark; ye barbarous waves forbear!
  Taunt not the anguish of a lover's brain,
Nor feebly emulate the soul's despair!
  For howling winds, and foaming seas, in vain
Assail the breast, when passion rages there!

                                 (1796)

133. XXIII. *Sappho's Conjectures*

To Etna's scorching sands my Phaon flies!
  False youth! can other charms attractive prove?
  Say, can Sicilian loves thy passions move,
Play round thy heart, and fix thy fickle eyes,
While in despair the Lesbian Sappho dies?
  Has Spring for thee a crown of poppies wove,
  Or dost thou languish in the Idalian grove,
Whose altar kindles, fanned by Lover's sighs?
  Ah! think, that while on Etna's shores you stray,
A fire, more fierce than Etna's, fills my breast;

Nor deck Sicilian nymphs with garlands gay,
While Sappho's brows with cypress wreaths are dressed;
   Let one kind word my weary woes repay,
Or, in eternal slumbers bid them rest.

(1796)

134. XXIV. Her Address to the Moon

O thou! meek Orb! that stealing o'er the dale
   Cheer'st with thy modest beams the noon of night!
   On the smooth lake diffusing silvery light,
Sublimely still, and beautifully pale!
What can thy cool and placid eye avail,
   Where fierce despair absorbs the mental sight,
   While inbred glooms the vagrant thoughts invite,
To tempt the gulf where howling fiends assail?
   O, Night! all nature owns thy tempered power;
Thy solemn pause, thy dews, thy pensive beam;
   Thy sweet breath whispering in the moonlight bower,
While fainting flow'rets kiss the wandering stream!
   Yet, vain is every charm! and vain the hour,
That brings to maddening love, no soothing dream!

(1796)

135. XXV. To Phaon

Can'st thou forget, O! Idol of my soul!
   Thy Sappho's voice, her form, her dulcet lyre!
   That melting every thought to fond desire,
Bade sweet delirium o'er thy senses roll?
Can'st thou, so soon, renounce the blessed control
   That calmed with pity's tears love's raging fire,
   While Hope, slow breathing on the trembling wire,
In every note with soft persuasion stole?
   Oh! Sovereign of my heart! return! return!
For me no spring appears, no summers bloom,
   No sunbeams glitter, and no altars burn!
The mind's dark winter of eternal gloom,
   Shows 'midst the waste a solitary urn,
A blighted laurel, and a moldering tomb!

(1796)

136. XXVI. Contemns Philosophy

Where antique woods o'erhang the mountain's crest,
   And mid-day glooms in solemn silence lour;
   Philosophy, go seek a lonely bower,
And waste life's fervid noon in fancied rest.

Go, where the bird of sorrow weaves her nest,
   Cooing, in sadness sweet, through night's dim hour;
   Go, cull the dewdrops from each potent flower
That med'cines to the cold and reasoning breast!
   Go, where the brook in liquid lapse steals by,
Scarce heard amidst the mingling echoes round,
   What time, the noon fades slowly down the sky,
And slumbering zephyrs moan, in caverns bound:
   Be these thy pleasures, dull Philosophy!
Nor vaunt the balm, to heal a lover's wound.

(1796)

137. XXVII. Sappho's Address to the Stars

Oh! ye bright Stars! that on the ebon fields
   Of heaven's vast empire, trembling seem to stand;
   'Till rosy morn unlocks her portal bland,
Where the proud Sun his fiery banner wields!
To flames, less fierce than mine, your luster yields,
   And powers more strong my countless tears command;
   Love strikes the feeling heart with ruthless hand,
And only spares the breast which dullness shields.
   Since, then, capricious nature but bestows
The fine affections of the soul, to prove
   A keener sense of desolating woes,
Far, far from me the empty boast remove;
   If bliss from coldness, pain from passion flows,
Ah! who would wish to feel, or learn to love?

(1796)

138. XXVIII. Describes the Fascinations of Love

Weak is the sophistry, and vain the art
   That whispers patience to the mind's despair!
   That bids reflection bathe the wounds of care,
While Hope, with pleasing phantoms, soothes their smart;
For memory still, reluctant to depart
   From the dear spot, once rich in prospects fair,
   Bids the fond soul enamored linger there,
And its least charm is grateful to the heart!
   He never loved, who could not muse and sigh,
Spangling the sacred turf with frequent tears,
   Where the small rivulet, that ripples by,
Recalls the scenes of past and happier years,
   When, on its banks he watched the speaking eye,
And one sweet smile o'erpaid an age of fears!

(1796)

139. XXIX. *Determines to Follow Phaon*

Farewell, ye towering cedars, in whose shade,
  Lulled by the nightingale, I sunk to rest,
  While spicy breezes hovered o'er my breast
To fan my cheek, in deepening tints arrayed;
While amorous insects, humming round me, played,
  Each flower forsook, of prouder sweets in quest;
  Of glowing lips, in humid fragrance dressed,
That mocked the sunny Hybla's vaunted aid!
  Farewell, ye limpid rivers! Oh! farewell!
No more shall Sappho to your grots repair;
  No more your white waves to her bosom swell,
Or your dank weeds, entwine her floating hair;
  As erst, when Venus in her sparry cell
Wept, to behold a brighter goddess there!

                                  (1796)

140. XXX. *Bids Farewell to Lesbos*

O'er the tall cliff that bounds the billowy main
  Shadowing the surge that sweeps the lonely strand,
  While the thin vapors break along the sand,
Day's harbinger unfolds the liquid plain.
The rude sea murmurs, mournful as the strain
  That love-lorn minstrels strike with trembling hand,
  While from their green beds rise the Siren band
With tongues aerial to repeat my pain!
  The vessel rocks beside the pebbly shore,
The foamy curls its gaudy trappings lave;
  Oh! Bark propitious! bear me gently o'er,
Breathe soft, ye winds; rise slow, O! swelling wave!
  Lesbos; these eyes shall meet thy sands no more:
I fly, to seek my lover, or my grave!

                                  (1796)

141. XXXI. *Describes her Bark*

Far o'er the waves my lofty bark shall glide,
  Love's frequent sighs the fluttering sails shall swell,
  While to my native home I bid farewell,
Hope's snowy hand the burnished helm shall guide!
Triton's shall sport amidst the yielding tide,
  Myriads of Cupids round the prow shall dwell,
  And Venus, throned within her opal shell,
Shall proudly o'er the glittering billows ride!
  Young dolphins, dashing in the golden spray,
Shall with their scaly forms illume the deep

Tinged with the purple flush of sinking day,
Whose flaming wreath shall crown the distant steep;
  While on the breezy deck soft minstrels play,
And songs of love, the lover soothe to sleep!

(1796)

142. XXXII. Dreams of a Rival

Blessed as the Gods! Sicilian Maid is he,
  The youth whose soul thy yielding graces charm;
  Who bound, O! thralldom sweet! by beauty's arm,
In idle dalliance fondly sports with thee!
Blessed as the Gods! that ivory throne to see,
  Throbbing with transports, tender, timid, warm!
  While round thy fragrant lips zephyrs swarm,
As opening buds attract the wandering bee!
  Yet, short is youthful passion's fervid hour;
Soon, shall another clasp the beauteous boy;
  Soon, shall a rival prove, in that gay bower,
The pleasing torture of excessive joy!
  The bee flies sickened from the sweetest flower;
The lightning's shaft, but dazzles to destroy!

(1796)

143. XXXIII. Reaches Sicily

I wake! delusive phantoms hence, away!
  Tempt not the weakness of a lover's breast;
  The softest breeze can shake the halcyon's nest,
And lightest clouds o'ercast the dawning ray!
'Twas but a vision! Now, the star of day
  Peers, like a gem on Etna's burning crest!
  Welcome, ye hills, with golden vintage dressed;
Sicilian forests brown, and valleys gay!
  A mournful stranger, from the Lesbian Isle,
Not strange, in loftiest eulogy of song!
  She, who could teach the stoic's cheek to smile,
Thaw the cold heart, and chain the wondering throng,
  Can find no balm, love's sorrows to beguile;
Ah! Sorrows known too soon! and felt too long!

(1796)

144. XXXIV. Sappho's Prayer to Venus

Venus! to thee, the Lesbian Muse shall sing,
  The song, which Mytilenian youths admired,
  When Echo, amorous of the strain inspired,
Bade the wild rocks with maddening plaudits ring!

Attend my prayer! O! Queen of rapture! bring
   To these fond arms, he, whom my soul has fired;
   From these fond arms removed, yet, still desired,
Though love, exulting, spreads his varying wing!
   Oh! source of every joy! of every care!
Blest Venus! Goddess of the zone divine!
   To Phaon's bosom, Phaon's victim bear;
So shall her warmest, tend'rest vows be thine!
   For Venus, Sappho shall a wreath prepare,
And Love be crowned, immortal as the Nine!

(1796)

145. XXXV. Reproaches Phaon

What means the mist opaque that veils these eyes;
   Why does yon threatening tempest shroud the day?
   Why does thy altar, Venus, fade away,
And on my breast the dews of horror rise?
Phaon is false! be dim, ye orient skies;
   And let black Erebus succeed your ray;
   Let clashing thunders roll, and lightnings play;
Phaon is false! and hopeless Sappho dies!
   "Farewell! my Lesbian love, you might have said,"
Such sweet remembrance had some pity proved,
   "Or coldly this, farewell, Oh! Lesbian maid!"
No task severe, for one so fondly loved!
   The gentle thought had soothed my wandering shade,
From life's dark valley, and its thorns removed!

(1796)

146. XXXVI. Her Confirmed Despair

Lead me, Sicilian Maids, to haunted bowers,
   While yon pale moon displays her faintest beams
   O'er blasted woodlands, and enchanted streams,
Whose banks infect the breeze with poisonous flowers.
Ah! lead me, where the barren mountain towers,
   Where no sounds echo, but the night-owl's screams,
   Where some lone spirit of the desert gleams,
And lurid horrors wing the fateful hours!
   Now goaded frenzy grasps my shrinking brain,
Her touch absorbs the crystal fount of woe!
   My blood rolls burning through each gasping vein;
Away, lost Lyre! unless thou can'st bestow
   A charm, to lull that agonizing pain,
Which those who never loved, can never know!

(1796)

147. XXXVII. Foresees her Death

When, in the gloomy mansion of the dead,
  This withering heart, this faded form shall sleep;
  When these fond eyes, at length shall cease to weep,
And earth's cold lap receive this feverish head;
Envy shall turn away, a tear to shed,
  And Time's obliterating pinions sweep
  The spot, where poets shall their vigils keep,
To mourn and wander near my freezing bed!
  Then, my pale ghost, upon the Elysian shore,
Shall smile, released from every mortal care;
  While, doomed love's victim to repine no more,
My breast shall bathe in endless rapture there!
  Ah! no! my restless shade would still deplore,
Nor taste that bliss, which Phaon did not share.

(1796)

148. XXXVIII. To a Sigh

Oh Sigh! thou steal'st, the herald of the breast,
  The lover's fears, the lover's pangs to tell;
  Thou bid'st with timid grace the bosom swell,
Cheating the day of joy, the night of rest!
Oh! lucid tears! with eloquence confessed,
  Why on my fading cheek unheeded dwell,
  Meek, as the dew-drops on the flowret's bell
By ruthless tempests to the green sod pressed.
  Fond sigh be hushed! congeal, O! slighted tear!
Thy feeble powers the busy Fates control!
  Or if thy crystal streams again appear,
Let them, like Lethe's, to oblivion roll:
  For Love the tyrant plays, when hope is near,
And she who flies the lover,—chains the soul!

(1796)

149. XXXIX. To the Muses

Prepare your wreaths, Aonian maids divine,
  To strew the tranquil bed where I shall sleep;
  In tears, the myrtle and the laurel steep,
And let Erato's hand the trophies twine.
No parian marble, there, with labored line,
  Shall bid the wandering lover stay to weep;
  There holy silence shall her vigils keep,
Save, when the nightingale such woes as mine
  Shall sadly sing; as twilight's curtains spread,
There shall the branching lotus widely wave,

Sprinkling soft showers upon the lily's head,
Sweet drooping emblem for a lover's grave!
And there shall Phaon pearls of pity shed,
To gem the vanquished heart he scorned to save!

(1796)

150. XL. Visions Appear to her in a Dream

On the low margin of a murmuring stream,
As rapt in meditation's arms I lay;
Each aching sense in slumbers stole away,
While potent fancy formed a soothing dream;
O'er the Leucadian deep, a dazzling beam
Shed the bland light of empyrean day!
But soon transparent shadows veiled each ray,
While mystic visions sprang athwart the gleam!
Now to the heaving gulf they seemed to bend,
And now across the sphery regions glide;
Now in mid-air, their dulcet voices blend,
"Awake! awake!" the restless phalanx cried,
"See ocean yawns the lover's woes to end,
Plunge the green wave, and bid thy griefs subside."

(1796)

151. XLI. Resolves to Take the Leap of Leucata

Yes, I will go, where circling whirlwinds rise,
Where threatening clouds in sable grandeur lour;
Where the blast yells, the liquid columns pour,
And maddening billows combat with the skies!
There, while the Demon of the tempest flies
On growing pinions through the troublous hour,
The wild waves gasp impatient to devour,
And on the rock the wakened vulture cries!
Oh! dreadful solace to the stormy mind!
To me, more pleasing than the valley's rest,
The woodland songsters, or the sportive kind,
That nip the turf, or prune the painted crest;
For in despair alone, the wretched find
That unction sweet, which lulls the bleeding breast!

(1796)

152. XLII. Her Last Appeal to Phaon

Oh! can'st thou bear to see this faded frame,
Deformed and mangled by the rocky deep?
Wilt thou remember, and forbear to weep,
My fatal fondness, and my peerless fame?

Soon o'er this heart, now warm with passion's flame,
  The howling winds and foamy waves shall sweep;
  Those eyes be ever closed in death's cold sleep,
And all of Sappho perish, but her name!
  Yet, if the Fates suspend their barbarous ire,
If days less mournful, Heaven designs for me!
  If rocks grow kind, and winds and waves conspire,
To bear me softly on the swelling sea;
  To Phoebus only will I tune my Lyre,
"What suits with Sappho, Phoebus suits with thee!"

                      (1796)

153. XLIII. Her Reflections on the Leucadian Rock Before She Perishes

While from the dizzy precipice I gaze,
  The world receding from my pensive eyes,
  High o'er my head the tyrant eagle flies,
Clothed in the sinking sun's transcendent blaze!
The meek-eyed moon, 'midst clouds of amber plays
  As o'er the purpling plains of light she hies,
  Till the last stream of living luster dies,
And the cool concave owns her tempered rays!
  So shall this glowing, palpitating soul,
Welcome returning Reason's placid beam,
  While o'er my breast the waves Lethean roll,
To calm rebellious Fancy's feverish dream;
  Then shall my lyre disdain love's dread control,
And loftier passions, prompt the loftier theme!

                      (1796)

154. XLIV. Conclusive

Here droops the muse! while from her glowing mind,
  Celestial Sympathy, with humid eye,
  Bids the light sylph capricious Fancy fly,
Time's restless wings with transient flowers to bind!
For now, with folded arms and head inclined,
  Reflection pours the deep and frequent sigh,
  O'er the dark scroll of human destiny,
Where gaudy buds and wounding thorns are twined.
  O! Sky-born Virtue! sacred is thy name!
And though mysterious Fate, with frown severe,
  Oft decorates thy brows with wreaths of Fame,
Bespangled o'er with sorrow's chilling tear!
  Yet shalt thou more than mortal raptures claim,
The brightest planet of the ETERNAL SPHERE!

                      (1796)

155. Laura to Petrarch

O solitary wand'rer! whither stray
  From the smooth path the dimpled pleasures love,
  From flowery meadow, and embowering grove,
Where hope and fancy smiling, lead the way!
To thee, I ween, full tedious seems the day;
  While lorn and slow the devious path you rove,
  Sighing soft sorrows on the garland wove
By young desire, of blossoms sweetly gay!
  Oh! blossoms! frail and fading! like the morn
Of love's first rapture! beauteous all, and pure,
  Deep hid beneath your charms lies misery's thorn,
To bid the feeling breast a pang endure!
  Then check thy wand'rings, weary and forlorn,
And find in friendship's balm sick passion's cure.

                                       (1806)

Ann Yearsley
(1752–1806)

Ann Yearsley had six children and sold milk and produce door to door. By
1783 her family was impoverished, and she brought her poetry to the atten-
tion of Hannah More, who dubbed her "the Milkwoman of Clifton near
Bristol" and helped Yearsley publish by subscription *Poems on Several Occa-
sions* (1785). *The Rural Lyre; a Volume of Poems* (1796) includes sonnets, lyrics,
elegies, epistles, and a fragment of an epic.

156. To _____

Lo! dreary Winter, howling o'er the waste,
Imprints the glebe, bids every channel fill—
His tears in torrents down the mountains haste,
His breath augments despair, and checks our will!
Yet thy pure flame through lonely night is seen,
To lure the shiv'ring pilgrim o'er the green—
He hastens on, nor heeds the pelting blast:
Thy spirit softly breathes—"The worst is past;
Warm thee, poor wand'rer, 'mid thy devious way!
On thy cold bosom hangs unwholesome air;
Ah! pass not this bright fire! Thou long may'st stray
Ere through the glens one other spark appear."

Thus breaks thy friendship on my sinking mind,
And lures me on, while sorrow dies behind.

                                       (1796)

William Beckford
(1760–1844)

Remembered chiefly as the author of *Vathek* (1786), one of the earliest gothic novels, William Beckford travelled extensively and lived extravagantly. He was also a member of Parliament. His burlesque of contemporary women's writing, *Azemia*, published under the pseudonym "Jacquetta Agneta Mariana Jenks," contains poetic parodies such as this sonnet penned by "a languishing fair one." As its title suggests, the sonnet is a parody of the type popularized by Charlotte Smith in her *Elegiac Sonnets,* which was tiresomely imitated throughout the 1780s and 1790s.

157. *Elegiac Sonnet to a Mopstick*

Straight remnant, of the spiry birchen bough,
  That o'er the streamlet wont perchance to quake
Thy many twinkling leaves, and, bending low,
  Beheld thy white rind dancing on the lake—
How doth thy present state, poor stick! awake
  My pathos—for, alas! even stript as thou
May be my beating breast, if e'er forsake
  Philisto this poor heart; and break his vow.

So musing on I fare, with many a sigh,
  And meditating then on times long past.
To thee, lorn pole! I look with tearful eye,
  As all beside the floor-soiled pail thou'rt cast,
And my sad thoughts, while I behold thee twirled,
Turn on the twistings of this troublous world.

                  (1797)

Charles Lloyd
(1775–1839)

The son of a prominent Quaker banker, Charles Lloyd wandered aimlessly as a young man until he became the tenant and pupil of Samuel Taylor Coleridge and the friend of Charles Lamb. The three published together a volume of poems in 1797 entitled, simply, *Poems.* Lloyd wrote many sonnets, several of which are highly emotional and metaphysical. Lloyd suffered from chronic depression and increasing mental disability and frequently quarreled with his friends. In addition to poetry, he published translations and one novel, *Isabel* (1809). Lloyd spent the latter part of his life in a French mental institution.

158. *'My pleasant home! where erst when sad and faint'*

My pleasant home! where erst when sad and faint
  I sought maternal friendship's sheltering arms,

My pleasant home! where is the reverenced saint
    Whose presence gave thee thy peculiar charms?
Ah me! when slow the accustomed doors unfold,
    No more her looks affectionate and mild
Beam on my burdened heart! O, still and cold
    The cherished spot where welcome sat and smiled!
My spirit pines not nursing fancied ill;
    'Tis not the feverish and romantic tie
      Which now I weep dissevered; not a form
That woke brief passion's desultory thrill:
    I mourn the cherisher of infancy!
      The dear protectress from life's morning storm!

                                                          (1797)

159. 'Oh, I have told thee every secret care'

Oh, I have told thee every secret care,
    And crept to thee when pale with sickliness!
Thou didst provide my morrow's simple fare,
    And with meek love my elfin wrongs redress.
My grandmother! when pondering all alone
    Fain would I list thy footstep! but my call
    Thou dost not hear; nor mark the tears that fall
From my dim eyes! No, thou art dead and gone!
How can I think that thou didst mildly spread
    Thy feeble arms, and clasp me o'er and o'er
Ere infant gratitude one tear could shed!
    How think of thee, to whom its little store
My bosom owes, nor tempted by despair
Mix busy anguish with imperfect prayer!

                                                           (1797)

160. Written at the Hotwells, near Bristol

Meek Friend! I have been traversing the steep
    Where when a frolic boy with patient eye
Thou heededst all my wand'rings, (I could weep
    To think perchance thy shade might hover nigh,
Marking thy altered child); how little then
    Dreamt I, that thou, a tenant of the grave,
    No more shouldst smile on me, when I might crave
Some little solace 'mid the hum of men!
Those times had joys which I no more shall know,
    And e'en their saddest moments now seem sweet:
Such comforts mingle with remembered woe!
    Now with this hope I prompt my onward feet,
That He, who took thee, pitying my lone heart,
Will reunite us where friends never part!

                                                           (1797)

161. 'Erst when I wandered far from those I loved'

Erst when I wandered far from those I loved,
   If weariness o'ertook me, if my heart
   Heaved big with sympathy, and ached t'impart
Its secret treasures, much have I been moved
Thinking of those most dear; and I have known
   It very sweet all feelingly to pour
   Of youthful fantasies the eccentric store
Through the warm line: nor didst thou seldom own
The tender gratulation, earliest friend!
   And now when heavily the lone hours roll
   Stealeth an image on my cheated soul
No other than thyself! and I would send
Tidings of love—till the mind starts from sleep
As it had heard thy knell!—I pause, and weep!

                                        (1797)

162. 'Oh, she was almost speechless!'

Oh, she was almost speechless! nor could hold
   Awakening converse with me! (I shall bless
   No more the modulated tenderness
Of that dear voice!) Alas, 'twas shrunk and cold
Her honored face! yet when I sought to speak,
   Through her half-opened eye-lids she did send
   Faint looks, that said "I would be yet thy friend!"
And (O my choked breast!) e'en on that shrunk cheek
I saw one slow tear roll! my hand she took,
   Placing it on her heart—I heard her sigh
   "'Tis too, too much!" 'Twas love's last agony!
I tore me from her! 'Twas her latest look,
Her latest accents—Oh my heart, retain
That look, those accents, till we meet again!

                                        (1797)

163. 'Whether thou smile or frown, thou beauteous face'

Whether thou smile or frown, thou beauteous face,
   Thy charms alike possess my throbbing heart,
   Nor canst thou gesture, look, or word impart
Fraught not with magic of enchanting grace:
Oh, could I once thy lovely form embrace!
   Die on thy lips, and, as fierce raptures dart,
   Breathe sighs that bid the mutual soul depart!
And with keen glances, keener glances chase!
   It may not be, Oh Love!—Thou gavest to me
A heart too prone thy raptures to adore!
The touch, the look, the sigh, are mine no more!

Love is departed, and in agony
The infatuated spirit must deplore
That after love no other joy can be.

(1819)

164. Metaphysical Sonnet

My soul's an atom in the world of mind,
  Hurled from its center by some adverse storm;
The attraction's gone, its movements that confined
  The impulse fled, that urged it to perform
Its destined office. Wandering through the void,
  Each due attrition, each excitement dead,
Its moral aim and action seem destroyed,
  And its *existence,* like its *functions,* fled.
Love was the parent orb from whence it drew
  Its moral being, hope its active force;
But Love's dear sun shall never shine anew;
  Nor Hope again direct my wandering course!
My life is nothing to mankind!—To me
Tis worse than nothing! *'Tis all agony!*

(1819)

Robert Southey
(1774–1843)

During his lifetime, Robert Southey was known as one of the "Lake Poets,"
which included William Wordsworth and Samuel Taylor Coleridge. While
a student at Oxford, he planned (but never realized) with Coleridge a utopian
community, which Coleridge called "Pantisocracy," to be established in
Pennsylvania, and wrote *Joan of Arc,* an epic poem celebrating democracy and
liberty. His sequence, *Poems on the Slave Trade,* expresses Southey's passionate
objection to England's involvement in the capture and selling into servitude
of native Africans. In 1813, he was appointed poet laureate.

165–170. Poems on the Slave Trade

I am innocent of this Blood, See ye to it!

165. I

Hold your mad hands! for ever on your plain
  Must the gorged vulture clog his beak with blood?
  For ever must your Niger's tainted flood
Roll to the ravenous shark his banquet slain?
Hold your mad hands! what demon prompts to rear
  The arm of Slaughter? on your savage shore
  Can hell-sprung Glory claim the feast of gore,

With laurels watered by the widow's tear
Wreathing his helmet crown? lift high the spear!
  And like the desolating whirlwind's sweep,
  Plunge ye yon bark of anguish in the deep;
For the pale fiend, cold-hearted Commerce there
Breathes his gold-gendered pestilence afar,
And calls, to share the prey, his kindred demon War.

(1797)

166. II

Why dost thou beat thy breast and rend thine hair,
  And to the deaf sea pour thy frantic cries?
  Before the gale the laden vessel flies;
The heavens all-favoring smile, the breeze is fair;
Hark to the clamors of the exulting crew!
  Hark how their thunders mock the patient skies!
  Why dost thou shriek and strain thy red-swol'n eyes
As the white sail dim lessens from thy view?
Go pine in want and anguish and despair,
  There is no mercy found in human-kind—
Go widow to thy grave and rest thee there!
  But may the god of justice bid the wind
Whelm that curst bark beneath the mountain wave,
And bless with liberty and death the slave!

(1797)

167. III

Oh he is worn with toil! the big drops run
  Down his dark cheek; hold—hold thy merciless hand,
  Pale tyrant! for beneath thy hard command
O'erwearied Nature sinks. The scorching sun,
As pitiless as proud prosperity,
  Darts on him his full beams; gasping he lies
  Arraigning with his looks the patient skies,
While that inhuman trader lifts on high
  The mangling scourge. Oh ye who at your ease
  Sip the blood-sweetened beverage! thoughts like these
Hap'ly ye scorn: I thank thee Gracious God!
  That I do feel upon my cheek the glow
Of indignation, when beneath the rod
  A sable brother writhes in silent woe.

(1797)

168. IV

'Tis night; the mercenary tyrants sleep
  As undisturbed as justice! but no more

The wretched slave, as on his native shore,
Rests on his reedy couch: he wakes to weep!
Though through the toil and anguish of the day
    No tear escaped him, not one suffering groan
    Beneath the twisted thong, he weeps alone
In bitterness; thinking that far away
Though the gay negroes join the midnight song,
    Though merriment resounds on Niger's shore,
She whom he loves far from the cheerful throng
    Stands sad, and gazes from her lowly door
With dim grown eye, silent and woe-begone,
    And weeps for him who will return no more.

                                       (1797)

169. V

Did then the bold slave rear at last the sword
    Of vengeance? drenched he deep its thirsty blade
In the cold bosom of his tyrant lord?
    Oh! who shall blame him? through the midnight shade
Still o'er his tortured memory rushed the thought
    Of every past delight; his native grove,
    Friendship's best joys, and liberty and love,
All lost for ever! then remembrance wrought
His soul to madness: round his restless bed
    Freedom's pale specter stalked, with a stern smile
    Pointing the wounds of slavery, the while
She shook her chains and hung her sullen head:
No more on Heaven he calls with fruitless breath,
But sweetens with revenge, the draught of death.

                                       (1797)

170. VI

High in the air exposed the slave is hung
    To all the birds of Heaven, their living food!
He groans not, though awaked by that fierce sun
    New torturers live to drink their parent blood!
He groans not, though the gorging vulture tear
    The quivering fiber! Hither gaze O ye
    Who tore this man from peace and liberty!
Gaze hither ye who weigh with scrupulous care
The right and prudent; for beyond the grave
    There is another world! and call to mind,
    Ere your decrees proclaim to all mankind
Murder is legalized, that there the slave
Before the Eternal, "thunder-tongued shall plead
Against the deep damnation of your deed."

                                       (1797)

171. To a Goose

If thou didst feed on western plains of yore;
Or waddle wide with flat and flabby feet
Over some Cambrian mountain's plashy moor;
Or find in farmer's yard a safe retreat
From gypsy thieves, and foxes sly and fleet;
If thy gray quills, by lawyer guided, trace
Deeds big with ruin to some wretched race,
Or love-sick poet's sonnet, sad and sweet,
Wailing the rigor of his lady fair;
Or if, the drudge of housemaid's daily toil,
Cobwebs and dust thy pinions white besoil,
Departed Goose! I neither know nor care.
But this I know, that we pronounced thee fine,
Seasoned with sage and onions, and port wine.

(1799)

172. Winter

A wrinkled, crabbed man they picture thee,
Old Winter, with a rugged beard as gray
As the long moss upon the apple-tree;
Blue-lipped, an ice-drop at thy sharp blue nose,
Close muffled up, and on thy dreary way,
Plodding alone through sleet and drifting snows.
They should have drawn thee by the high-heaped hearth,
Old Winter! seated in thy great armed chair,
Watching the children at their Christmas mirth;
Or circled by them as thy lips declare
Some merry jest or tale of murder dire,
Or troubled spirit that disturbs the night,
Pausing at times to rouse the moldering fire,
Or taste the old October brown and bright.

(1799)

Edward Gardner
(fl. 1770–98)

Edward Gardner was the friend of Thomas Chatterton and published a variety of essays and poems. His volume *Miscellanies, in Prose and Verse* (1798) includes, among other curiosities, several sonnets and an essay on Anna Seward's poetical novel *Louisa* (1784). His life is now largely obscure.

173. Written in Tintern Abbey, Monmouthshire

Admiring stranger, that with ling'ring feet,
Enchained by wonder, pauses on this green;

Where thy enraptured sight the dark woods meet,
  Ah! rest awhile, and contemplate the scene.

These hoary pillars clasped by ivy round,
  This hallowed floor by holy footsteps trod,
The mold'ring choir by spreading moss embrowned,
  Where fasting saints devoutly hymned their God.

Unpitying Time, with slow but certain sweep,
  Has laid, alas! their ancient splendor low:
Yet here let pilgrims, while they muse and weep,
  Think on the lesson that from hence may flow.
Like theirs, how soon may be the tottering state
Of man,—the temple of a shorter date.

(1798)

174. To Love

Ah dear associate of youth's tender days,
  When round my heart my Laura's charms entwined:
When ardent sighs quick blew the kindling rays,
  That flashed the flames of frenzy on the mind.

Art thou of human kind the dreadful curse?
  For sure thy poisons cauterize the soul;
Or of contentment sweet the soothing nurse,
  When o'er the swelling heart thy mighty raptures roll.

O thou art both, for midst the pangs of pain,
  Warm hope and joy in quick succession flow,
And floods of bliss too mighty to sustain,
  A moment check the bitter waves of woe.
Still varying Goddess, still we bow to thee,
Thou daughter bland of Sensibility.

(1798)

Joseph Hucks

(d. 1800)

Joseph Hucks was a close friend of Samuel Taylor Coleridge, with whom he made a walking tour through Wales, recorded in Hucks's *Pedestrian Tour through North Wales* (1795). During their walk, Hucks contributed to the conception of Coleridge and Southey's utopian scheme, "Pantisocracy." He was educated at Eton and St. Catherine's Hall, Cambridge. His sonnet "To Freedom" demonstrates something of the revolutionary fervor for democracy characteristic of the 1790s. He died while still a young man.

175. To Freedom

On Gallia's land I saw thy faded form,
    Dim through the midnight mist—the rock thy bed—
The livid lightning flashed, and the wild storm
    Fell blasting, keen, and loud, around thy head,
And Peace sat by, and poured forth many a tear.
    To other realms I marked thy mournful flight,
    While slowly bursting from the clouds of night,
Gleamed the pale moon upon thy blunted spear.
    Though exiled still from Europe's purple plain,
    Oh! fly not, Freedom! from our happier shore;
The tyrant's frown, or anarchy's wild train,
    Too long do Gallia's harassed sons deplore:
But never *from old Ocean's favorite isle,*
Freedom! withdraw thy renovating smile.

                                      (1798)

Anna Seward
(1742–1809)

Anna Seward's *Elegy on Captain Cook* (1780) won applause from Samuel Johnson. When her friend Major John Andrè was hanged in America as a traitor for conspiring with Benedict Arnold, she published a long elegy, *Monody on the Death of Major Andrè* (1781), which won her instant fame. *Louisa, a Poetical Novel in Four Epistles* (1784), a highly experimental novel in verse, went through five editions; *Llangollen Vale* (1796) commemorates female friendship. Seward's Miltonic *Original Sonnets on Various Subjects; and Odes Paraphrased from Horace* (1799) demonstrate technical prowess by adhering to strict rules of sonnet form. Walter Scott edited Seward's *Poetical Works* (1810). Jane West called her "the British Sappho."

176. 'When Life's realities the Soul perceives'

When Life's realities the Soul perceives
    Vain, dull, perchance corrosive, if she glows
    With rising energy, and open throws
    The golden gates of genius, she achieves
His fairy clime delighted, and receives
    In those gay paths, decked with the thornless rose,
    Blest compensation.—Lo! with altered brows
    Lours the false world, and the fine spirit grieves;
No more young Hope tints with her light and bloom
    The darkening scene.—Then to ourselves we say,
    Come, bright Imagination, come! relume
Thy orient lamp; with recompensing ray

Shine on the mind, and pierce its gathering gloom
With all the fires of intellectual day!

(1799)

177. To a Friend, Who Thinks Sensibility a Misfortune

Ah, thankless! canst thou envy him who gains
   The Stoic's cold and indurate repose?
   Thou! with thy lively sense of bliss and woes!—
   From a false balance of life's joys and pains
Thou deem'st him happy.—Placed 'mid fair domains,
   Where full the river down the valley flows,
   As wisely might'st thou with thy home had rose
On the parched surface of unwatered plains,
For that, when long the heavy rain descends,
   Bursts over guardian banks their whelming tide!—
   Seldom the wild and wasteful flood extends,
But, spreading plenty, verdure, beauty wide,
   The cool translucent stream perpetual bends,
   And laughs the vale as the bright waters glide.

(1799)

178. 'By Derwent's rapid stream as oft I strayed'

By Derwent's rapid stream as oft I strayed,
   With Infancy's light step and glances wild,
   And saw vast rocks, on steepy mountains piled,
   Frown o'er the umbrageous glen; or pleased surveyed
The cloudy moonshine in the shadowy glade,
   Romantic Nature to the enthusiast child
   Grew dearer far than when serene she smiled,
   In uncontrasted loveliness arrayed.
But O! in every scene, with sacred sway,
   Her graces fire me; from the bloom that spreads
   Resplendent in the lucid morn of May,
To the green light the little glow-worm sheds
   On mossy banks, when midnight glooms prevail,
   And softest silence broods o'er all the dale.

(1799)

179. 'Seek not, my Lesbia, the sequestered dale'

Seek not, my Lesbia, the sequestered dale,
   Or bear thou to its shades a *tranquil* heart;
   Since rankles most in *solitude* the smart
   Of injured charms and talents, when they fail
To meet their due regard;—nor e'en prevail
   Where most they wish to please:—Yet, since thy part
   Is large in Life's chief blessings, why desert

Sullen the world?—Alas! how many wail
Dire loss of the best comforts Heaven can grant!
  While they the bitter tear in secret pour,
  Smote by the death of Friends, Disease, or Want,
Slight wrongs if thy self-valuing soul deplore,
  Thou but resemblest, in thy lonely haunt,
  Narcissus pining on the watery shore.

                                 (1799)

180. *To Honora Sneyd*

Honora, should that cruel time arrive
  When 'gainst my truth thou should'st my errors poise,
  Scorning remembrance of our vanished joys;
  When for the love-warm looks, in which I live,
But cold respect must greet me, that shall give
  No tender glance, no kind regretful sighs;
  When thou shalt pass me with averted eyes,
  Feigning thou see'st me not, to sting, and grieve,
And sicken my sad heart, I could not bear
  Such dire eclipse of thy soul-cheering rays;
  I could not learn my struggling heart to tear
From thy loved form, that through my memory strays;
  Nor in the pale horizon of despair
  Endure the wintry and the darkened days.

                                 (1799)

181. *'Ingratitude, how deadly is thy smart'*

Ingratitude, how deadly is thy smart
  Proceeding from the form we fondly love!
  How light, compared, all *other* sorrows prove!
  Thou shed'st a *night* of woe, from whence depart
The gentle beams of patience, that the heart
  'Mid *lesser* ills, illume.—*Thy* victims rove
  Unquiet as the ghost that haunts the grove
  Where Murder spilt the life-blood.—O! thy dart
Kills *more* than life,—e'en all that makes life dear;
  Till we "the sensible of pain" would change
  For frenzy, that defies the bitter tear;
Or wish, in kindred callousness, to range
  Where moon-eyed Idiocy, with fallen lip,
  Drags the loose knee, and intermitting step.

                                 (1799)

182. *To* ———

Farewell, false Friend!—our scenes of kindness close!
  To cordial looks, to sunny smiles farewell!

To sweet consolings, that can grief expel,
And every joy soft sympathy bestows!
For altered looks, where truth no longer glows,
   Thou hast prepared my heart;—and it was well
   To bid thy pen the unlooked for story tell,
   Falsehood avowed, that shame, nor sorrow knows.—
O! when we meet,—(to meet we're destined, try
   To avoid it as thou may'st) on either brow,
   Nor in the stealing consciousness of eye,
Be seen the slightest trace of what, or how
   We once were to each other;—nor one sigh
   Flatter with weak regret a broken vow!

                                         (1799)

183. December Morning

I love to rise ere gleams the tardy light,
   Winter's pale dawn;—and as warm fires illume,
   And cheerful tapers shine around the room,
   Through misty windows bend my musing sight
Where, round the dusky lawn, the mansions white,
   With shutters closed, peer faintly through the gloom,
   That slow recedes; while yon gray spires assume,
   Rising from their dark pile, an added height
By indistinctness given.—Then to decree
   The grateful thoughts to God, ere they unfold
   To friendship, or the Muse, or seek with glee
Wisdom's rich page!—O, hours! more worth than gold,
   By whose blest use we lengthen life, and free
   From drear decays of age, outlive the old!

                                         (1799)

184. 'In every breast affection fires, there dwells'

In every breast affection fires, there dwells
   A secret consciousness to what degree
   They are themselves beloved.—We hourly see
   The involuntary proof, that either quells,
Or ought to quell false hopes,—or sets us free
   From pained distrust;—but, O, the misery!
   Weak self-delusion timidly repels
   The lights obtrusive—shrinks form all that tells
Unwelcome truths, and vainly seeks repose
   For startled fondness, in the opiate balm,
   Of kind profession, though, perchance, it flows
To hush complaint—O! in belief's clear calm,
   Or 'mid the lurid clouds of doubt, we find
   Love rise the sun, or comet of the mind.

                                         (1799)

185. *To Mr. Henry Cary, On the Publication of his Sonnets*

Praised be the poet, who the sonnet's claim,
  Severest of the orders that belong
  Distinct and separate to the Delphic Song,
  Shall venerate, nor its appropriate name
Lawless assume. Peculiar is its frame,
  From him derived, who shunned the city throng,
  And warbled sweet thy rocks and streams among,
  Lonely Valclusa!—and that heir of fame,
Our greater Milton, hath, by many a lay
  Formed on that arduous model, fully shown
  That English verse may happily display
Those strict energic measures, which alone
  Deserve the name of sonnet, and convey
  A grandeur, grace and spirit, all their own.

(1799)

186. *To a Young Lady, Purposing to Marry a Man of Immoral Character in the Hope of his Reformation*

Time, and thy charms, thou fanciest will redeem
  Yon aweless libertine from rooted vice.
  Misleading thought! has he not paid the price,
  His taste for virtue?—Ah, the sensual stream
Has flowed too long.—What charms can so entice,
  What frequent guilt so pall, as not to shame
  The rash belief, presumptuous and unwise,
  That crimes habitual will forsake the frame?—
Thus, on the river's bank, in fabled lore,
  The rustic stands; sees the stream swiftly go,
  And thinks he soon shall find the gulf below
A channel dry, which he may safe pass o'er.—
  Vain hope!—it flows—and flows—and yet will flow,
  Volume decreaseless, to the *final hour.*

(1799)

187. *To the Poppy*

While summer roses all their glory yield
  To crown the votary of love and joy,
  Misfortune's victim hails, with many a sigh,
  Thee, scarlet Poppy of the pathless field,
Gaudy, yet wild and lone; no leaf to shield
  Thy flaccid vest, that, as the gale blows high,
  Flaps, and alternate folds around thy head.—
So stands in the long grass a love-crazed maid,
  Smiling aghast; while stream to every wind
  Her garish ribbons, smeared with dust and rain;

But brain-sick visions cheat her tortured mind,
And bring false peace. Thus, lulling grief and pain,
Kind dreams oblivious from thy juice proceed,
Thou flimsy, showy, melancholy weed.

(1799)

188. *On a Lock of Miss Sarah Seward's Hair Who Died in her Twentieth Year*

My Angel Sister, though thy lovely form
   Perished in youth's gay morning, yet is mine
   This precious ringlet!—still the soft hairs shine,
   Still glow the nut-brown tints, all bright and warm
With sunny gleam!—Alas! each kindred charm
   Vanished long since; deep in the silent shrine
   Withered to shapeless dust!—and of their grace
   Memory alone retains the faithful trace.—
Dear lock, had thy sweet owner lived, ere now
   Time on her brow had faded thee!—My care
   Screened from the sun and dew thy golden glow;
And thus her early beauty dost thou wear,
   Thou *all* of that fair frame my love could save
   From the resistless ravage of the *grave!*

(1799)

189. *'On the damp margin of the sea-beat shore'*

On the damp margin of the sea-beat shore
   Lonely at eve to wander;—or reclined
   Beneath a rock, what time the rising wind
   Mourns o'er the waters, and, with solemn roar,
Vast billows into caverns surging pour,
   And back recede alternate; while combined
   Loud shriek the sea-fowls, harbingers assigned,
   Clamorous and fearful, of the stormy hour;
To listen with deep thought those awful sounds;
   Gaze on the boiling, the tumultuous waste,
   Or promontory rude, or craggy mounds
Staying the furious main, delight has cast
   O'er my rapt spirit, and my thrilling heart,
   Dear as the softer joys green vales impart.

(1799)

190. *Written December 1790*

Lyre of the sonnet, that full many a time
   Amused my lassitude, and soothed my pains,

When graver cares forbade the *lengthened* strains,
  To thy brief bound, and oft-returning chime
A long farewell!—the splendid forms of rhyme
  When Grief in lonely orphanism reigns,
  Oppress the drooping Soul.—Death's dark domains
  Throw mournful shadows o'er the Aonian clime;
For in their silent borne my filial bands
  Lie all dissolved;—and swiftly wasting pour
From my frail glass of life, health's sparkling sands.
Sleep then, my Lyre, thy tuneful tasks are o'er,
  Sleep! for my heart bereaved, and listless hands
  Wake with rapt touch thy glowing strings no more!

                                                     (1799)

Jane West
(1758–1852)

Even when her children were small, Jane West published books of poetry, including *Miscellaneous Poems Written at an Early Period in Life* (1786), *An Elegy on the Death of the Right Honourable Edmund Burke* (1797), and *The Mother, a Poem in Five Books* (1809), as well as plays and novels. She also wrote conduct books and essays. West's novel *A Gossip's Story* (1796) was the main source for Jane Austen's *Sense and Sensibility*. A political conservative, West maintained that her housework took precedence over her writing. Her anti-Jacobinism is explicit in her second novel, *A Tale of the Times* (1799), whose villain is a supporter of the French Revolution. In 1833, she brought out a volume of *Sacred Poems*.

191. To May

Come May, the empire of the earth assume,
  Be crowned with flowers as universal queen;
  Take from fresh budded groves their tender green
Bespangled with Pomona's richest bloom,
And form thy vesture. Let the sun illume
  The dew-drops glittering in the blue serene,
  And let them hang, like orient pearls, between
Thy locks besprent with Flora's best perfume.
Attend your sovereign's steps, ye balmy gales!
  O'er her ambrosial floods of fragrance pour;
Let livelier verdure animate the vales,
  And brighter hues embellish every flower;
And hark, the concert of the woodland hails,
  All gracious May! thy presence, and thy power.

                                                     (1799)

Ann Home Hunter
(1742–1821)

First cousin of poet and playwright Joanna Baillie, Anne Home Hunter lived in London and was married to the distinguished surgeon John Hunter, with whom she had four children. She was the friend of Hester Lynch Piozzi and Elizabeth Carter and of Joseph Haydn, who set to music her poems "Dear to my Heart as Life's Warm Streams" and "My Mother Bids me Bind my Hair." A collection of her work, *Poems,* was published in 1802 and went into a second edition the following year. She faced poverty after her husband's death until she sold what became the Hunterian Museum to the British government.

192. Winter

Behold the gloomy tyrant's awful form
Binding the captive earth in icy chains;
His chilling breath sweeps o'er the watery plains,
Howls in the blast, and swells the rising storm.

See from its center bends the rifted tower,
Threat'ning the lowly vale with frowning pride,
O'er the scared flocks that seek its sheltering side,
A fearful ruin o'er their heads to pour.

While to the cheerful hearth and social board
Content and ease repair, the sons of want
Receive from niggard fate their pittance scant;
And where some shed bleak covert may afford,
Wan poverty, amidst her meager host
Casts round her haggard eyes, and shivers at the frost.

(1802)

Eliza Kirkham Mathews
(1772–1802)

Eliza (or Elizabeth) Kirkham Mathews published *Poems* (1796) by subscription under her birth name, Strong. She worked for a time as a teacher in Swansea, Wales, and contributed to the *Monthly Mirror.* In 1797, she married Charles Mathews, a well-known comedian and actor. With her husband's work keeping him frequently away on extended trips, she wrote several novels, a stage adaptation, children's books, and many poems. She also struggled with the couple's financial problems and battled tuberculosis. In 1801, she published *What Has Been,* a tale whose heroine finds that writing a novel cannot support her family. A collection of her *Poems,* including sonnets, elegies, and odes, was published by subscription in 1802, the year of her death.

193. The Indian

Alone, unfriended, on a foreign shore,
  Behold an hapless, melancholy maid,
Begging her scanty fare from door to door,
  With piteous voice, and humbly bended head.
Alas! her native tongue is known to few;
  Her manners and her garb excite surprise;
The vulgar stare to see her bid adieu;
  Her tattered garments fix their curious eyes.
Cease, cease your laugh, ye thoughtless vain;
Why sneer at yon poor Indian's pain?
'Tis nature's artless voice that speaks:—
Behold! the tear, bedew her cheeks!
Imploring actions,—bursting sighs,
Reveal enough to British eyes!

(1802)

William Cowper
(1731–1800)

William Cowper suffered from acute depression as well as recurring attacks of mental illness, and attempted suicide several times. He felt isolated and spurned by providence—a theme that appears in his major works, such as "The Castaway" (1803). A bright spot in his life was his friendship with Mary Unwin. They became engaged, but his recurring mental illness and her poor health prevented the marriage from taking place. Cowper's works, including *The Task* (1785), were canonical during the Romantic era.

194. To Mrs. Unwin

Mary! I want a lyre with other strings;
Such aid from Heaven, as some have feigned they drew!
An eloquence scarce given to mortals, new,
And undebased by praise of meaner things!
That ere through age or woe I shed my wings,
I may record thy worth, with honor due,
In verse as musical, as thou art true,
Verse, that immortalizes whom it sings!

But thou hast little need: There is a book
By seraphs writ with beams of heavenly light,
On which the eyes of God not rarely look;
A chronicle of actions just and bright!

There all thy deeds, my faithful Mary, shine,
And since thou own'st that praise, I spare thee mine.

(1803)

195. To George Romney, Esq.

Romney! expert infallible to trace,
On chart or canvas, not the form alone,
And 'semblance, but, however, faintly shown,
The mind's impression too on every face,
With strokes that time ought never to erase:
Thou hast so penciled mine, that though I own
The subject worthless, I have never known
The artist shining with superior grace.

But this I mark, that symptoms none of woe
In thy incomparable work appear:
Well! I am satisfied, it should be so,
Since, on maturer thought, the course is clear;

For in my looks what sorrow could'st thou see,
While I was Hayley's guest, and sat to thee?

(1803)

Henry Kirke White
(1785–1806)

Henry Kirke White's literary ambitions, it was said, drove him to an early grave. His poetry lived after him, earning the praise of Lord Byron and Robert Southey. Charmed by White's unsuccessful 1803 volume, *Clifton Grove*, Southey had encouraged White in his literary endeavors. After White's death in 1806, Southey assembled his works for a posthumous edition that remained popular for the first half of the nineteenth century.

196. 'Give me a cottage on some Cambrian wild'

Give me a cottage on some Cambrian wild,
    Where, far from cities, I may spend my days:
And, by the beauties of the scene beguiled,
    May pity man's pursuits, and shun his ways.
While on the rock I mark the browsing goat,
    List to the mountain torrent's distant noise,
Or the hoarse bittern's solitary note,
    I shall not want the world's delusive joys;
But, with my little scrip, my book, my lyre,
    Shall think my lot complete, nor covet more;
And when, with time, shall wane the vital fire,

I'll raise my pillow on the desert shore,
And lay me down to rest where the wild wave
Shall make sweet music o'er my lonely grave.

(1803)

197. The Winter Traveler

God help thee, Traveler, on thy journey far;
  The wind is bitter keen,—the snow o'erlays
  The hidden pits, and dangerous hollow-ways,
And darkness will involve thee.—No kind star
To-night will guide thee, Traveler,—and the war
  Of winds and elements, on thy head will break,
  And in thy agonizing ear the shriek,
Of spirits howling on their stormy car,
Will often ring appalling—I portend
  A dismal night—and on my wakeful bed
  Thoughts, Traveler, of thee, will fill my head,
And him, who rides where winds and waves contend,
And strives, rude cradled on the seas, to guide
His lonely bark through the tempestuous tide.

(1803)

Mrs. B. Finch
(fl. 1805)

Finch's 126-page book, *Sonnets, and Other Poems: To Which are Added Tales in Prose,* was published in London in 1805 by Blacks and Parry. Its contents suggest that she was born in the country, wrote from a place called "Duncroft Cottage," was the mother of at least one son, and was interested in botany. However, her first name, along with other biographical details, is now obscure.

198. Written in a Shrubbery Towards the Decline of Autumn

See, o'er its withering leaves, the musk-rose bend,
  And scarce a purple aster paints the glade;
Yet, cease awhile, ye ruffling winds! to rend
  This variegated canopy of shade.
Here, autumn's touch the rich dark brown bestows,
  There, mixed with paler leaves of yellow hue,
The shining holly's scarlet fruitage glows,
  And crimson berries stud the deep-green yew.
Thou radiant orb! whose mild declining ray
  Now gilds with gayer tinge this loved retreat,
Yet, lingering, still prolong the golden day.—
  How vain the wish! no more thy glories meet

My dazzled eye; but from the lakes arise
Blue mists, and twilight gray involves the blushing skies.

(1805)

199. Written in a Winter's Morning

Though storms and tempests mark thy gloomy reign,
    Stern winter! still the poet's eye shall find
Full many a charm to linger in thy train—
Spread round thy frozen panoply of snow;
    In icy chains, each brook and streamlet bind;
Still unappalled the Christmas rose shall blow,
And beauteous crocuses their golden bloom
    Disclose, ere yet thy ruthless reign be past;
And bright mezereon breathe its faint perfume,
    Amid the rigors of thy northern blast:
Whilst on the leafless lime pale mistletoe
    Its wax-like berries hangs, and green of sickly cast.
And the sweet redbreast, from his laurel bower,
Warbles his vespers clear, at twilight's sober hour.

(1805)

Anna Maria Smallpiece
(fl. 1805)

Joseph Johnson, the radical publisher of books by Maria Edgeworth, Anna
Letitia Barbauld, and Mary Wollstonecraft, brought out Anna Maria Small-
piece's 182-page volume *Original Sonnets, and Other Small Poems* in 1805.
She spent her childhood in Woburn, Bedfordshire and traveled to Cornwall,
London, Devonshire, and abroad, but little else is known about her.

200. Written in Ill Health

Ah! what avails, when sinking down to sleep,
That silken curtains shade the languid eye?
On beds of down how many wake to weep,
And break the calm of night with sorrow's sigh!
O! then, thou poor, ne'er at thy lot repine,
If o'er thy straw-stuffed bed no trappings play;
More pure thy sleep, and calmer dreams are thine,
Than those who waste in luxury their day.
If o'er thy cheek the loose-zoned goddess, Health,
With coral finger, spread her rosy hues,
Far art thou blessed, beyond the joys of wealth,
And all the joys the busy crowd pursues.
Nor more would I at little ills repine,
Were her full eye, and sparkling luster mine.

(1805)

201. 'The veil's removed, the gaudy, flimsy veil'

The veil's removed, the gaudy, flimsy veil,
That shrouded thy false heart, and now I see,
With friendship pure, it never beat for me.
Fool! that I was, to listen to the tale.
Well, be it so—this pleasure must prevail,
Though at thy falsehood much my heart has grieved,
Thou canst not say, I e'er thy hopes deceived.
This still my solace; should all others fail,
What now remains of life I will employ
In bliss less fragile; Nature's charms sublime,
Her hills and woodlands wild, reechoing joy,
Her blushing spring, and summer's flowery prime,
Though winter for awhile her sweets destroy,
They still return, on wings of faithful time.

(1805)

William Wordsworth
(1770–1850)

Over the course of roughly fifty years, Wordsworth wrote well over 500 sonnets. His first published poem was a sonnet and his sonnet sequence *The River Duddon* was among the most successful and admired works he ever published. Many of his best sonnets appeared in *Poems, In Two Volumes* (1807). While Wordsworth evidently admired the sonnets of Charlotte Smith, Anna Seward, and Helen Maria Williams, his poetic allegiance lay most strongly with Milton. Wordsworth's prodigious output of sonnets demonstrates a remarkable variety of subjects and concerns, ranging from the political to the personal to the philosophical to the topographical. He succeeded Robert Southey as poet laureate in 1843.

202. On Seeing Miss Helen Maria Williams Weep at a Tale of Distress

She wept—Life's purple tide began to flow
In languid streams through every thrilling vein;
Dim were my swimming eyes—my pulse beat slow,
And my full heart was swelled to dear delicious pain.
Life left my loaded heart, and closing eye;
A sigh recalled the wand'rer to my breast;
Dear was the pulse of life, and dear the sigh
That called the wand'rer home, and home to rest.
That tear proclaims—in thee each virtue dwells,
And bright will shine in misery's midnight hour;
As the soft star of dewy evening tells
What radiant fires were drowned by day's malignant power

That only wait the darkness of the night
To cheer the wand'ring wretch with hospitable light.

(1787)

203. 1801

I grieved for Buonaparte, with a vain
And an unthinking grief! the vital blood
Of that man's mind—what can it be? What food
Fed his first hopes? What knowledge could he gain?
'Tis not in battles that from youth we train
The Governor who must be wise and good,
And temper with the sternness of the brain
Thoughts motherly, and meek as womanhood.
Wisdom doth live with children round her knees:
Books, leisure, perfect freedom, and the talk
Man holds with week-day man in the hourly walk
Of the mind's business: these are the degrees
By which true Sway doth mount; this is the stalk
True Power doth grow on; and her rights are these.

(1802)

204. '"With how sad steps, O Moon thou climb'st the sky"'

"With how sad steps, O Moon thou climb'st the sky,
How silently, and with how wan a face!"
Where art thou? Thou whom I have seen on high
Running among the clouds a wood–nymph's race?
Unhappy nuns, whose common breath's a sigh
Which they would stifle, move at such a pace!
The Northern Wind, to call thee to the chase,
Must blow tonight his bugle horn. Had I
The power of Merlin, Goddess! this should be:
And all the stars, now shrouded up in heaven,
Should sally forth to keep thee company.
What strife would then be yours, fair creatures, driv'n
Now up, now down, and sparkling in your glee!
But, Cynthia, should to thee the palm be giv'n,
Queen both for beauty and for majesty.

(1807)

205. 'Nuns fret not at their convent's narrow room'

Nuns fret not at their convent's narrow room;
And hermits are contented with their cells;
And students with their pensive citadels;
Maids at the wheel, the weaver at his loom,

Sit blithe and happy; bees that soar for bloom,
High as the highest peak of Furness Fells,
Will murmur by the hour in foxglove bells:
In truth, the prison, unto which we doom
Ourselves, no prison is: and hence to me,
In sundry moods, 'twas pastime to be bound
Within the Sonnet's scanty plot of ground:
Pleased if some souls (for such there needs must be)
Who have felt the weight of too much liberty,
Should find short solace there, as I have found.

(1807)

206. 'How sweet it is, when mother Fancy rocks'

How sweet it is, when mother Fancy rocks
The wayward brain, to saunter through a wood!
An old place, full of many a lovely brood,
Tall trees, green arbors, and ground flowers in flocks;
And Wild rose tip-toe upon hawthorn stocks,
Like to a bonny lass, who plays her pranks
At wakes and fairs with wandering mountebanks,
When she stands cresting the clown's head, and mocks
The crowd beneath her. Verily I think,
Such place to me is sometimes like a dream
Or map of the whole world: thoughts, link by link,
Enter through ears and eyesight, with such gleam
Of all things, that at last in fear I shrink,
And leap at once from the delicious stream.

(1807)

207. 'Where lies the land to which yon ship must go?'

Where lies the land to which yon ship must go?
Festively she puts forth in trim array;
As vigorous as a lark at break of day:
Is she for tropic suns, or polar snow?
What boots the enquiry? Neither friend nor foe
She cares for; let her travel where she may,
She finds familiar names, a beaten way
Ever before her, and a wind to blow.
Yet still I ask, what haven is her mark?
And, almost as it was when ships were rare,
From time to time, like pilgrims, here and there
Crossing the waters; doubt, and something dark,
Of the old sea some reverential fear,
Is with me at thy farewell, joyous bark!

(1807)

208. *Composed after a Journey across the Hamilton Hills, Yorkshire*

Ere we had reached the wished-for place, night fell:
We were too late at least by one dark hour,
And nothing could we see of all that power
Of prospect, whereof many thousands tell.
The western sky did recompense us well
With Grecian temple, minaret, and bower;
And, in one part, a minster with its tower
Substantially distinct, a place for bell
Or clock to toll from. Many a glorious pile
Did we behold, sights that might well repay
All disappointment! and, as such, the eye
Delighted in them; but we felt, the while,
We should forget them: they are of the sky,
And from our earthly memory fade away.

(1807)

209. *'These words were uttered in a pensive mood'*

. . . . . . *they are of the sky,*
And from our earthly memory fade away.

These words were uttered in a pensive mood,
Even while mine eyes were on that solemn sight:
A contrast and reproach to gross delight,
And life's unspiritual pleasures daily wooed!
But now upon this thought I cannot brood:
It is unstable, and deserts me quite;
Nor will I praise a cloud, however bright,
Disparaging Man's gifts, and proper food.
The grove, the sky-built temple, and the dome,
Though clad in colors beautiful and pure,
Find in the heart of man no natural home:
The immortal Mind craves objects that endure:
These cleave to it; from these it cannot roam,
Nor they from it: their fellowship is secure.

(1807)

210. *'With ships the sea was sprinkled far and nigh'*

With ships the sea was sprinkled far and nigh,
Like stars in heaven, and joyously it showed;
Some lying fast at anchor in the road,
Some veering up and down, one knew not why.
A goodly vessel did I then espy
Come like a giant from a haven broad;
And lustily along the bay she strode,
Her tackling rich, and of apparel high.

This ship was nought to me, nor I to her,
Yet I pursued her with a lover's look;
This ship to all the rest did I prefer:
When will she turn, and whither? She will brook
No tarrying; where she comes the winds must stir:
On went she, and due north her journey took.

(1807)

211. *Composed Upon Westminster Bridge, Sept. 3, 1803*

Earth has not any thing to show more fair:
Dull would he be of soul who could pass by
A sight so touching in its majesty:
This city now doth like a garment wear
The beauty of the morning; silent, bare,
Ships, towers, domes, theaters, and temples lie
Open unto the fields, and to the sky;
All bright and glittering in the smokeless air.
Never did sun more beautifully steep
In his first splendor valley, rock, or hill;
Ne'er saw I, never felt, a calm so deep!
The river glideth at his own sweet will:
Dear God! the very houses seem asleep;
And all that mighty heart is lying still!

(1807)

212. *'Methought I saw the footsteps of a throne'*

Methought I saw the footsteps of a throne
Which mists and vapors from mine eyes did shroud,
Nor view of him who sate thereon allowed;
But all the steps and ground about were strown
With sights the ruefullest that flesh and bone
Ever put on; a miserable crowd,
Sick, hale, old, young, who cried before that cloud,
"Thou art our king, O Death! to thee we groan."
I seemed to mount those steps; the vapors gave
Smooth way; and I beheld the face of one
Sleeping alone within a mossy cave,
With her face up to heaven; that seemed to have
Pleasing remembrance of a thought foregone;
A lovely beauty in a summer grave!

(1807)

213. *'The world is too much with us'*

The world is too much with us; late and soon,
Getting and spending, we lay waste our powers:
Little we see in Nature that is ours;

We have given our hearts away, a sordid boon!
This sea that bares her bosom to the moon;
The winds that will be howling at all hours
And are up-gathered now like sleeping flowers;
For this, for every thing, we are out of tune;
It moves us not—Great God! I'd rather be
A Pagan suckled in a creed outworn;
So might I, standing on this pleasant lea,
Have glimpses that would make me less forlorn
Have sight of Proteus coming from the sea;
Or hear old Triton blow his wreathed horn.

(1807)

214. 'It is a beauteous evening, calm and free'

It is a beauteous evening, calm and free;
The holy time is quiet as a nun
Breathless with adoration; the broad sun
Is sinking down in its tranquillity;
The gentleness of heaven is on the Sea:
Listen! the mighty Being is awake,
And doth with his eternal motion make
A sound like thunder—everlastingly.
Dear Child! dear Girl! that walkest with me here,
If thou appear'st untouched by solemn thought,
Thy nature is not therefore less divine:
Thou liest in Abraham's bosom all the year;
And worshipp'st at the Temple's inner shrine,
God being with thee when we know it not.

(1807)

215. Composed by the Sea-Side, near Calais, August, 1802

Fair star of evening, splendor of the west,
Star of my country! on the horizon's brink
Thou hangest, stooping, as might seem, to sink
On England's bosom; yet well pleased to rest,
Meanwhile, and be to her a glorious crest
Conspicuous to the nations. Thou, I think,
Should'st be my country's emblem; and should'st wink,
Bright Star! with laughter on her banners, dressed
In thy fresh beauty. There! that dusky spot
Beneath thee, it is England; there it lies.
Blessings be on you both! one hope, one lot,
One life, one glory! I, with many a fear
For my dear country, many heartfelt sighs,
Among men who do not love her linger here.

(1807)

216. To Toussaint L'Ouverture

Toussaint, the most unhappy Man of Men!
Whether the rural milk-maid by her cow
Sing in thy hearing, or thou liest now
Alone in some deep dungeon's earless den,
O miserable chieftain! where and when
Wilt thou find patience? Yet die not; do thou
Wear rather in thy bonds a cheerful brow:
Though fallen thyself, never to rise again,
Live, and take comfort. Thou hast left behind
Powers that will work for thee; air, earth, and skies;
There's not a breathing of the common wind
That will forget thee; thou has great allies;
Thy friends are exultations, agonies,
And love, and Man's unconquerable mind.

(1807)

217. London, 1802

Milton! thou should'st be living at this hour:
England hath need of thee: she is a fen
Of stagnant waters: altar, sword and pen,
Fireside, the heroic wealth of hall and bower,
Have forfeited their ancient English dower
Of inward happiness. We are selfish men;
Oh! raise us up, return to us again;
And give us manners, virtue, freedom, power.
Thy soul was like a star and dwelt apart:
Thou hadst a voice whose sound was like the sea;
Pure as the naked heavens, majestic, free,
So didst thou travel on life's common way,
In cheerful godliness; and yet thy heart
The lowliest duties on itself did lay.

(1807)

218. October, 1803

When, looking on the present face of things,
I see one Man, of Men the meanest too!
Raised up to sway the World, to do, undo,
With mighty nations for his underlings,
The great events with which old story rings
Seem vain and hollow; I find nothing great;
Nothing is left which I can venerate;
So that almost a doubt within me springs
Of Providence, such emptiness at length
Seems at the heart of all things. But, great God!

I measure back the steps which I have trod,
And tremble, seeing, as I do, the strength
Of such poor instruments, with thoughts sublime
I tremble at the sorrow of the time.

(1807)

219. 'Surprised by joy—impatient as the wind'

Surprised by joy—impatient as the wind
I turned to share the transport—Oh! with whom
But thee, long buried in the silent tomb,
That spot which no vicissitude can find?
Love, faithful love, recalled thee to my mind—
But how could I forget thee?—Through what power,
Even for the least division of an hour,
Have I been so beguiled as to be blind
To my most grievous loss?—That thought's return
Was the worst pang that sorrow ever bore,
Save one, one only, when I stood forlorn,
Knowing my heart's best treasure was no more;
That neither present time, nor years unborn
Could to my sight that heavenly face restore.

(1815)

220–252. The River Duddon
A Series of Sonnets

The River Duddon rises upon Wrynose Tell, on the
confines of Westmorland, Cumberland, and Lancashire;
and, serving as a boundary to the two latter counties, for
the space of about twenty-five miles, enters the Irish sea,
between the isle of Walney and the lordship of Millum.

220. I

Not envying shades which haply yet may throw
A grateful coolness round that rocky spring,
Bandusia, once responsive to the string
Of the Horatian lyre with babbling flow;
Careless of flowers that in perennial blow
Round the moist marge of Persian fountains cling;
Heedless of Alpine torrents thundering
Through icy portals radiant as heaven's bow;
I seek the birth-place of a native Stream.—
All hail ye mountains, hail thou morning light!
Better to breathe upon this aery height

Than pass in needless sleep from dream to dream;
Pure flow the verse, pure, vigorous, free, and bright,
For Duddon, long-loved Duddon, is my theme!

(1820)

221. II

Child of the clouds! remote from every taint
Of sordid industry thy lot is cast;
Thine are the honors of the lofty waste;
Not seldom, when with heat the valleys faint,
Thy hand-maid Frost with spangled tissue quaint
Thy cradle decks; —to chant thy birth, thou hast
No meaner poet than the whistling blast,
And Desolation is thy Patron-saint!
She guards thee, ruthless Power! who would not spare
Those mighty forests, once the bison's screen,
Where stalked the huge deer to his shaggy lair
Through paths and alleys roofed with somber green,
Thousand of years before the silent air
Was pierced by whizzing shaft of hunter keen!

(1820)

222. III

How shall I paint thee?—Be this naked stone
My seat while I give way to such intent;
Pleased could my verse, a speaking monument,
Make to the eyes of men thy features known.
But as of all those tripping lambs not one
Outruns his fellows, so hath nature lent
To thy beginning nought that doth present
Peculiar grounds for hope to build upon.
To dignify the spot that gives thee birth,
No sign of hoar Antiquity's esteem
Appears, and none of modern fortune's care;
Yet thou thyself hast round thee shed a gleam
Of brilliant moss, instinct with freshness rare;
Prompt offering to thy foster-mother, Earth!

(1820)

223. IV

Take, cradled nursling of the mountain, take
This parting glance, no negligent adieu!
A Protean change seems wrought while I pursue
The curves, a loosely-scattered chain doth make;
Or rather thou appear'st a glistering snake,

Silent, and to the gazer's eye untrue,
Thridding with sinuous lapse the rushes, through
Dwarf willows gliding, and by the ferny brake.
Starts from a dizzy steep the undaunted rill
Robed instantly in garb of snow-white foam;
And laughing dares the adventurer, who hath clomb
So high, a rival purpose to fulfill;
Else let the dastard backward wend, and roam,
Seeking less bold achievement, where he will!

(1820)

224. V

Sole listener, Duddon! to the breeze that played
With thy clear voice, I caught the fitful sound
Wafted o'er sullen moss and craggy mound,
Unfruitful solitudes, that seemed to upbraid
The sun in heaven!—but now, to form a shade
For Thee, green alders have together wound
Their foliage; ashes flung their arms around;
And birch-trees risen in silver colonnade.
And thou hast also tempted here to rise,
'Mid sheltering pines, this cottage rude and gray;
Whose ruddy children, by the mother's eyes
Carelessly watched, sport through the summer day,
Thy pleased associates:—light as endless May
On infant bosoms lonely Nature lies.

(1820)

225. VI. Flowers

Ere yet our course was graced with social trees
It lacked not old remains of hawthorn bowers,
Where small birds warbled to their paramours;
And, earlier still, was heard the hum of bees;
I saw them ply their harmless robberies,
And caught the fragrance which the sundry flowers,
Fed by the stream with soft perpetual showers,
Plenteously yielded to the vagrant breeze.
There bloomed the strawberry of the wilderness;
The trembling eye-bright showed her sapphire blue,
The thyme her purple like the blush of even;
And, if the breath of some to no caress
Invited, forth they peeped so fair to view,
All kinds alike seemed favorites of Heaven.

(1820)

226. VII

"Change me, some God, into that breathing rose!"
The love-sick stripling fancifully sighs,
The envied flower beholding, as it lies
On Laura's breast, in exquisite repose;
Or he would pass into her bird, that throws
The darts of song from out its wiry cage;
Enraptured,—could he for himself engage
The thousandth part of what the nymph bestows,
And what the little careless innocent
Ungraciously receives. Too daring choice!
There are whose calmer mind it would content
To be an unculled flow'ret of the glen,
Fearless of plough and scythe; or darkling wren,
That tunes of Duddon's banks her slender voice.

(1820)

227. VIII

What aspect bore the man who roved or fled,
First of his tribe, to this dark dell—who first
In this pellucid current slaked his thirst?
What hopes came with him? what designs were spread
Along his path? His unprotected bed
What dreams encompassed? Was the intruder nursed
In hideous usages, and rites accursed,
That thinned the living and disturbed the dead?
No voice replies;—the earth, the air is mute;
And thou, blue streamlet, murmuring yield'st no more
Than a soft record that whatever fruit
Of ignorance thou might'st witness heretofore,
Thy function was to heal and to restore,
To soothe and cleanse, not madden and pollute!

(1820)

228. IX. The Stepping-Stones

The struggling rill insensibly is grown
Into a brook of loud and stately march,
Crossed ever and anon by plank and arch;
And, for like use, lo! what might seem a zone
Chosen for ornament; stone matched with stone
In studied symmetry, with interspace
For the clear waters to pursue their race
Without restraint.—How swiftly have they flown!
Succeeding—still succeeding! Here the child

Puts, when the high-swol'n flood runs fierce and wild,
His budding courage to the proof;—and here
Declining manhood learns to note the sly
And sure encroachments of infirmity,
Thinking how fast time runs, life's end how near!

                                                        (1820)

229. X. The Same Subject

Not so that pair whose youthful spirits dance
With prompt emotion, urging them to pass;
A sweet confusion checks the shepherd-lass;
Blushing she eyes the dizzy flood askance,—
To stop ashamed—too timid to advance;
She ventures once again—another pause!
His outstretched hand he tauntingly withdraws—
She sues for help with piteous utterance!
Chidden she chides again; the thrilling touch
Both feel when he renews the wished-for aid:
Ah! if their fluttering hearts should stir too much,
Should beat too strongly, both may be betrayed.
The frolic loves who, from yon high rock, see
The struggle, clap their wings for victory!

                                                        (1820)

230. XI. The Faery Chasm

No fiction was it of the antique age:
A sky-blue stone, within this sunless cleft,
Is of the very foot-marks unbereft
Which tiny elves impressed;—on that smooth stage
Dancing with all their brilliant equipage
In secret revels—haply after theft
Of some sweet babe, flower stolen, and coarse weed left,
For the distracted mother to assuage
Her grief with, as she might!—But, where, oh where
Is traceable a vestige of the notes
That ruled those dances, wild in character?
—Deep underground?—Or in the upper air,
On the shrill wind of midnight? or where floats
O'er twilight fields the autumnal gossamer?

                                                        (1820)

231. XII. Hints for the Fancy

On, loitering Muse!—The swift stream chides us—on!
Albeit his deep-worn channel doth immure
Objects immense, portrayed in miniature,

Wild shapes for many a strange comparison!
Niagaras, Alpine passes, and anon
Abodes of Naiads, calm abysses pure,
Bright liquid mansions, fashioned to endure
When the broad oak drops, a leafless skeleton,
And the solidities of mortal pride,
Palace and tower, are crumbled into dust!
—The Bard who walks with Duddon for his guide,
Shall find such toys of Fancy thickly set:—
Turn from the sight, enamored Muse—we must;
Leave them—and, if thou canst, without regret!

(1820)

232. XIII. Open Prospect

Hail to the fields—with dwellings sprinkled o'er,
And one small hamlet, under a green hill
Clustered with barn and byer, and spouting mill!
A glance suffices,—should we wish for more,
Gay June would scorn us;—but when bleak winds roar
Through the stiff lance-like shoots of pollard ash,
Dread swell of sound! loud as the gusts that lash
The matted forests of Ontario's shore
By wasteful steel unsmitten, then would I
Turn into port,—and, reckless of the gale,
Reckless of angry Duddon sweeping by,
While the warm hearth exalts the mantling ale,
Laugh with the generous household heartily,
At all the merry pranks of Donnerdale!

(1820)

233. XIV

O Mountain Stream! the shepherd and his cot
Are privileged inmates of deep solitude;
Nor would the nicest anchorite exclude
A field or two of brighter green, or plot
Of tillage-ground, that seemeth like a spot
Of stationary sunshine:—thou hast viewed
These only, Duddon! with their paths renewed
By fits and starts, yet this contents thee not.
Thee hath some awful spirit impelled to leave,
Utterly to desert, the haunts of men,
Though simple thy companions were and few;
And through this wilderness a passage cleave
Attended but by thy own voice, save when
The clouds and fowls of the air thy way pursue!

(1820)

234. XV

From this deep chasm—where quivering sunbeams play
Upon its loftiest crags—mine eyes behold
A gloomy niche, capacious, blank, and cold;
A concave free from shrubs and mosses gray;
In semblance fresh, as if, with dire affray,
Some statue, placed amid these regions old
For tutelary service, thence had rolled,
Startling the flight of timid yesterday!
Was it by mortals sculptured?—weary slaves
Of slow endeavor! or abruptly cast
Into rude shape by fire, with roaring blast
Tempestuously let loose from central caves?
Or fashioned by the turbulence of waves,
Then, when o'er highest hills the deluge past?

(1820)

235. XVI. American Tradition

Such fruitless questions may not long beguile
Or plague the fancy, mid the sculptured shows
Conspicuous yet where Oroonoko flows;
There would the Indian answer with a smile
Aimed at the White Man's ignorance, the while
Of the Great Waters telling, how they rose,
Covered the plains, and wandering where they chose,
Mounted through every intricate defile,
Triumphant.—Inundation wide and deep,
O'er which his fathers urged, to ridge and steep
Else unapproachable, their buoyant way;
And carved, on mural cliff's undreaded side,
Sun, moon, and stars, and beast of chase or prey;
Whate'er they sought, shunned, loved, or deified!

(1820)

236. XVII. Return

A dark plume fetch me from yon blasted yew,
Perched on whose top the Danish Raven croaks;
Aloft, the imperial Bird of Rome invokes
Departed ages, shedding where he flew
Loose fragments of wild wailing that bestrew
The clouds, and thrill the chambers of the rocks,
And into silence hush the timorous flocks,
That slept so calmly while the nightly dew
Moistened each fleece, beneath the twinkling stars:
These couched mid that lone camp on Hardknot's height,

Whose guardians bent the knee to Jove and Mars:
These near that mystic round of Druid frame,
Tardily sinking by its proper weight
Deep into patient Earth, from whose smooth breast it came!

(1820)

237. XVIII. Seathwaite Chapel

Sacred Religion, "mother of form and fear,"
Dread Arbitress of mutable respect,
New rites ordaining when the old are wrecked,
Or cease to please the fickle worshipper;
If one strong wish may be embosomed here,
Mother of Love! for this deep vale, protect
Truth's holy lamp, pure source of bright effect,
Gifted to purge the vapory atmosphere
That seeks to stifle it;—as in those days
When this low pile a Gospel teacher knew,
Whose good works formed an endless retinue:
Such priest as Chaucer sang in fervent lays;
Such as the heaven-taught skill of Herbert drew;
And tender Goldsmith crowned with deathless praise!

(1820)

238. XIX. Tributary Stream

My frame hath often trembled with delight
When hope presented some far-distant good,
That seemed from heaven descending, like the flood
Of yon pure waters, from their aery height,
Hurrying with lordly Duddon to unite;
Who, mid a world of images impressed
On the calm depth of his transparent breast,
Appears to cherish most that torrent white,
The fairest, softest, liveliest of them all!
And seldom hath ear listened to a tune
More lulling than the busy hum of noon,
Swoln by that voice—whose murmur musical
Announces to the thirsty fields a boon
Dewy and fresh, till showers again shall fall.

(1820)

239. XX. The Plain of Donnerdale

The old inventive poets, had they seen,
Or rather felt, the entrancement that detains
Thy waters, Duddon! mid these flow'ry plains—
The still repose, the liquid lapse serene,

Transferred to bowers imperishably green,
Had beautified Elysium! But these chains
Will soon be broken;—a rough course remains,
Rough as the past; where thou, of placid mien,
Innocuous as a firstling of a flock,
And countenanced like a soft cerulean sky,
Shalt change thy temper; and, with many a shock
Given and received in mutual jeopardy,
Dance like a Bacchanal from rock to rock,
Tossing her frantic thyrsus wide and high!

(1820)

240. XXI

Whence that low voice?—A whisper from the heart,
That told of days long past when here I roved
With friends and kindred tenderly beloved;
Some who had early mandates to depart,
Yet are allowed to steal my path athwart
By Duddon's side; once more do we unite,
Once more beneath the kind Earth's tranquil light;
And smothered joys into new being start.
From her unworthy seat, the cloudy stall
Of Time, breaks forth triumphant Memory;
Her glistening tresses bound, yet light and free
As golden locks of birch, that rise and fall
On gales that breathe too gently to recall
Aught of the fading year's inclemency!

(1820)

241. XXII. Tradition

A love-lorn maid, at some far-distant time,
Came to this hidden pool, whose depths surpass
In crystal clearness Dian's looking-glass;
And, gazing, saw that rose, which from the prime
Derives its name, reflected as the chime
Of echo doth reverberate some sweet sound:
The starry treasure from the blue profound
She longed to ravish;—shall she plunge, or climb
The humid precipice, and seize the guest
Of April, smiling high in upper air?
Desperate alternative! what fiend could dare
To prompt the thought?—Upon the steep rock's breast
The lonely primrose yet renews its bloom,
Untouched memento of her hapless doom!

(1820)

242. XXIII. *Sheep Washing*

Sad thoughts, avaunt!—the fervor of the year,
Poured on the fleece-encumbered flock, invites
To laving currents, for prelusive rites
Duly performed before the dales-men shear
Their panting charge. The distant mountains hear,
Hear and repeat, the turmoil that unites
Clamor of boys with innocent despites
Of barking dogs, and bleatings from strange fear.
Meanwhile, if Duddon's spotless breast receive
Unwelcome mixtures as the uncouth noise
Thickens, the pastoral river will forgive
Such wrong; nor need *we* blame the licensed joys
Though false to Nature's quiet equipoise:
Frank are the sports, the stains are fugitive.

(1820)

243. XXIV. *The Resting-Place*

Mid-noon is past;—upon the sultry mead
No zephyr breathes, no cloud its shadow throws:
If we advance unstrengthened by repose,
Farewell the solace of the vagrant reed.
This nook, with woodbine hung and straggling weed,
Tempting recess as ever pilgrim chose,
Half grot, half arbor, proffers to enclose
Body and mind, from molestation freed,
In narrow compass—narrow as itself:
Or if the Fancy, too industrious elf,
Be loath that we should breathe awhile exempt
From new incitements friendly to our task,
There wants not stealthy prospect, that may tempt
Loose idless to forego her wily mask.

(1820)

244. XXV

Methinks 'twere no unprecedented feat
Should some benignant minister of air
Lift, and encircle with a cloudy chair,
The One for whom my heart shall ever beat
With tenderest love;—or, if a safer seat
Atween his downy wings be furnished, there
Would lodge her, and the cherished burden bear
O'er hill and valley to this dim retreat!
Rough ways my steps have trod; too rough and long
For her companionship; here dwells soft ease:

With sweets that she partakes not some distaste
Mingles, and lurking consciousness of wrong;
Languish the flowers; the waters seem to waste
Their vocal charm; their sparklings cease to please.

(1820)

245. XXVI

Return, content! for fondly I pursued,
Even when a child, the streams—unheard, unseen;
Through tangled woods, impending rocks between;
Or, free as air, with flying inquest viewed
The sullen reservoirs whence their bold brood,
Pure as the morning, fretful, boisterous, keen,
Green as the salt-sea billows, white and green,
Poured down the hills, a choral multitude!
Nor have I tracked their course for scanty gains;
They taught me random cares and truant joys,
That shield from mischief and preserve from stains
Vague minds, while men are growing out of boys;
Maturer Fancy owes to their rough noise
Impetuous thoughts that brook not servile reins.

(1820)

246. XXVII. Journey Renewed

I rose while yet the cattle, heat-oppressed,
Crowded together under rustling trees,
Brushed by the current of the water-breeze;
And for *their* sakes, and love of all that rest,
On Duddon's margin, in the sheltering nest;
For all the startled scaly tribes that slink
Into his coverts, and each fearless link
Of dancing insects forged upon his breast;
For these, and hopes and recollections worn
Close to the vital seat of human clay;
Glad meetings—tender partings—that upstay
The drooping mind of absence, by vows sworn
In his pure presence near the trysting thorn;
I thanked the leader of my onward way.

(1820)

247. XXVIII

No record tells of lance opposed to lance,
Horse charging horse mid these retired domains;
Nor that their turf drank purple from the veins
Of heroes fall'n, or struggling to advance,

Till doubtful combat issued in a trance
Of victory, that struck through heart and reins,
Even to the inmost seat of mortal pains,
And lightened o'er the pallid countenance.
Yet, to the loyal and the brave, who lie
In the blank earth, neglected and forlorn,
The passing Winds memorial tribute pay;
The Torrents chant their praise, inspiring scorn
Of power usurped,—with proclamation high,
And glad acknowledgment of lawful sway.

(1820)

248. XXIX

Who swerves from innocence, who makes divorce
Of that serene companion—a good name,
Recovers not his loss; but walks with shame,
With doubt, with fear, and haply with remorse.
And oft-times he, who, yielding to the force
Of chance-temptation, ere his journey end,
From chosen comrade turns, or faithful friend,
In vain shall rue the broken intercourse.
Not so with such as loosely wear the chain
That binds them, pleasant river! to thy side:—
Through the rough copse wheel thou with hasty stride,
I choose to saunter o'er the grassy plain,
Sure, when the separation has been tried,
That we, who part in love, shall meet again.

(1820)

249. XXX

The Kirk of Ulpha to the pilgrim's eye
Is welcome as a star, that doth present
Its shining forehead through the peaceful rent
Of a black cloud diffused o'er half the sky;
Or as a fruitful palm-tree towering high
O'er the parched waste beside an Arab's tent;
Or the Indian tree whose branches, downward bent,
Take root again, a boundless canopy.
How sweet were leisure! could it yield no more
Than mid that wave-washed churchyard to recline,
From pastoral graves extracting thoughts divine;
Or there to pace, and mark the summits hoar
Of distant moonlit mountains faintly shine,
Soothed by the unseen river's gentle roar.

(1820)

250. XXXI

Not hurled precipitous from steep to steep;
Lingering no more mid flower-enameled lands
And blooming thickets; nor by rocky bands
Held;—but in radiant progress toward the Deep
Where mightiest rivers into powerless sleep
Sink, and forget their nature;—*now* expands
Majestic Duddon, over smooth flat sands,
Gliding in silence with unfettered sweep!
Beneath an ampler sky a region wide
Is opened round him;—hamlets, towers, and towns,
And blue-topped hills, behold him from afar;
In stately mien to sovereign Thames allied,
Spreading his bosom under Kentish downs,
With commerce freighted or triumphant war.

(1820)

251. XXXII

But here no cannon thunders to the gale;
Upon the wave no haughty pendants cast
A crimson splendor; lowly is the mast
That rises here, and humbly spread the sail;
While less disturbed than in the narrow Vale
Through which with strange vicissitudes he passed,
The wanderer seeks that receptacle vast
Where all his unambitious functions fail.
And may thy poet, cloud-born stream! be free,
The sweets of earth contentedly resigned,
And each tumultuous working left behind
At seemly distance, to advance like thee,
Prepared, in peace of heart, in calm of mind
And soul, to mingle with Eternity!

(1820)

252. XXXIII. *Conclusion*

I thought of thee, my partner and my guide,
As being past away.—Vain sympathies!
For, *backward,* Duddon! as I cast my eyes,
I see what was, and is, and will abide;
Still glides the stream, and shall for ever glide;
The Form remains, the Function never dies;
While *we,* the brave, the mighty, and the wise,
We Men, who in our morn of youth defied
The elements, must vanish;—be it so!
Enough, if something from our hands have power

To live, and act, and serve the future hour;
And if, as toward the silent tomb we go,
Through love, through hope, and faith's transcendent dower,
We feel that we are greater than we know.

(1820)

253. *Mutability*

From low to high doth dissolution climb,
And sinks from high to low, along a scale
Of awful notes, whose concord shall not fail;
A musical but melancholy chime,
Which they can hear who meddle not with crime,
Nor avarice, nor over-anxious care.
Truth fails not; but her outward forms that bear
The longest date do melt like frosty rime,
That in the morning whitened hill and plain
And is no more; drop like the tower sublime
Of yesterday, which royally did wear
Its crown of weeds, but could not even sustain
Some casual shout that broke the silent air,
Or the unimaginable touch of Time.

(1822)

254. *'Scorn not the Sonnet'*

Scorn not the Sonnet; critic, you have frowned,
Mindless of its just honors;—with this key
Shakespeare unlocked his heart; the melody
Of this small lute gave ease to Petrarch's wound;
A thousand times this pipe did Tasso sound;
Camöens soothed with it an exile's grief;
The Sonnet glittered a gay myrtle leaf
Amid the cypress with which Dante crowned
His visionary brow: a glow-worm lamp,
It cheered mild Spenser, called from Faery-land
To struggle through dark ways; and when a damp
Fell round the path of Milton, in his hand
The thing became a trumpet, whence he blew
Soul-animating strains—alas, too few!

(1827)

255. *Steamboats, Viaducts, and Railways*

Motions and Means, on land and sea at war
With old poetic feeling, not for this,
Shall ye, by poets even, be judged amiss!
Nor shall your presence, howsoe'er it mar

The loveliness of Nature, prove a bar
To the mind's gaining that prophetic sense
Of future change, that point of vision whence
May be discovered what in soul ye are.
In spite of all that beauty may disown
In your harsh features, Nature doth embrace
Her lawful offspring in man's art; and Time,
Pleased with your triumphs o'er his brother Space,
Accepts from your bold hands the proffered crown
Of hope, and smiles on you with cheer sublime.

(1835)

256. 'Most sweet it is with unuplifted eyes'

Most sweet it is with unuplifted eyes
To pace the ground, if path be there or none,
While a fair region round the traveler lies
Which he forbears again to look upon;
Pleased rather with some soft ideal scene,
The work of Fancy, or some happy tone
Of meditation, slipping in between
The beauty coming and the beauty gone.
If Thought and Love desert us, from that day
Let us break off all commerce with the Muse;
With Thought and Love companions of our way,
Whate'er the senses take or may refuse,
The Mind's internal Heaven shall shed her dews
Of inspiration on the humblest lay.

(1835)

257. On the Projected Kendal and Windermere Railway

Is then no nook of English ground secure
From rash assault? Schemes of retirement sown
In youth, and mid the busy world kept pure
As when their earliest flowers of home were blown,
Must perish;—how can they this blight endure?
And must he too the ruthless change bemoan
Who scorns a false utilitarian lure
Mid his paternal fields at random thrown?
Baffle the threat, bright scene, from Orrest-head
Given to the pausing traveler's rapturous glance:
Plead for thy peace, thou beautiful romance
Of nature; and, if human hearts be dead,
Speak, passing winds; ye torrents, with your strong
And constant voice, protest against the wrong.

(1845)

Mathilda Betham

(1776–1852)

Mathilda Betham's first book, *Elegies, and Other Small Poems* (1797), had a wide and enthusiastic critical reception. Admirers of her poetry included Robert Southey, Charles Lamb, and Samuel Taylor Coleridge, who praised her poetic ability in his poem "To Mathilda Betham, from a Stranger" (1802). She also was well-known as a conversationalist and as a painter of miniatures. To supplement her income, she gave dramatic readings of Shakespeare. In 1804, she published a landmark work of feminist scholarship, *A Biographical Dictionary of the Celebrated Women of Every Age and Country.* Sometime between 1818 and 1820, she suffered a mental breakdown.

258. 'Urge me no more!'

Urge me no more! nor think, because I seem
Tame and unsorrowing in the world's rude strife,
That anguish and resentment have not life
Within the heart that ye so quiet deem:
In this forced stillness only, I sustain
My thought and feeling, wearied out with pain!
Floating as 'twere upon some wild abyss,
Whence, silent Patience, bending o'er the brink,
Would rescue them with strong and steady hand,
And join again, by that connecting link,
Which now is broken:——O, respect her care!
Respect her in this fearful self-command!
No moment teems with greater woe than this,
Should she but pause, or falter in despair!

(1808)

259. To a Llangollen Rose, the Day after It Had Been Given by Miss Ponsonby

Soft blushing flower! my bosom grieves,
To view thy sadly drooping leaves:
For, while their tender tints decay,
The rose of Fancy fades away!
As pilgrims, who, with zealous care,
Some little treasured relic bear,
To reassure the doubtful mind,
When pausing memory looks behind;
I, from a more enlightened shrine,
Had made this sweet memento mine:
But, lo! its fainting head reclines;
It folds the pallid leaf, and pines,

As mourning the unhappy doom,
Which tears it from so sweet a home!

(1808)

Susan Evance
(fl. 1808–18)

The life of Susan Evance, afterwards Hooper, is now obscure. Reviews of her 1808 *Poems* were generally favorable. The *British Critic* praised the "elegance and sensibility" of the poems, among them many sonnets, but worried that real misfortune might have inspired their melancholy. James Clarke, the editor of Evance's *Poems,* remarks in his preface on the similarities between Evance's sonnets and those of Charlotte Smith, particularly in their melancholy tone and intense expression of emotion. Her last book, published in 1818, received little attention; she had dropped out of sight by the 1820s.

260. *To Melancholy*

When wintry tempests agitate the deep,
    On some lone rock I love to sit reclined;
And view the sea-birds on wild pinions sweep,
    And hear the roaring of the stormy wind,
That, rushing through the caves with hollow sound,
    Seems like the voices of those viewless forms
Which hover wrapped in gloomy mist around,
    Directing in their course the rolling storms.
Then, Melancholy! thy sweet power I feel,
    For there thine influence reigns o'er all the scene;
Then o'er my heart thy "mystic transports" steal,
    And from each trifling thought my bosom wean.
My raptured spirit soars on wing sublime
Beyond the narrow bounds of space or time!

(1808)

261. *Written in a Ruinous Abbey*

As 'mid these moldering walls I pensive stray,
    With moss and ivy rudely overgrown,
I love to watch the last pale glimpse of day,
    And hear the rising winds of evening moan.

How loud the gust comes sweeping o'er the vale!
    Now faintly murmurs midst those distant trees;
The owl begins her melancholy wail,
    Filling with shrieks the pauses of the breeze.

Fancy, thy wildest dreams engage my mind—
    I gaze on forms which not to earth belong;
I see them riding on the passing wind,
    And hear their sadly-sweet, expressive song.
Wrapped in the dear though visionary sound,
In spells of rapture all my soul is bound!

                                                        (1808)

262. To a Violet

Spring's sweet attendant! modest simple flower,
    Whose soft retiring charms the woods adorn,
How often have I wandered at that hour,
    When first appear the rosy tints of morn,
To the wild brook—there, upon mossy ground,
    Thy velvet form all beautiful to view;
To catch thy breath that steals delicious round,
    And mark thy pensive smile through tears of dew:
But then I sigh that other violets bloom,
    Unseen, in wilds where footstep never trod,
Find unadmired, unnoticed, there a tomb,
    And mingle silent with the grassy sod;
Ah, so the scattered flowers of genius rise;
    These bloom to charm—that, hid—neglected dies.

                                                        (1808)

263. To the Clouds

O ye who ride upon the wandering gale,
    And silently, yet swiftly pass away—
    I love to view you, when the glimmering ray
Of early morning tints your forms so pale,
Or when meek twilight gleams above the steep,
    As in fantastic changeful shapes ye fly
    Far in the west,—when smiles the summer sky,
Or when rough wintry winds with fury sweep
Along the hill your darkly-frowning forms,
    All desolate and gloomy as my heart.
    Ah! could I but from this sad earth depart
And wander careless as the roving storms
Amidst your shadowy scenes—borne by the wind,
Far I would fly, and leave my woes behind!

                                                        (1808)

264. Written in Ill Health at the Close of Spring

Where are the tearful smiles of youthful Spring,
    That nursed the budding leaves and infant flowers?

Ah! vanished—like those dear regretted hours
That fled away on Pleasure's fairy wing,
When Hope light scattered o'er my glowing way
　　Her rose-buds of delight.—The cooling breeze,
　　The wily sportive warblers of the trees,
And garlands sweet that made the woods so gay,
All, all are gone.—Spring will return again,
　　But never more for me its charms shall bloom,
　　For me then slumbering in the dreary tomb
The birds will sing and flow'rets blow in vain;
While gentle gales, the budding trees that wave,
Will breathe their lonely sighs across my grave.

(1808)

265. Written at Netley Abbey

Why should I fear the spirits of the dead?
　　What if they wander at the hour of night,
Amid these sacred walls, with silent tread,
　　And dimly visible to mortal sight!
What if they ride upon the wandering gale,
　　And with low sighs alarm the listening ear;
Or swell a deep, a sadly-sounding wail,
　　Like solemn dirge of death! why should I fear?
No! seated on some fragment of rude stone,
　　While through the ash-trees waving o'er my head
The wild winds pour their melancholy moan,
　　My soul, by fond imagination led,
Shall muse on days and years for ever flown,
　　And hold mysterious converse with the dead!

(1808)

Martha Hanson
(fl. 1809)

Martha Hanson published by subscription with the firm J. Mawman and T. Lake a two-volume poetry collection entitled *Sonnets and Other Poems* (1809). The contents reveal that she spent her childhood near Hurstpier-point, Sussex, and that the poems were penned at Belle-vue House. She also clearly admired two other prominent sonneteers—Mary Robinson and Charlotte Smith.

266. To Fancy

Fancy! to thee, I pour a votive strain,
　　Who kindly cheer'st the lonely midnight hour,
　　For oft thy airy and fantastic power,

To my sad bosom, soothes the throb of pain.
When balmy sleep, on downy wing, retires
  (Like the false friend who far from sorrow flies)
  Stealing his poppies from my watchful eyes,
And leaves me, racked with fever's quenchless fires;
Then Fancy! thy soft melody I hear,
  Around my couch, in soothing cadence play;
  And round me throngs thy train of visions gay,
Attired in every hue, that paints the year.
Ah gentle Goddess! thy mild fire impart,
Its genial warmth revives my grief-chilled heart.

                                                      (1809)

267. Occasioned by Reading Mrs. M.[ary] Robinson's Poems

Daughter of Genius! while thy tuneful lays
  Lift my warm spirit from its mortal clay,
  And bid it soar to realms of endless day,
In vain I seek thy matchless power to praise.
Though in the regions of the silent grave,
  The tyrant Death has laid thy beauties low,
  Around thy urn a lasting wreath shall blow,
Which still the wintry storms of fate shall brave.
The Muses culled its never fading flowers:
  Which emblematic of thy heavenly strain,
  To Time's last moment shall unchanged remain,
(Nor feel base envy's sting, detraction's powers)
And bloom for ever, round thy sacred name,
'Graved by the fingers of eternal fame.

                                                      (1809)

268. 'How proudly Man usurps the power to reign'

How proudly Man usurps the power to reign,
  In every climate of the world is known,
  From the cold regions of the Northern Zone,
To where the South extends his boundless main.
Yet in this wide expanse, no realm we find,
  To boast a Woman, who the yoke disdained;
  And with intrepid soul, that freedom claimed,
Which Heaven impartial, gave all human kind.
With soul too proud, to bear the servile chain,
  Or to usurping Man, submissive bow,
  Though poorest of the names, record can show,
Ages unborn, with wonder, shall proclaim
The pride of one unyielding Female thine,
Dear native England! and the name be mine.

                                                      (1809)

269. To Mrs. Charlotte Smith

Sweet Poetess! as pensive oft I stray,
   Amid the wilds thy steps were wont to trace,
   Thy charmful strains impart a touching grace,
To each rude scene, where thou hast waked thy lay.
Some sweet enchantment soothes my soul to rest,
   As memory oft, thy tuneful verse recalls,
   While evening's pearly tear unheeded falls
On every vermeil floret's fragrant breast.
Sweet Poetess! around thy honored brow,
   A wreath of simple flowers, I fain would twine;
   But when its blooms are intermixed with thine,
(Where Poesy's most cultured blossoms glow)
To thee, its wild buds could no praise impart,
Thy proudest trophy, is the feeling heart.

                                     (1809)

Mary F. Johnson
(fl. 1810; d. 1863)

Mary F. Johnson's *Original Sonnets, and Other Poems,* penned at Wroxhall
Farm, Isle of Wight, was published in 1810 by Longmans. In her introduc-
tion, she calls her poems "the first attempt of a secluded, unknown and inex-
perienced female" who wrote these "spontaneous effusion[s] of solitude and
leisure" without having thought about publication until a male friend en-
couraged her. In addition to Miltonic, Spenserian, and irregular sonnets, the
volume contains eight odes. A handwritten inscription in one copy says that
Johnson later married George Moncrieff, younger brother of Sir Harry
Moncrieff, and died in 1863, having lost a daughter, Georgiana, nine months
earlier.

270. Thunder Storm

Loud, louder still, resounds the thundering peal;
   The troubled deep reflects the vivid flash;
   Their bounds with deepened roar the white waves dash,
And yon black, billowy clouds their slow course wheel.
Mournful, amid the elemental crash,
   Their hollow, broken groans the raised winds deal,
The sighing copses, bending to their lash,
   Scarcely the frighted, moaning herd conceal.
Let fear, within the closet's gloom, deter
   Them whose weak hearts amid the tempest shrink:
May I, whene'er these awful scenes occur,
   Stand on this clefted rock's indented brink;

Here with the genius of the storm confer,
   And let my soul from grandeur's fountain drink.

(1810)

271. Second Evening

Exists there one, who carelessly can view
   The vivid glory of the sun's last gleams
On the green wave reflect a vermeil hue,
   And upward cast pale heat-portending beams?
When the white cliff receives the ruddy glow,
   And splendid flushes smooth its craggy side;
When the glazed windows of the warship throw
   A sparkling radiance o'er the crimsoned tide;
When rising Venus sheds her light of love,
   Fresh from the main, as erst the Goddess rose;
When in his circuit shines the belted Jove,
   And further orbs their twinkling sparks disclose:
Then lightly soars the meditative mind,
   And leaves this little world and all its cares behind.

(1810)

272. The Village Maid

Marked you, by yon thatched farm that skirts the down—
   Though, but for neatness, could she draw your eye—
A maid, in apron white, and russet gown,
   Who drove her kine, and passed, low courts'ying, by?
She, in whose grange her cares and pleasures lie;
Whose wishes never, in their loftiest flights,
   Beyond the confines of her station fly;
She, in whose taste the wake or feast unites,
   Of mortal gladness, the supreme delights—
Who all of fame concenters, in the boast
That hers, of dairies, is esteemed the most;
   She, of her sex, my envy most excites.
I would, like hers, my soaring spirit found
Its limits in my station's narrow round.

(1810)

273. Invocation to the Spirit Said to Haunt Wroxall Down

The solemn moon-beams fall, soft dews distill,
   While now in pensive mood I lonely walk;
Come sullen spirit of the breezy hill,
   Convince a skeptic, and before me stalk.
Skimm'st thou by night the heath's impurpled bloom,
   To view the rocks abrupt, and white sailed bark,

While Luna's rays the sea and coast illume,
  Gilding stacked farm, woods, meads, and mansioned park?
Wast thou a bard enkindling martial rage?
  Wast thou a mighty chief in combat slain,
Still doomed to haunt this once embattled stage,
  And guard the barrowed urns from aught profane?
Come, what thou wast, and what thou art reveal,
Show me what spirits are, and tell me what they feel.

(1810)

274. *The Idiot Girl*

Start not at her, who, in fantastic guise,
  Comes wildly chanting in a dirge-like tone,
With big tears trembling in her vacant eyes,
  And uncoifed tresses by the breezes blown.
Recoil not from the harmless idiot maid,
  Who often from a rugged beldame creeps
To yon deserted cottage in the shade,
  And its fallen stones, to guard the entrance, heaps.
There was the home where passed her early years
  With parents now withdrawn to final rest,
Who proved how infant helplessness endears;
  And of a numerous offspring loved her best.
Now wails she, as she rudely blocks the door,
"They both are in, and will come out no more."

(1810)

275. *The Widow's Remarriage*

While her fond heart against the deed rebels,
  While to her buried lord her hopes ascend,
Maternal love the widow's vows impels,
  To gain her only child one fostering friend.
True to the memory of her former love,
  Rather a victim than a bride she seems;
Her feigned and cheerless smiles deep sighs reprove;
  From her dim eye the tear unbidden streams;
Sorrow conflicts with duty in her breast.
  The mournful privilege of grief destroyed,
Too feelingly her glowing looks attest
  Esteem can never fill affection's void;
And prove, that, in the heart which loved indeed,
No second choice can to the first succeed.

(1810)

Mary Tighe
(1772–1810)

Mary Tighe's tour de force, *Psyche; or the Legend of Love*, a six-canto dream-like allegory in Spenserian stanzas, was privately printed in 1805 for friends and family. In 1811, a year after her death from tuberculosis, her brother-in-law, William Tighe, edited and published *Psyche, with Other Poems*. All of the most important journals reviewed it, to wide acclaim. Like *Psyche*, Tighe's sonnets demonstrate great technical facility and contain unusually rich imagery. Her influence on the poetry of John Keats is well documented.

276. *Written at Scarborough. August, 1799*

As musing pensive in my silent home
  I hear far off the sullen ocean's roar,
    Where the rude wave just sweeps the level shore,
Or bursts upon the rocks with whitening foam,
I think upon the scenes my life has known;
  On days of sorrow, and some hours of joy;
    Both which alike time could so soon destroy!
And now they seem a busy dream alone;
While on the earth exists no single trace
  Of all that shook my agitated soul,
    As on the beach new waves for ever roll
And fill their past forgotten brother's place:
  But I, like the worn sand, exposed remain
  To each new storm which frets the angry main.

(1811)

277. *'As one who late hath lost a friend adored'*

As one who late hath lost a friend adored,
  Clings with sick pleasure to the faintest trace
  Resemblance offers in another's face,
Or sadly gazing on that form deplored,
Would clasp the silent canvas to his breast:
  So muse I on the good I have enjoyed,
  The wretched victim of my hopes destroyed;
On images of peace I fondly rest,
Or in the page, where weeping fancy mourns,
  I love to dwell upon each tender line,
  And think the bliss once tasted still is mine;
While cheated memory to the past returns,
  And, from the present leads my shivering heart
  Back to those scenes from which it wept to part.

(1811)

278. 'When glowing Phoebus quits the weeping earth'

When glowing Phoebus quits the weeping earth,
  What splendid visions rise upon the sight!
  Fancy, with transient charms and colors bright,
To changing forms in Heaven's gay scene gives birth:
But soon the melting beauties disappear,
  And fade like those which in life's early bloom
  Hope bade me prize; and the approaching gloom,
These tints of sadness, and these shades of fear,
  Resemble most that melancholy hour
  Which, with a silent and resistless power,
Shrouded my joy's bright beam in shadowy night:
  Till memory marks each scene which once shone gay;
As the dark plains, beneath the moon's soft light,
  Again revealed, reflect a mellowing ray.

                                                    (1811)

279. Written in Autumn

O Autumn! how I love thy pensive air,
  Thy yellow garb, thy visage sad and dun!
  When from the misty east the laboring Sun
Bursts through thy fogs, that gathering round him, dare
Obscure his beams, which, though enfeebled, dart
  On the cold, dewy plains a luster bright:
  But chief, the sounds of thy reft woods delight;
Their deep, low murmurs to my soul impart
A solemn stillness, while they seem to speak
  Of Spring, of Summer now for ever past,
  Of drear, approaching Winter, and the blast
Which shall ere long their soothing quiet break:
  Here, when for faded joys my heaving breast
  Throbs with vain pangs, here will I love to rest.

                                                    (1811)

280. 'Poor, fond deluded heart!'

Poor, fond deluded heart! wilt thou again
  Listen, enchanted, to the siren song
  Of treacherous Pleasure? Ah, deceived too long,
Cease now at length to throb with wishes vain!
Ah, cease her paths bewildering to explore!
  Betrayed so oft! yet recollect the woe
  Which waits on disappointment; taught to know
By sad experience, wilt thou not give o'er
  To rest, deluded, on the fickle wing
  Which Fancy lends thee in her airy flight,

But to seduce thee to some giddy height,
And leave thee there a poor forsaken thing.
  Hope warbles once again, Truth pleads in vain,
  And my charmed soul sinks vanquished by her strain.

(1811)

281. *Written at Rossana. November 18, 1799*

Oh, my rash hand! what hast thou idly done?
  Turn from its humble bank the last poor flower
  That patient lingered to this wintry hour:
Expanding cheerly to the languid sun
It flourished yet, and yet it might have blown,
  Had not thy sudden desolating power
  Destroyed what many a storm and angry shower
Had pitying spared. The pride of summer gone,
  Cherish what yet in faded life can bloom;
And if domestic love still sweetly smiles,
If sheltered by thy cot he yet beguiles
  Thy winter's prospect of its dreary gloom,
Oh, from the spoiler's touch thy treasure screen,
To bask beneath contentment's beam serene!

(1811)

282. *Written at the Eagle's Nest, Killarney. July 26, 1800*

Here let us rest, while with meridian blaze
  The sun rides glorious 'mid the cloudless sky,
  While o'er the lake no cooling Zephyrs fly,
But on the liquid glass we dazzled gaze,
And fainting ask for shade: lo! where his nest
  The bird of Jove has fixed: the lofty brow,
  With arbutus and fragrant wild shrubs dressed,
  Impendent frowns, nor will approach allow:
Here the soft turf invites; here magic sounds
  Celestially respondent shall enchant,
While Melody from yon steep wood rebounds
  In thrilling cadence sweet. Sure, life can grant
No brighter hours than this; and memory oft
Shall paint this happiest scene with pencil soft.

(1811)

283. *Written at Killarney. July 29, 1800*

How soft the pause! the notes melodious cease,
  Which from each feeling could an echo call;
  Rest on your oars; that not a sound may fall
To interrupt the stillness of our peace:

The fanning west-wind breathes upon our cheeks
   Yet glowing with the sun's departed beams.
   Through the blue heavens the cloudless moon pours streams
Of pure resplendent light, in silver streaks
Reflected on the still, unruffled lake.
   The Alpine hills in solemn silence frown,
   While the dark woods night's deepest shades embrown.
And now once more that soothing strain awake!
Oh, ever to my heart, with magic power,
Shall those sweet sounds recall this rapturous hour!

                                    (1811)

284. To Death

O thou most terrible, most dreaded power,
   In whatsoever form thou meetest the eye!
   Whether thou biddest thy sudden arrow fly
In the dread silence of the midnight hour;
Or whether, hovering o'er the lingering wretch
   Thy sad cold javelin hangs suspended long,
   While round the couch the weeping kindred throng
With hope and fear alternately on stretch;
Oh, say, for me what horrors are prepared?
   Am I now doomed to meet thy fatal arm?
   Or wilt thou first from life steal every charm,
And bear away each good my soul would guard?
That thus, deprived of all it loved, my heart
From life itself contentedly may part.

                                    (1811)

285. 'Can I look back, and view with tranquil eye'

Can I look back, and view with tranquil eye
   The course of my sad life? what vain desires
   Have kindled in my heart consuming fires!
That heart accustomed each extreme to try
Of hope and chilling fear. What torturing dreams
   Have vexed my soul with phantoms of despair,
   Which wearied now regrets its wasted care!
Repentant shame its former anguish deems
Unworthy of that sacred spark of life
From heaven received! Exhausted in the strife
   To thee Oh God! my sinking soul would turn,
To thee devote the remnant of my years;
Oh thou! who seest my sorrows, calm my fears,
   Nor let thy wrath against thy creature burn!

                                    (1811)

286. 1802

Thy summer's day was long, but couldst thou think
  Deluded fool, it would for ever last?
  Thy sun indeed mid shrouding clouds, is fast
Declining, and must soon for ever sink.
But from the long foreboded gloom to shrink.
  Thus in the hopeless depths of languor cast,
  Declares thy brighter hours were idly past
In thoughtless folly. Didst thou never think
That all thy fond heart prized must pass away?
  And all those sparkling joys, even when most bright
Were but as heavy drops which trembling play
  On the breeze-shaken leaf? Couldst thou delight
With calm security through all the day?
  Nor seek a shelt'ring bower for sure approaching night?

(1811)

Leigh Hunt
(1784–1859)

Leigh Hunt was a controversial journalist, political liberal, critic, and poet. In 1808, he and his older brother, John, founded and edited the radical weekly newspaper, the *Examiner,* which published literature and political commentary, including early poems by John Keats and Percy Bysshe Shelley, whom Hunt introduced to one another and with whom he participated in famous sonnet-writing competitions. Hunt's major works include the *Story of Rimini* (1816), *Lord Byron and Some of His Contemporaries* (1825), and his *Autobiography* (1850). His poems "Abou Ben Adhem" and "Jenny Kissed Me" appeared widely in anthologies. In 1822, he and Byron and Shelley started a magazine entitled the *Liberal.* He also coedited an anthology of sonnets, the *Book of the Sonnet,* published posthumously in 1867.

287. To Hampstead

Sweet upland, to whose walks with fond repair
  Out of thy western slope I took my rise
  Day after day, and on these feverish eyes
Met the moist fingers of the bathing air,—
If health, unearned of thee, I may not share,
  Keep it, I pray thee, where my memory lies,
  In thy green lanes, brown dells, and breezy skies,
Till I return, and find thee doubly fair.

Wait then my coming, on that lightsome land,
  Health, and the joy that out of nature springs,

And freedom's air-blown locks:—but stay with me,
Friendship, frank entering with the cordial hand,
And honor, and the Muse with growing wings,
And love domestic, smiling equably.

(1813)

288. To Hampstead

Winter has reached thee once again at last;
  And now the rambler, whom thy groves yet please,
  Feels on his housewarm lips the thin air freeze;
While in his shrugging neck the resolute blast
Comes edging; and the leaves, in heaps down cast,
  He shuffles with his hastening foot, and sees
  The cold sky whitening through the wiry trees,
And sighs to think his loitering noons have passed.

And do I love thee less to paint thee so?
  No; this the season is of beauty still
    Doubled at heart;—of smoke with whirling glee
Uptumbling ever from the blaze below,—
  And home remembered most,—and oh, loved hill,
    The second, and the last, away from thee!

(1814)

289. On the Grasshopper and Cricket

Green little vaunter in the sunny grass,
  Catching your heart up at the feel of June,
  Sole voice left stirring midst the lazy noon,
When even the bees lag at the summoning brass;—
And you, warm little housekeeper, who class
  With those who think the candles come too soon,
  Loving the fire, and with your tricksome tune
Nick the glad silent movements as they pass;—
Oh sweet and tiny cousins, that belong,
  One to the fields, the other to the hearth,
Both have your sunshine; both though small are strong
  At your clear hearts; and both were sent on earth
To sing in thoughtful ears this natural song,
  —In doors and out,—summer and winter,—Mirth.

(1817)

290. To Percy Shelley, on the Degrading Notions of Deity

What wonder, Percy, that with jealous rage
  Men should defame the kindly and the wise,
  When in the midst of the all-beauteous skies,

And all this lovely world, that should engage
Their mutual search for the old golden age,
They seat a phantom, swelled into grim size
Out of their own passions and bigotries,
And then, for fear, proclaim it meek and sage!
And this they call a light and a revealing!
Wise as the clown, who plodding home at night
In autumn, turns at call of fancied elf,
And sees upon the fog, with ghastly feeling,
A giant shadow in its imminent might,
Which his own lanthorn throws up from himself.

(1818)

291. To the Same

Yet, Percy, not for this, should he whose eye
Sees loveliness, and the unselfish joy
Of justice, turn him, like a peevish boy,
At hindrances and thwartings; and deny
Wisdom's divinest privilege, constancy;
That which most proves him free from the alloy
Of useless earth,—least prone to the decoy
That clamors down weak pinions from the sky.
The Spirit of Beauty, though by solemn quires
Hourly blasphemed, stoops not from its calm end,
And forward breathing love, but ever on
Rolls the round day, and calls the starry fires
To their glad watch. Therefore, high-hearted friend,
Be still with thine own task in unison.

(1818)

292. To John Keats

'Tis well you think me truly one of those,
Whose sense discerns the loveliness of things;
For surely as I feel the bird that sings
Behind the leaves, or dawn as it up grows,
Or the rich bee rejoicing as he goes,
Or the glad issue of emerging springs,
Or overhead the glide of a dove's wings,
Or turf, or trees, or, midst of all, repose.
And surely as I feel things lovelier still,
The human look, and the harmonious form
Containing woman, and the smile in ill,
And such a heart as Charles's, wise and warm,—
As surely as all this, I see, ev'n now,
Young Keats, a flowering laurel on your brow.

(1818)

293. The Nile

It flows through old hushed Egypt and its sands,
Like some grave mighty thought threading a dream,
And times and things, as in that vision, seem
Keeping along it their eternal stands,—
Caves, pillars, pyramids, the shepherd bands
That roamed through the young world, the glory extreme
Of high Sesostris, and that southern beam,
The laughing queen that caught the world's great hands.
Then comes a mightier silence, stern and strong,
As of a world left empty of its throng,
And the void weighs on us; and then we wake,
And hear the fruitful stream lapsing along
Twixt villages, and think how we shall take
Our own calm journey on for human sake.

(1818)

Mary Bryan
(fl. 1815)

Mary Bryan's highly original, moody, and plaintive poems, published in
Sonnets and Metrical Tales (1815), reflect the financial and emotional difficul-
ties of her life as a widow with six children. In her preface, however, she re-
jects the piteous mode popularized by Charlotte Smith. Many of her poems
were written to her husband during their separations, although he later for-
bade her to write. She endured financial disaster, her husband's mental and
physical illness and death, and her own serious health problems. For a decade
after her husband's death, she took charge of the family's printing business.

294. The Maniac

"My own Maria!—Ah my own—my own!"
Withheld my steps in such entreating tone,
I turned—so meek a form I could not fear,
I pressed the extended hand and bathed it with a tear.—
I stood as I could never leave that place,
Yet would have spoken, would have turned away:—
"My own Maria!"—gazing on my face,
As one long lost to him, did that lorn maniac say.
I could not speak—so lovely was the joy
The maniac showed, 'twere cruel to destroy;
And I had seen him look so lost in woe,
That if I were not his—I could not tell him so.
"My own Maria!"—with such tender grace,

Repeated oft—that now the maniac grew
Dear and more dear; till urged to leave the place,
I could not speak—I could not *look* adieu—
Lest I had seen him in his wild despair,
And hastened to that prisoned maniac's cell,
And left the world to dwell for ever there—
Few in that sordid world I loved so well:
And often since that hour, thou poor unknown,
In memory's tenderest thoughts, I have been all thine own!

(1815)

295. *To My Brother*

O, thou art far away from me—dear boy!
So fond affection loves to call thee still;
Recalling hours that oft my bosom thrill,
When in our native haunts thou wert my joy.
Where now in distant climates dost thou stray?
When in the ardor of thy boyish pride,
Thou wert a faithless truant from my side;
Soon thou return'st to chase my fears away.
How have I marked thee oft, with wonder there,
Climb the tall elm, and prayed and prayed again
Thou would'st such dangerous heights forbear,
And gazed, with upraised eyes, that sued in vain:
Gained the proud height—prompt to descend and smile,
And love the very tear thou chid'st the while.

(1815)

296. *To My Brother*

Once in our customed walk a wounded bird,
With feeble effort fluttering awhile,
Fell at my feet; unknowing of its hurt,
"Poor thing, 'tis sick," I said, and laid it on
My bosom; it could not rest for pain;
So tenderly I gave it to thy care.—"Look—
Ah it bleeds! we cannot save nor ease it,—
See its torn wing—its shattered panting breast—
It writhes its little limbs with grievous pain;
And now its dim eyes close—quite close—it dies!
Poor pretty bird!—Could he who did this deed,
Have seen thy lingering life in torture thus
Expire, I know he would forbear to kill."—
"Nay, nay, dear Mary! thou hast much to learn."

(1815)

297. To —— ——

O thou unknown disturber of my rest,
Ceaseless intruder, life-consuming foe;
Proud o'er my fall, and in my sorrow, blest,
Destroyer of a love thou ne'er canst know—
And life with love—O leave me—spare me now—
On that blessed moment while I fondly dwell,
When kind some pitying Genii heard my vow
And as my trembling fingers touched the spell,
Propitious to my wish bestowed the skill
That gave,—O more than wealth, or fame could give;
My Henry gave, by Fate's resistless will,
And snatched from death and made it bliss to live,
To live for him, and at Love's sanctioned shrine
Pledge my devoted heart, and clasp that treasure mine.

(1815)

298. To —— ——

O timeless guest!—so soon returned art thou,
Hope's sickly gleam with cruel haste to quench,
To mock the prayer, and scorn the trembling vow,
I feel thy fatal power and vainly bid thee hence.—
Still, still thou com'st in dreadful guise to me,
Howe'er to others fair thy form appear;
Not shapeless things with midnight witchery
Could so appall my soul—so chill my breast, with fear!
—Now fateful is thy look!—thou lead'st me,—where?
O well, thou lead'st me to my destined place,
And bid'st me close my eyes for ever there.
Nor view thee wrapped in Henry's dear embrace:
Yes—proud one, haste thee to the nuptial shrine,
I sleep in death's cold arms—ere Henry sleep in thine.

(1815)

George Gordon, Lord Byron
(1788–1824)

The publication of the first two cantos of *Childe Harold's Pilgrimage* (1812), a reflective travelogue in Spenserian stanzas, made Lord Byron an overnight sensation. His divorce and scandalous liaisons forced his exile from England in 1816. On the continent, he wrote many of his most famous works, including the verse drama *Manfred* (1817) and the mock epic *Don Juan* (1819-24). Byron wrote few sonnets and despised Petrarch, of whom he writes in *Don Juan* 3.8, "Think you, if Laura had been Petrarch's wife, / He would have written sonnets all his life?"

299. On Chillon

Eternal spirit of the chainless mind!
   Brightest in dungeons, Liberty! thou art,
   For there thy habitation is the heart—
The heart which love of thee alone can bind;
And when thy sons to fetters are consigned—
   To fetters, and the damp vault's dayless gloom,
   Their country conquers with their martyrdom,
And Freedom's fame finds wings on every wind.
Chillon! thy prison is a holy place,
   And thy sad floor an altar—for 'twas trod,
Until his very steps have left a trace
   Worn, as if thy cold pavement were a sod,
By Bonnivard!—May none those marks efface!
   For they appeal from tyranny to God.

                                  (1816)

300. 'Rousseau—Voltaire—our Gibbon—and de Staël'

Rousseau—Voltaire—our Gibbon—and de Staël—
   Leman! these names are worthy of thy shore,
   Thy shore of names like these! wert thou no more,
Their memory thy remembrance would recall:
To them thy banks were lovely as to all,
   But they have made them lovelier, for the lore
   Of mighty minds doth hallow in the core
Of human hearts the ruin of a wall
   Where dwelt the wise and wondrous; but by *thee*
How much more, Lake of Beauty! do we feel,
   In sweetly gliding o'er thy crystal sea,
The wild glow of that not ungentle zeal,
   Which of the heirs of immortality
Is proud, and makes the breath of glory real!

                                  (1816)

John Keats
(1795–1821)

John Keats's first published poem, like Wordsworth's, was a sonnet: "To Soli-tude" appeared in John and Leigh Hunt's newpaper, the *Examiner,* in 1816. Keats continued to write sonnets throughout his short career, variously ex-perimenting with new forms and practicing old ones. Keats's sonnets are lush, impassioned and psychological, informed by a sense of the poet's own short lifespan troped by the brief duration of the form itself. His long, ornate early poem "Endymion" (1818) inspired savage reviews. He wrote his finest poems, including "The Eve of St. Agnes," "Lamia," "La Belle Dame sans

Merci," and a series of remarkable odes in the last few years of his life. He was
only twenty-six when he died of tuberculosis in Rome.

301. To Solitude

O Solitude! if I must with thee dwell,
  Let it not be among the jumbled heap
  Of murky buildings; —climb with me the steep,
Nature's observatory—whence the dell,
Its flowery slopes—its rivers crystal swell,
  May seem a span: let me thy vigils keep
  'Mongst boughs pavilioned; where the deer's swift leap
Startles the wild bee from the fox-glove bell.
Ah! fain would I frequent such scenes with thee;
  But the sweet converse of an innocent mind,
  Whose words are images of thoughts refined,
Is my soul's pleasure; and it sure must be
  Almost the highest bliss of human kind,
When to thy haunts two kindred spirits flee.

(1816)

302. On First Looking into Chapman's Homer

Much have I traveled in the realms of gold,
  And many goodly states and kingdoms seen;
  Round many western islands have I been
Which bards in fealty to Apollo hold.
Oft of one wide expanse had I been told,
  That deep-browed Homer ruled as his demesne;
  Yet did I never breathe its pure serene
Till I heard Chapman speak out loud and bold:
Then felt I like some watcher of the skies
  When a new planet swims into his ken;
Or like stout Cortez when with eagle eyes
  He stared at the Pacific—and all his men
Looked at each other with a wild surmise—
  Silent, upon a peak in Darien.

(1816)

303. To ★ ★ ★ ★ ★ ★

Had I a man's fair form, then might my sighs
  Be echoed swiftly through that ivory shell
  Thine ear, and find thy gentle heart; so well
Would passion arm me for the enterprise:
But ah! I am no knight whose foeman dies;

No cuirass glistens on my bosom's swell;
  I am no happy shepherd of the dell
  Whose lips have trembled with a maiden's eyes.
Yet must I dote upon thee,—call thee sweet,
  Sweeter by far than Hybla's honeyed roses
    When steeped in dew rich to intoxication.
Ah! I will taste that dew, for me 'tis meet,
  And when the moon her pallid face discloses,
    I'll gather some by spells, and incantation.

(1817)

304. *Written on the Day that Mr. Leigh Hunt Left Prison*

What though, for showing truth to flattered state,
  Kind Hunt was shut in prison, yet has he,
  In his immortal spirit, been as free
As the sky-searching lark, and as elate.
Minion of grandeur! think you he did wait?
  Think you he naught but prison walls did see,
  Till, so unwilling, thou unturnd'st the key?
Ah, no! far happier, nobler was his fate!
In Spenser's halls he strayed, and bowers fair,
  Culling enchanted flowers; and he flew
With daring Milton through the fields of air:
  To regions of his own his genius true
Took happy flights. Who shall his fame impair
  When thou art dead, and all thy wretched crew?

(1817)

305. *'How many bards gild the lapses of time!'*

How many bards gild the lapses of time!
  A few of them have ever been the food
  Of my delighted fancy,—I could brood
Over their beauties, earthly, or sublime:
And often, when I sit me down to rhyme,
  These will in throngs before my mind intrude:
  But no confusion, no disturbance rude
Do they occasion; 'tis a pleasing chime.
So the unnumbered sounds that evening store;
  The songs of birds—the whispering of the leaves—
  The voice of waters—the great bell that heaves
With solemn sound,—and thousand others more,
  That distance of recognizance bereaves,
Make pleasing music, and not wild uproar.

(1817)

306. *To a Friend Who Sent Me Some Roses*

As late I rambled in the happy fields,
  What time the sky-lark shakes the tremulous dew
  From his lush clover covert;—when anew
Adventurous knights take up their dinted shields:
I saw the sweetest flower wild nature yields,
  A fresh-blown musk-rose; 'twas the first that threw
  Its sweets upon the summer: graceful it grew
As is the wand that queen Titania wields.
And, as I feasted on its fragrancy,
  I thought the garden-rose it far excelled:
But when, O Wells! thy roses came to me
  My sense with their deliciousness was spelled:
Soft voices had they, that with tender plea
  Whispered of peace, and truth, and friendliness unquelled.

(1817)

307. *'Keen, fitful gusts are whisp'ring here and there'*

Keen, fitful gusts are whisp'ring here and there
  Among the bushes half leafless, and dry;
  The stars look very cold about the sky,
And I have many miles on foot to fare.
Yet feel I little of the cool bleak air,
  Or of the dead leaves rustling drearily,
  Or of those silver lamps that burn on high,
Or of the distance from home's pleasant lair:
For I am brimful of the friendliness
  That in a little cottage I have found;
Of fair-haired Milton's eloquent distress,
  And all his love for gentle Lycid drowned;
Of lovely Laura in her light green dress,
  And faithful Petrarch gloriously crowned.

(1817)

308. *'To one who has been long in city pent'*

To one who has been long in city pent,
  'Tis very sweet to look into the fair
  And open face of heaven,—to breathe a prayer
Full in the smile of the blue firmament.
Who is more happy, when, with heart's content,
  Fatigued he sinks into some pleasant lair
  Of wavy grass, and reads a debonair
And gentle tale of love and languishment?
Returning home at evening, with an ear
  Catching the notes of Philomel,—an eye

Watching the sailing cloudlet's bright career,
    He mourns that day so soon has glided by:
E'en like the passage of an angel's tear
    That falls through the clear ether silently.

                                            (1817)

309. *On Leaving Some Friends at an Early Hour*

Give me a golden pen, and let me lean
    On heaped up flowers, in regions clear, and far;
    Bring me a tablet whiter than a star,
Or hand of hymning angel, when 'tis seen
The silver strings of heavenly harp atween:
    And let there glide by many a pearly car,
    Pink robes, and wavy hair, and diamond jar,
And half-discovered wings, and glances keen.
The while let music wander round my ears,
    And as it reaches each delicious ending,
        Let me write down a line of glorious tone,
And full of many wonders of the spheres:
    For what a height my spirit is contending!
        'Tis not content so soon to be alone.

                                            (1817)

310. *Addressed to Haydon*

Highmindedness, a jealousy for good,
    A loving-kindness for the great man's fame,
    Dwells here and there with people of no name,
In noisome alley, and in pathless wood:
And where we think the truth least understood,
    Oft may be found a "singleness of aim,"
    That ought to frighten into hooded shame
A money mongering, pitiable brood.
How glorious this affection for the cause
    Of steadfast genius, toiling gallantly!
What when a stout unbending champion awes
    Envy, and malice to their native sty?
Unnumbered souls breathe out a still applause,
    Proud to behold him in his country's eye.

                                            (1817)

311. *Addressed to the Same*

Great spirits now on earth are sojourning;
    He of the cloud, the cataract, the lake,
    Who on Helvellyn's summit, wide awake,
Catches his freshness from archangel's wing:

He of the rose, the violet, the spring,
  The social smile, the chain for freedom's sake:
  And lo!—whose steadfastness would never take
A meaner sound than Raphael's whispering.
And other spirits there are standing apart
  Upon the forehead of the age to come;
These, these will give the world another heart,
  And other pulses. Hear ye not the hum
Of mighty workings?——
  Listen awhile ye nations, and be dumb.

(1817)

312. On the Grasshopper and Cricket

The poetry of earth is never dead:
  When all the birds are faint with the hot sun,
  And hide in cooling trees, a voice will run
From hedge to hedge about the new-mown mead;
That is the Grasshopper's—he takes the lead
  In summer luxury,—he has never done
  With his delights; for when tired out with fun
He rests at ease beneath some pleasant weed.
The poetry of earth is ceasing never:
  On a lone winter's evening, when the frost
    Has wrought a silence, from the stove there shrills
The Cricket's song, in warmth increasing ever,
  And seems to one in drowsiness half lost,
    The Grasshopper's among some grassy hills.

(1817)

313. To Kosciusko

Good Kosciusko, thy great name alone
  Is a full harvest whence to reap high feeling;
  It comes upon us like the glorious pealing
Of the wide spheres—an everlasting tone.
And now it tells me, that in the worlds unknown,
  The names of heroes, burst from clouds concealing,
  And changed to harmonies, for ever stealing
Through cloudless blue, and round each silver throne.
It tells me too, that on a happy day,
  When some good spirit walks upon the earth,
  Thy name with Alfred's, and the great of yore
Gently commingling, gives tremendous birth
To a loud hymn, that sounds far, far away
  To where the great God lives for evermore.

(1817)

314. 'Happy is England! I could be content'

Happy is England! I could be content
   To see no other verdure than its own;
   To feel no other breezes than are blown
Through its tall woods with high romances blent:
Yet do I sometimes feel a languishment
   For skies Italian, and an inward groan
   To sit upon an Alp as on a throne,
And half forget what world or worldling meant.
Happy is England, sweet her artless daughters;
   Enough their simple loveliness for me,
     Enough their whitest arms in silence clinging:
Yet do I often warmly burn to see
     Beauties of deeper glance, and hear their singing,
And float with them about the summer waters.

                                   (1817)

315. 'After dark vapors have oppressed our plains'

After dark vapors have oppressed our plains
   For a long dreary season, comes a day
   Born of the gentle South, and clears away
From the sick heavens all unseemly stains.
The anxious month, relieving from its pains,
   Takes as a long lost right the feel of May:
   The eyelids with the passing coolness play
Like rose leaves with the drip of summer rains.

The calmest thoughts come round us; as of leaves
   Budding—fruit ripening in stillness—autumn suns
Smiling at eve upon the quiet sheaves—
     Sweet Sappho's cheek—a smiling infant's breath—
   The gradual sand that through an hour-glass runs—
     A woodland rivulet—a poet's death.

                                   (1817)

316. To Haydon, with a Sonnet Written on Seeing the Elgin Marbles

Haydon! forgive me that I cannot speak
   Definitively on these mighty things;
   Forgive me that I have not eagle's wings—
That what I want I know not where to seek:
And think that I would not be overmeek
   In rolling out upfollowed thunderings,
   Even to the steep of Heliconian springs,
Were I of ample strength for such a freak—
Think too, that all those numbers should be thine;

Whose else? In this who touch thy vesture's hem?
For when men stared at what was most divine
  With browless idiotism—o'erwise phlegm—
Thou hadst beheld the Hesperean shine
  Of their star in the East, and gone to worship them.

                                                    (1817)

317. On Seeing the Elgin Marbles

My spirit is too weak—Mortality
  Weighs heavily on me like unwilling sleep,
  And each imagined pinnacle and steep
Of godlike hardship tells me I must die
Like a sick eagle looking at the sky.
  Yet 'tis a gentle luxury to weep
  That I have not the cloudy winds to keep
Fresh for the opening of the morning's eye.
Such dim-conceived glories of the brain
  Bring round the heart an undescribable feud;
So do these wonders a most dizzy pain,
  That mingles Grecian grandeur with the rude
Wasting of old time—with a billowy main—
  A sun—a shadow of a magnitude.

                                                    (1817)

318. To Ailsa Rock

Hearken, thou craggy ocean-pyramid,
  Give answer by thy voice—the sea fowls' screams!
  When were thy shoulders mantled in huge streams?
When from the sun was thy broad forehead hid?
How long is't since the mighty Power bid
  Thee heave to airy sleep from fathom dreams—
  Sleep in the lap of thunder or sunbeams—
Or when gray clouds are thy cold coverlid?
Thou answer'st not; for thou art dead asleep.
  Thy life is but two dead eternities,
The last in air, the former in the deep!
  First with the whales, last with the eagle-skies!
Drowned wast thou till an earthquake made thee steep,
  Another cannot wake thy giant size!

                                                    (1818)

319. To a Cat

Cat! who hast passed thy grand climacteric,
  How many mice and rats hast in thy days
  Destroyed?—How many tit-bits stolen? Gaze

With those bright languid segments green, and prick
Those velvet ears—but pr'ythee do not stick
   Thy latent talons in me—and upraise
   Thy gentle mew—and tell me all thy frays
Of fish and mice, and rats and tender chick.
Nay, look not down, nor lick thy dainty wrists—
For all the wheezy asthma,—and for all
Thy tail's tip is nicked off—and though the fists
Of many a maid have given thee many a maul,
Still is that fur as soft as when the lists
In youth thou enter'dst on glass-bottled wall.

                                             (1830)

320. 'If by dull rhymes our English must be chained'

If by dull rhymes our English must be chained,
   And, like Andromeda, the sonnet sweet
   Fettered, in spite of pained loveliness;
Let us find out, if we must be constrained,
   Sandals more interwoven and complete
To fit the naked foot of poesy;
Let us inspect the lyre, and weigh the stress
Of every chord, and see what may be gained
   By ear industrious, and attention meet;
Misers of sound and syllable, no less
Than Midas of his coinage, let us be
   Jealous of dead leaves in the bay wreath crown;
So, if we may not let the Muse be free,
   She will be bound with garlands of her own.

                                             (1836)

321. On Fame

Fame, like a wayward girl, will still be coy
   To those who woo her with too slavish knees,
But makes surrender to some thoughtless boy,
   And dotes the more upon a heart at ease;
She is a gypsy,—will not speak to those
   Who have not learnt to be content without her;
A jilt, whose ear was never whispered close,
   Who thinks they scandal her who talk about her;
A very gypsy is she, Nilus-born,
   Sister-in-law to jealous Potiphar;
Ye love-sick bards! repay her scorn for scorn;
   Ye artists lovelorn! madmen that ye are!
Make your best bow to her and bid adieu,
Then, if she likes it, she will follow you.

                                             (1837)

322. 'Bright star! would I were steadfast as thou art'

Bright star! would I were steadfast as thou art—
  Not in lone splendor hung aloft the night,
And watching, with eternal lids apart,
  Like Nature's patient sleepless eremite,
The moving waters at their priestlike task
  Of pure ablution round earth's human shores,
Or gazing on the new soft fallen mask
  Of snow upon the mountains and the moors—
No—yet still steadfast, still unchangeable,
  Pillowed upon my fair love's ripening breast,
To feel for ever its soft fall and swell,
  Awake for ever in a sweet unrest,
Still, still to hear her tender-taken breath,
And so live ever—or else swoon to death.

                           (1838)

323. 'The day is gone, and all its sweets are gone!'

The day is gone, and all its sweets are gone!
  Sweet voice, sweet lips, soft hand, and softer breast,
Warm breath, light whisper, tender semi-tone,
  Bright eyes, accomplished shade, and lang'rous waist!
Faded the flower and all its budded charms,
  Faded the sight of beauty from my eyes,
Faded the shape of beauty from my arms,
  Faded the voice, warmth, whiteness, paradise—
Vanished unseasonably at shut of eve,
  When the dusk holiday—or holinight
Of fragrant-curtained love begins to weave
  The woof of darkness thick, for hid delight;
But, as I've read love's missal through today,
He'll let me sleep, seeing I fast and pray.

                           (1838)

324. To Sleep

O soft embalmer of the still midnight!
  Shutting, with careful fingers and benign,
Our gloom-pleased eyes, embowered from the light,
  Enshaded in forgetfulness divine;
O soothest Sleep! if so it please thee, close,
  In midst of this thine hymn, my willing eyes,
Or wait the amen, ere thy poppy throws
  Around my bed its lulling charities;
Then save me, or the passed day will shine
  Upon my pillow, breeding many woes;

Save me from curious conscience, that still lords
   Its strength, for darkness burrowing like a mole;
Turn the key deftly in the oiled wards,
   And seal the hushed casket of my soul.

(1838)

325. 'O Chatterton! how very sad thy fate!'

O Chatterton! how very sad thy fate!
Dear child of sorrow—son of misery!
How soon the film of death obscured that eye,
Whence genius mildly flashed, and high debate.
How soon that voice, majestic and elate,
Melted in dying numbers! Oh! how nigh
Was night to thy fair morning. Thou didst die
A half-blown flow'ret which cold blasts amate.
But this is past: thou art among the stars
Of highest Heaven: to the rolling spheres
Thou sweetly singest: naught thy hymning mars,
Above the ingrate world and human fears.
On earth the good man base detraction bars
From thy fair name, and waters it with tears.

(1848)

326. 'O thou! whose face hath felt the winter's wind'

O thou! whose face hath felt the winter's wind,
Whose eye has seen the snow-clouds hung in mist,
And the black elm-tops among the freezing stars:
To thee the spring will be a harvest-time.
O thou! whose only book has been the light
Of supreme darkness which thou feddest on
Night after night, when Phoebus was away,
To thee the spring will be a triple morn.
O fret not after knowledge!—I have none,
And yet my song comes native with the warmth.
O fret not after knowledge—I have none,
And yet the evening listens. He who saddens
At thought of idleness cannot be idle,
And he's awake who thinks himself asleep.

(1848)

327. 'When I have fears that I may cease to be'

When I have fears that I may cease to be
   Before my pen has gleaned my teeming brain,
Before high-piled books, in charact'ry,
   Hold like rich garners the full-ripened grain;

When I behold, upon the night's starred face,
  Huge cloudy symbols of a high romance,
And think that I may never live to trace
  Their shadows, with the magic hand of chance;
And when I feel, fair creature of an hour!
  That I shall never look upon thee more,
Never have relish in the faery power
  Of unreflecting love!—then on the shore
Of the wide world I stand alone, and think
Till love and fame to nothingness do sink.

                                     (1848)

328. 'Why did I laugh tonight?'

Why did I laugh tonight? No voice will tell:
  No God, no Demon of severe response,
Deigns to reply from Heaven or from Hell.
  Then to my human heart I turn at once.
Heart! Thou and I are here sad and alone;
  I Say, why did I laugh? O mortal pain!
O Darkness! Darkness! ever must I moan,
  To question Heaven and Hell and Heart in vain.
Why did I laugh? I know this being's lease,
  My fancy to its utmost blisses spreads;
Yet would I on this very midnight cease,
  And the world's gaudy ensigns see in shreds;
Verse, Fame, and Beauty are intense indeed,
But Death intenser—Death is Life's high mead.

                                     (1848)

329. 'I cry your mercy—pity—love!—aye, love!'

I cry your mercy—pity—love!—aye, love!
  Merciful love that tantalizes not,
One-thoughted, never-wandering, guileless love,
  Unmasked, and being seen—without a blot!
O! let me have thee whole,—all—all—be mine!
  That shape, that fairness, that sweet minor zest
Of love, your kiss,—those hands, those eyes divine,
  That warm, white, lucent, million-pleasured breast,—
Yourself—your soul—in pity give me all,
  Withhold no atom's atom or I die,
Or living on perhaps, your wretched thrall,
  Forget, in the mist of idle misery,
Life's purposes,—the palate of my mind
Losing its gust, and my ambition blind!

                                     (1848)

Percy Bysshe Shelley
(1792-1822)

The modest number of sonnets Percy Bysshe Shelley composed during his brief literary career reflect remarkable stylistic diversity, justifying Wordsworth's assessment of him as "one of the best artists of us all" in terms of "workmanship of style." Shelley's sonnets reflect, too, many of his strongest political and philosophical views, from the pained dismay he expresses at Wordsworth's increased conservativism in "To Wordsworth," to the apocalyptic litany he chants in condemnation of George III's debilitated government in "England in 1819." His passionate and unconventional views led to controversy during his lifetime. Shelley spent the final years of his life in Europe, where he produced such important works as *Prometheus Unbound* (1820), "Ode to the West Wind" (1820), and *Epipsychidion* (1821).

330. To Wordsworth

Poet of Nature, thou hast wept to know
That things depart which never may return:
Childhood and youth, friendship and love's first glow,
Have fled like sweet dreams, leaving thee to mourn.
These common woes I feel. One loss is mine
Which thou too feel'st, yet I alone deplore.
Thou wert as a lone star, whose light did shine
On some frail bark in winter's midnight roar:
Thou hast like to a rock-built refuge stood
Above the blind and battling multitude:
In honored poverty thy voice did weave
Songs consecrate to truth and liberty,—
Deserting these, thou leavest me to grieve,
Thus having been, that thou shouldst cease to be.

(1816)

331. Feelings of a Republican on the Fall of Bonaparte

I hated thee, fallen tyrant! I did groan
To think that a most unambitious slave,
Like thou, shouldst dance and revel on the grave
Of Liberty. Thou mightst have built thy throne
Where it had stood even now: thou didst prefer
A frail and bloody pomp which time has swept
In fragments towards oblivion. Massacre,
For this I prayed, would on thy sleep have crept,
Treason and Slavery, Rapine, Fear, and Lust,
And stifled thee, their minister. I know
Too late, since thou and France are in the dust,
That virtue owns a more eternal foe

Than force or fraud: old Custom, legal Crime,
And bloody Faith the foulest birth of time.

(1816)

332. Ozymandias

I met a traveler from an antique land
Who said: Two vast and trunkless legs of stone
Stand in the desert. Near them, on the sand,
Half sunk, a shattered visage lies, whose frown,
And wrinkled lip, and sneer of cold command,
Tell that its sculptor well those passions read
Which yet survive, stamped on these lifeless things,
The hand that mocked them and the heart that fed;
And on the pedestal these words appear:
"My name is Ozymandias, king of kings:
Look on my works, ye Mighty, and despair!"
Nothing beside remains. Round the decay
Of that colossal wreck, boundless and bare,
The lone and level sands stretch far away.

(1818)

333. Ode to the West Wind

I

O wild West Wind, thou breath of Autumn's being,
Thou, from whose unseen presence the leaves dead
Are driven, like ghosts from an enchanter fleeing,

Yellow, and black, and pale, and hectic red,
Pestilence-stricken multitudes: O, thou,
Who chariotest to their dark wintry bed

The winged seeds, where they lie cold and low,
Each like a corpse within its grave, until
Thine azure sister of the spring shall blow

Her clarion o'er the dreaming earth, and fill
(Driving sweet buds like flocks to feed in air)
With living hues and odors plain and hill:

Wild Spirit, which art moving everywhere;
Destroyer and preserver; hear, O hear!

II

Thou on whose stream, 'mid the steep sky's commotion,
Loose clouds like earth's decaying leaves are shed,
Shook from the tangled boughs of Heaven and Ocean,

Angels of rain and lightning: there are spread
On the blue surface of thine airy surge,
Like the bright hair uplifted from the head

Of some fierce Mænad, even from the dim verge
Of the horizon to the zenith's height
The locks of the approaching storm. Thou dirge

Of the dying year, to which this closing night
Will be the dome of a vast sepulchre,
Vaulted with all thy congregated might

Of vapors, from whose solid atmosphere
Black rain, and fire, and hail will burst: O, hear!

III

Thou who didst waken from his summer dreams
The blue Mediterranean, where he lay,
Lulled by the coil of his crystalline streams,

Beside a pumice isle in Baiæ's bay,
And saw in sleep old palaces and towers
Quivering within the wave's intenser day,

All overgrown with azure moss and flowers
So sweet, the sense faints picturing them! Thou
For whose path the Atlantic's level powers

Cleave themselves into chasms, while far below
The sea-blooms and the oozy woods which wear
The sapless foliage of the ocean, know

Thy voice, and suddenly grow gray with fear,
And tremble and despoil themselves: O, hear!

IV

If I were a dead leaf thou mightest bear;
If I were a swift cloud to fly with thee;
A wave to pant beneath thy power, and share

The impulse of thy strength, only less free
Than thou, O, uncontrollable! If even
I were as in my boyhood, and could be

The comrade of thy wanderings over heaven,
As then, when to outstrip thy skiey speed
Scarce seemed a vision; I would ne'er have striven

As thus with thee in prayer in my sore need.
Oh! lift me as wave, a leaf, a cloud!
I fall upon the thorns of life! I bleed!

A heavy weight of hours has chained and bowed
One too like thee: tameless, and swift, and proud.

V

Make my thy lyre, even as the forest is:
What if my leaves are falling like its own!
The tumult of thy mighty harmonies

Will take from both a deep, autumnal tone,
Sweet though in sadness. Be thou, spirit fierce,
My spirit! Be thou me, impetuous one!

Drive my dead thoughts over the universe
Like withered leaves to quicken a new birth!
And, by the incantation of this verse,

Scatter, as from an unextinguished hearth
Ashes and sparks, my words among mankind!
Be through my lips to unawakened earth

The trumpet of a prophecy! O, Wind,
If Winter comes, can Spring be far behind?

(1820)

334. Political Greatness

Nor happiness, nor majesty, nor fame,
Nor peace, nor strength, nor skill in arms or arts,
Shepherd those herds whom tyranny makes tame;
Verse echoes not one beating of their hearts,
History is but the shadow of their shame,
Art veils her glass, or from the pageant starts
As to oblivion their blind millions fleet,
Staining that Heaven with obscene imagery
Of their own likeness. What are numbers knit
By force or custom? Man who man would be,
Must rule the empire of himself; in it
Must be supreme, establishing his throne
On vanquished will, quelling the anarchy
Of hopes and fears, being himself alone.

(1824)

335. 'Lift not the painted veil'

Lift not the painted veil which those who live
Call Life: though unreal shapes be pictured there,
And it but mimic all we would believe
With colors idly spread:—behind, lurk Fear
And Hope, twin destinies; who ever weave
The shadows, which the world calls substance, there.

I knew one who had lifted it—he sought,
For his lost heart was tender, things to love
But found them not, alas! nor was there aught
The world contains, the which he could approve.
Through the unheeding many he did move,
A splendor among shadows, a bright blot
Upon this gloomy scene, a Spirit that strove
For truth, and like the Preacher found it not.

(1824)

336. England in 1819

An old, mad, blind, despised, and dying king,—
Princes, the dregs of their dull race, who flow
Through public scorn—mud from a muddy spring,—
Rulers, who neither see, nor feel, nor know,
But leech-like to their fainting country cling,
Till they drop, blind in blood, without a blow,—
A people starved and stabbed in the untilled field,—
An army, which liberticide and prey
Makes as a two-edged sword to all who wield,
Golden and sanguine laws which tempt and slay,—
Religion Christless, Godless—a book sealed;
A Senate—Time's worst statute unrepealed,—
Are graves, from which a glorious Phantom may
Burst, to illumine our tempestuous day.

(1839)

Jane Alice Sargant
(fl. 1817–21)

Jane Alice Sargant wrote novels and plays as well as *Sonnets and Other Poems*, a 120-page volume published by subscription by Hatchard in 1817. A second edition quickly followed. In 1821 Sargant brought out *Extracts from the Pilgrimage of St. Caroline: With Notes, by an Englishwoman,* published by the London firm W. Wright.

337. 'Lo, on her dying couch, the sufferer lies'

'Lo, on her dying couch, the sufferer lies,
  While meager poverty stands shivering by,
  And pallid want, with nearly-closed eye,
And conscious guilt, that heaves unbidden sighs!
Fast down her cheeks fall penitential tears,
  To Heaven she turns, and now she meekly prays;
Her breast alternate throbs with hopes and fears,
  Which now depress, and now sweet comfort raise.
Go, base deceiver, view the dreadful scene—
  Go, view the victim that thine arts betrayed;
Who, but for thee, had blest with virtue been;
  Who, but for thee, had ne'er from honor strayed.
And keen remorse shall wake a pang of woe,
That only crimes like thine can ever know.

                                         (1817)

338. 'How gladly would I lay my aching head'

How gladly would I lay my aching head,
  Beneath these stately chestnuts' deepened shade,
Where the bright morning sun-beams ne'er have played
  Nor smiled as though in scorn upon the dead!
Methinks I here could peacefully repose,
  While these majestic boughs should o'er me wave;
And find at last a solace to my woes,
  Within an humble, but a welcome grave.
No stone be o'er me seen with praises vain,
  And useless pomp to lure the careless eye;
The spot be known but to the village swain,
  Whose uncorrupted heart may breathe a sigh;
And though no tear his ruddy cheek bedew,
He yet my lowly bed with flowers may strew.

                                          (1817)

Thomas Doubleday
(1790–1870)

Well known for his integrity and compassion for the laboring class, Thomas
Doubleday was active in Whig politics as well as literature. Once he was ac-
cused of but never prosecuted for sedition. *His Sixty-Five Sonnets* (1818) was
a popular success. He also wrote political and economic tracts, dramas, and a
biography of Sir Robert Peele.

339. 'Poppies, that scattered o'er this arid plain'

Poppies, that scattered o'er this arid plain,
  Display the barrenness ye cannot cure,

Though little may your sickly flowers allure,
Their juice deserves because it aids the strain,
For not alone it lulls our harshest pain,
    While, in the dangerous or the indulgent hour,
    The Turk still seeks it, but its wondrous power
Can bring to bear the poet's barren brain;
And in blessed service, like a knight of old,
    It conquers but the monsters of the mind:
        Oh! poppy-flowers, as rude weeds round ye press,
E'en you look beauteous, 'mong their colors cold:
    So, mid the prickly cares of life, we find
        The sweetest hours—those of forgetfulness.

                                                (1818)

340. 'No walk today;—November's breathings toss'

No walk today;—November's breathings toss
    The vaporous clouds in masses; fitter suit
    The intercourse of minds, social dispute,
And wit's pure fire purging the mental dross;—
—So, come, my friend; let those delights engross
    The present hour; and when their voice is mute
    Then let thy mellow-tongued, persuasive flute,
With its sweet utterance, well supply their loss.—
Thou shalt have tea, not wine; wine shall not sing
    With siren pleadings to the unfettered blood;
    Snug is the shuttered room; the fire is good;
Thy flute its tide of softest sounds shall bring:
    While quiet pleasure, with a halcyon's wing,
        Broods and luxuriates on the gentle flood!

                                                (1818)

341. 'Friends, when my latest bed of rest is made'

Friends, when my latest bed of rest is made,
    No empty bowls must ring my funeral knell,
    But bumpers rouse the gay song's wildest swell,
While soft you lay me in my vineyard's shade;
And press the ripe grapes till they weep and aid
    The rites for one that loved them still so well;
    A goblet on my grave its place may tell;
And thus would I be mourned, and thus be laid.
My vines, close twining round, shall keep away
    The rains, for water ever pained my sight;
Haply, as mild departs the autumnal day,
    The nightingale, amid their clusters bright,
May sit, and sweetly pour for him the lay,
    Whose song, like hers, was heard so oft at night.

                                                (1818)

Horace Smith
(1779–1849)

Percy Bysshe Shelley saw great irony in the fact that his friend Horace Smith, whom he considered the most generous of men, was also a successful stock-broker. With his brother James, Smith published the highly successful literary parody *Rejected Addresses* (1812), which lampooned Southey, Wordsworth, and Scott. He wrote his sonnet "Ozymandias" in competition with Shelley and was also the author of a popular novel, *Brambletye House* (1826).

342. Ozymandias

In Egypt's sandy silence, all alone,
  Stands a gigantic leg, which far off throws
  The only shadow that the desert knows:—
"I am great Ozymandias," saith the stone,
  "The King of Kings; this mighty City shows
The wonders of my hand."—The city's gone,—
  Nought but the leg remaining to disclose
The site of this forgotten Babylon.

We wonder,—and some hunter may express
Wonder like ours, when through the wilderness
  Where London stood, holding the wolf in chase,
He meets some fragment huge, and stops to guess
  What powerful but unrecorded race
Once dwelt in that annihilated place.

(1818)

John Clare
(1793–1864)

John Clare's first volume, *Poems Descriptive of Rural Life and Scenery* (1820), was a literary sensation. Of laboring-class origins, Clare was known as a "peasant poet" who had little formal education, who had worked as a farm laborer, and who had no literary pretentions. His aim was to capture the ordinary experience of rural life in a natural idiom. This he did, much as Burns had some decades before. His fame was short-lived, however; he spent the last twenty-five years of his life suffering from severe mental illness and confined to an institution. There, he wrote much of his best poetry, which remained largely unpublished until the twentieth century.

343. The Primrose

Welcome, pale Primrose! starting up between
  Dead matted leaves of ash and oak, that strew
  The every lawn, the wood, and spinney through,

Mid creeping moss and ivy's darker green;
  How much thy presence beautifies the ground:
How sweet thy modest, unaffected pride
Glows on the sunny bank, and wood's warm side.
  And where thy fairy flowers in groups are found,
The school-boy roams enchantedly along,
  Plucking the fairest with a rude delight:
While the meek shepherd stops his simple song,
  To gaze a moment on the pleasing sight;
O'erjoyed to see the flowers that truly bring
The welcome news of sweet returning Spring.

(1820)

344. The Gypsy's Evening Blaze

To me how wildly pleasing is that scene
  Which doth present, in evening's dusky hour,
A group of Gypsies, centered on the green,
  In some warm nook where Boreas has no power;
Where sudden starts the quivering blaze behind
  Short, shrubby bushes, nibbled by the sheep,
  That mostly on these short sward pastures keep;
Now lost, now seen, now bending with the wind:
And now the swarthy Sybil kneels reclined;
  With proggling stick she still renews the blaze,
  Forcing bright sparks to twinkle from the flaze.
When this I view, the all-attentive mind
  Will oft exclaim (so strong the scene pervades),
  "Grant me this life, thou Spirit of the Shades!"

(1820)

345. To an Hour-Glass

Old-fashioned uncouth measurer of the day,
  I love to watch thy filtering burden pass;
Though some there are that live would bid thee stay;
  But these view reasons through a different glass
From him, Time's meter, who addresses thee.
  The world has joys which they may deem as such;
The world has wealth to season vanity,
  And wealth is theirs to make their vainness much:
But small to do with joys and Fortune's fee
Hath he, Time's chronicler, who welcomes thee.
  So jog thou on, through hours of doomed distress;
So haste thou on the glimpse of hopes to come;
  As every sand-grain counts a trouble less,
As every drained glass leaves me nearer home.

(1821)

346. To an Angry Bee

Malicious insect, little vengeful bee,
   With venom-sting thou'rt whirling round and round
A harmless head that ne'er meant wrong to thee,
   And friendship's hand it is thou'dst wish to wound:
Cool thy revenge, and judge thy foes aright;
   The hardened neatherd and the sweet-toothed boy—
Thy moss-wrapped treasures, if but in their sight,
   Soon would they all thy honeyed lives destroy:
But delve the cowslip-peep in labor free,
And dread no pilferer of thy hoards in me.—
   Thus man to man oft takes a friend for foe,
And spurns a blessing when it's in his power,
   Mistakes real happiness for worldly woe,
Crops sorrow's weed, and treads on pleasure's flower.

                                                       (1821)

347. The Last of April

Old April wanes, and her last dewy morn
   Her death-bed steeps in tears:—to hail the May
New blooming blossoms 'neath the sun are born,
   And all poor April's charms are swept away.
The early primrose, peeping once so gay,
   Is now choked up with many a mounting weed,
   And the poor violet we once admired
Creeps in the grass unsought for—flowers succeed,
   Gaudy and new, and more to be desired,
   And of the old the school-boy seemeth tired.
So with us all, poor April, as with thee!
   Each hath its day;—the future brings my fears:
Friends may grow weary, new flowers rising be,
   And my last end, like thine, be steeped in tears.

                                                       (1821)

348. Winter

The small wind whispers through the leafless hedge
   Most sharp and chill, where the light snowy flakes
Rest on each twig and spike of withered sedge,
   Resembling scattered feathers;—vainly breaks
The pale split sunbeam through the frowning cloud,
   On Winter's frowns below—from day to day
Unmelted still he spreads his hoary shroud,
   In dithering pride on the pale traveler's way,
Who, croodling, hastens from the storm behind
Fast gathering deep and black, again to find

His cottage-fire and corner's sheltering bounds;
Where, haply, such uncomfortable days
    Make musical the wood-sap's frizzling sounds,
And hoarse loud bellows puffing up the blaze.

                                   (1821)

349. To the Memory of John Keats

The world, its hopes, and fears, have passed away;
    No more its trifling thou shalt feel or see;
Thy hopes are ripening in a brighter day,
    While these left buds thy monument shall be.
When Rancor's aims have past in nought away,
    Enlarging specks discerned in more than thee,
And beauties 'minishing which few display,—
    When these are past, true child of Poesy,
Thou shalt survive—Ah, while a being dwells,
    With soul, in Nature's joys, to warm like thine,
With eye to view her fascinating spells,
    And dream entranced o'er each form divine,
Thy worth, Enthusiast, shall be cherished here,—
Thy name with him shall linger, and be dear.

                                   (1821)

350. Rural Scenes

I never saw a man in all my days—
    One whom the calm of quietness pervades—
Who gave not woods and fields his hearty praise,
    And felt a happiness in summer shades.
There I meet common thoughts, that all may read
    Who love the quiet fields:—I note them well,
Because they give me joy as I proceed,
    And joy renewed, when I their beauties tell
In simple verse, and unambitious songs,
    That in some mossy cottage haply may
Be read, and win the praise of humble tongues
    In the green shadows of some after-day.
For rural fame may likeliest rapture yield
To hearts, whose songs are gathered from the field.

                                   (1835)

351. The Shepherd's Tree

Huge elm, with rifted trunk all notched and scarred,
    Like to a warrior's destiny! I love
To stretch me often on thy shadowed sward,
    And hear the laugh of summer leaves above;

Or on thy buttressed roots to sit, and lean
  In careless attitude, and there reflect
On times, and deeds, and darings that have been—
  Old castaways, now swallowed in neglect;
While thou art towering in thy strength of heart,
  Stirring the soul to vain imaginings,
In which life's sordid being hath no part.
  The wind of that eternal ditty sings
Humming of future things, that burn the mind
To leave some fragment of itself behind.

                                        (1835)

352. The Wren

Why is the cuckoo's melody preferred,
  And nightingale's rich songs so madly praised
In poets' rhymes! Is there no other bird
  Of Nature's minstrelsy, that oft hath raised
One's heart to ecstasy and mirth as well?
  I judge not how another's taste is caught,
With mine are other birds that bear the bell,
  Whose song hath crowds of happy memories brought:—
Such the wood robin, singing in the dell;
  And little wren, that many a time hath sought
Shelter from showers, in huts, where I did dwell
  In early spring, the tenant of the plain,
Tending my sheep; and still they come to tell
  The happy stories of the past again.

                                          (1835)

353. The Wryneck's Nest

That summer bird its oft-repeated note
  Chirps from the dottrel ash, and in the hole
The green woodpecker made in years remote,
  It makes its nest. When peeping idlers stroll
In anxious plundering moods, they by and by
  The wryneck's curious eggs, as white as snow,
While squinting in the hollow tree, espy.
  The sitting bird looks up with jetty eye,
And waves her head in terror to and fro,
  Speckled and veined with various shades of brown;
  And then a hissing noise assails the clown.
Quickly, with hasty terror in his breast,
  From the tree's knotty trunk he slides adown,
And thinks the strange bird guards a serpent's nest.

                                          (1835)

354. Nutting

The Sun had stooped, his westward clouds to win,
Like weary traveler seeking for an inn;
When from the hazelly wood we glad descried
The ivied gateway by the pasture side.
Long had we sought for nuts amid the shade,
Where Silence fled the rustle that we made;
When torn by briars, and brushed by sedges rank,
We left the wood, and on the velvet bank
Of short sward pasture-ground we sat us down,
To shell our nuts before we reached the town.
The near-hand stubble-field, with mellow glower,
Showed the dimmed blaze of poppies still in flower;
And sweet the mole-hills were we sat upon—
Again the thyme's in bloom, but where is Pleasure gone?

(1835)

355. Shadows

The fairest summer hath its sudden showers;
    The clearest sky is never without clouds;
And in the painted meadow's host of flowers
    Some lurking weed a poisonous death enshrouds.
Sweet days, that upon golden sunshine spring,
    A gloomy night in mourning waits to stain;
The honey-bees are girt with sharpest sting,
    And sweetest joys oft breed severest pain.
While like to autumn's storms, sudden and brief,
Mirth's parted lips oft close in silent grief,
    Amid this checkered life's disastrous state,
    Still Hope lives green amid the desolate;
As Nature, in her happy livery, waves
O'er ancient ruins, palaces, and graves.

(1835)

356. A Woodland Seat

Within this pleasant wood, beside the lane,
    Let's sit, and rest us from the burning sun,
And hide us in the leaves, and entertain
    An hour away;—to watch the wood-brook run
Through heaps of leaves, drop dribbling after drop,
    Pining for freedom, till it climbs along
In eddying fury o'er the foamy top;
    And then loud laughing sings its wimpling song,
Kissing the misty dewberry by its side,
    With eager salutations, and in joy;

Making the flag-leaves dance in graceful pride,
    Giving and finding joy.—Here we employ
An hour right profitably, thus to see
Life may meet joys where few intruders be.

(1835)

Samuel Rogers
(1763–1855)

Samuel Rogers was a successful poet, well-known for his passion for art
and his witty conversation, some of which Alexander Dyce recorded in his
Recollections (1856) and G. H. Powell recalled in his *Reminiscences* (1859).
Rogers's most popular work was the topographical poem *The Pleasures of
Memory* (1792). For many years, Rogers was the host of famous London lit-
erary breakfasts.

357. To the Fragment of a Statue of Hercules, Commonly Called the Torso

And dost thou still, thou mass of breathing stone,
    (Thy giant limbs to night and chaos hurled)
Still sit as on the fragment of a world;
    Surviving all, majestic and alone?
What though the Spirits of the North, that swept
Rome from the earth, when in her pomp she slept,
Smote thee with fury, and thy headless trunk
Deep in the dust mid tower and temple sunk;
Soon to subdue mankind 'twas thine to rise,
Still, still unquelled thy glorious energies!
Aspiring minds, with thee conversing, caught
Bright revelations of the Good they sought;
By thee that long-lost spell in secret given,
To draw down Gods, and lift the soul to Heaven!

(1820)

Thomas Lovell Beddoes
(1803–49)

Frequently compared to that of his contemporary Edgar Allan Poe, Thomas
Lovell Beddoes' poetry reveals a macabre obsession with death and the su-
pernatural. Beddoes was best-known as a dramatist, particularly for *Death's
Jest-Book, or The Fool's Tragedy,* published posthumously in 1850. He also
studied medicine, specializing in anatomy. After leading a restless, solitary life,
he committed suicide in 1849.

358. To Night

So thou art come again, old black-winged night,
    Like a huge bird, between us and the sun,

Hiding, with out-stretched form, the genial light;
　And still, beneath thine icy bosom's dun
And cloudy plumage, hatching fog-breathed blight,
　And embryo storms, and crabbed frosts, that shun
Day's warm caress. The owls from ivied loop
　Are shrieking homage, as thou cowerest high,
Like sable crow pausing in eager stoop
　On the dim world thou gluttest thy clouded eye,
Silently waiting latest time's fell whoop,
　When thou shalt quit thine eyrie in the sky,
To pounce upon the world with eager claw,
And tomb time, death, and substance in thy maw.

(1821)

Charles Johnston
(d. 1823)

Charles Johnston's life is obscure. Joanna Baillie (1762–1851) included these sonnets in *A Collection of Poems, Chiefly Manuscript, and From Living Authors* (1823). But she notes in her preface that, despite the title of the volume, Johnston "has sunk into an early grave."

359. 'I know thee not, bright creature, ne'er shall know'

I know thee not, bright creature, ne'er shall know;
　Thy course and mine lie far and far away;
　Yet heaven this once has given me to survey
Those charms that seldom may be seen below.
We part as soon as met, but where I go
　Thy form shall ever be; upon thy way
　Shall heaven, for thou art heaven's, its mildest ray
Shed ever bright; yet though disease and woe
　Thy cheek consume not, Time will have his prey,
And I may meet and know thee not again.
　But what lives in the mind shall not decay.
And thus shall mine thy form divine retain,
　In all the freshness of youth's dawning day,
When thou may'st be no more, and earth laments in vain.

(1823)

360. 'Spirit of evil, with which the earth is rife'

Spirit of evil, with which the earth is rife,
Revenge, Revenge! thee all abjure and blame,
Yet, when their hour is come, invoke thy name.
　Base men for thee in secret bare the knife;
　The brave partake the peril and the strife;

The weak, the sword more sure of justice claim;
The strong, when they have blasted power and fame,
    Give to their foe in scorn the curse of life—
The keenest, bitterest vengeance—for these all
    Are only shapes thou tak'st to goad the mind,
Turning the heart's pure, generous blood to gall;
    And thus, Revenge, thou stalk'st through all the kind,
Till might nations madden at thy call,
    And earth is waste, and seas incarnardined.

                                                    (1823)

Elizabeth Cobbold
(1767–1824)

Born Eliza Knipe, she published at the age of nineteen, *Poems on Various Subjects* (1783) and her first critical success four years later, *Six Narrative Poems,* dedicated to her friend Sir Joshua Reynolds. She published a two-volume novel in 1791 and the next year married the successful Ipswich brewer John Cobbold. His fourteen children combined with the seven they eventually had together meant that most of her time was spent parenting and running the household. Even so, she became an amateur naturalist and in 1800 published a burlesque *Mince Pye; an Heroic Epistle.* In 1812, she founded the Society for Clothing the Infant Poor. For almost two decades, she hosted a Valentine's eve party and composed verse valentines for each of eighty guests, published as *Cliff Valentines* (1813–4). Her collected *Poems* were published in 1825.

361–363. Sonnets of Laura

Lately discovered in a Casket enclosed in a Tomb at
Avignon, supposed to be that of Petrarch's Laura,
and now first translated into English.

361. I. Reproach

Ah! little cause has Petrarch to complain,
    Since thus he boasts his wound, thus vaunts the smart,
While Laura struggles to conceal the pain
    Derived from silence and a bursting heart:
For dear she holds the Poet and his lay:
    But this avowal meets no human ear,
Nor shall the conscious eye of tell-tale day
    Behold her shed the unavailing tear.
For this, with watchful and incessant care
    She tries each varied art, each strange disguise
While cold indifference marks her studied air,

Smiles on her cheek, and lords it o'er her sighs.
The world shall sympathize with Petrarch's woe,
While night and silence only Laura's know.

(1825)

362. II. The Veil

What weak remonstrance!—how I joy to find
    The well invented fraud thy faith deceive!
The veil that shades the face obscures the mind,
    And love is ever fearful to believe;
Else had my cheerful and unguarded smile,
    The pleasure that I felt when you were nigh,
The welcome gay, the look devoid of guile,
    The tear of rapture springing to my eye,
Told a fond tale that you should never learn,
    Of fears I would not for the world reveal,
Of hopes I almost tremble to discern;
    Of bliss my heart would from itself conceal.
Come, blessed veil! thy friendly aid I claim,
Guard of my pride, my honor, and my fame.

(1825)

363. III. Absence

What boots it that thy steps to distant shores
    In search of quiet or oblivion stray,
While here thy verse enthusiastic pours,
    While every morn presents the wonted lay?
'Twas not the beauty of thy manly form,
    'Twas not the luster of thy sparkling eye,
That bade my heart to fond affection warm,
    That in my tranquil bosom woke the sigh:
No, 'twas that rich and ever varying mind,
    With every just and generous feeling fraught,
That ardent love, by sentiment refined,
    That spoke in every look, and every thought.
Then while I view these graces in thy strain,
Vain is thy journey, and its distance vain.

(1825)

364. On Some Violets Planted in My Garden by a Friend

Catherine, though not from fortune's glittering stores
    Thou hadst a gift to offer, yet 'twas thine
A tender sweetness in thy gift to pour,
    That gave thy heart's expression best to mine.
    The violets, o'er yon western bank that twine,

To thy protecting hand their station owe;
   In brighter tints may proud exotics shine,
But none with fresher native fragrance blow:
Even as thy violets in my garden grow,
   So shall thy friendship in my bosom live,
Its rooting fibres round my heart-strings throw,
   And sweetness to each pure sensation give,
Still flourish there unfading, and defy
The changing climate and the stormy sky.

                                            (1825)

John F. M. Dovaston
(1782–1852)

After having worked briefly as a newspaper theatre critic, John F. M. Dov-aston inherited his father's estate in 1808 and was then free to pursue a life as a writer and naturalist. His *Fitz-Gwarine* (1812) and *British Melodies* (1817) were popular. These two sonnets from *Poems, Legendary, Incidental and Humorous* (1825) reflect how enduring as subjects rivers and the sonnet form itself were.

365. 'Streamlet! methinks thy lot resembles mine'

Streamlet! methinks thy lot resembles mine,
   For thou art wayward, and delight'st to run
Through dingles wild, where writhen roots entwine;
   The haunts that power and pride are like to shun;
Or if by chance they cross thy playful stream
   They mark thee not, nor seek to know thy source,
   For men have never mapped thy modest course,
Nor thought worth while to give thee even a name.
Yet art thou not unloved; for on thy brink
   The primrose blossoms early, and the bird
   Of orange bill down thy deep glen is heard
By some lone youth that pauses there to think
That he o'er life's sequestered vales, like thee,
Though not unmournful, runs right merrily.

                                            (1825)

366. 'There are who say the sonnet's meted maze'

There are who say the sonnet's meted maze
   Is all too fettered for the poet's powers,
   Compelled to crowd his flush and airy flowers,
Like pots of tall imperials, ill at ease.
Or should some tiny thought his fancy seize,
   A violet on a vase's top it towers,
   And 'mid the mass of leaves he round it showers

Its little cap and tippet scarce can raise.
Others assert the sonnet's proper praise,
  Like petaled flowers, to each its due degree,
The king-cup five, the pilewort eight bright rays,
  The speedwell four, the green-tipped snowdrop three:
So 'mid the bard's all-petaled sorts is seen
The sonnet—simple flow'ret of fourteen.

                                 (1825)

Sarah Hamilton
(c. 1769–1843)

Sarah Hamilton published four books in quick succession in London during the mid- to late-1820s, beginning with *Sonnets, Tour to Matlock, Recollections of Scotland, and Other Poems* (1825). According to an obituary in the *Gentleman's Magazine*, she was the youngest daughter of the physician Robert Hamilton of Lynn, Norfolk, and she died at Leamington. She published in 1826 a translation of a six-book poem the *Art of War* by Frederick III, King of Prussia. Perhaps reflecting a growing reputation, her last book, *Alfred the Great, a Drama, in Five Acts,* was published in 1829 by the distinguished firm Longman, Rees, Orme, Brown, and Green.

367. *Farewell to France*

Supposed to be repeated by Mary, Queen of Scots, from the deck of the ship which was to convey her to Scotland.

O land of elegance, where every grace
Resides—where science fills the polished mind,
How sad the bitter contrast I must find
  In barren Scotia's rude and frowning face!
  Oft, when away, shall memory love to trace
Thy smiling hillocks and thy flowery vales,
Thy groves, where feathered songsters tell their tales,
  Thy purple vines, thy cheerful peasant race,
  Thy court—but, ah! fond memory naught avails:
No more shall I of that gay court be queen!
For ever then farewell each long-loved scene.
  And, see, the cruel wind now swells the sails!
I go, with feeble power to meet the storm,
Where hate and furious zeal my native shores deform.

                                 (1825)

368. *The Poppy*

Light weed, whose poisoned scent with sickly power
Bears on the nerves which seek the morning air,
As thou, dire poppy, thy sleek head dost rear

Amid the yellow corn, thou fatal flower!
To soothe the sorrows of the midnight hour
The children of distress to thee repair,
But ah! too oft do wretched mortals dare
    Through thee to flee from life which cares devour.
    The coward mind, which shrinks beneath its woes,
Seeks in thy juice a cure for worldly grief,
But oh! how impotent the sad relief,
    Which bids the guilty victim's tomb unclose!
Yet thou canst mitigate disease's pain,
And with thy balm assuage the fevered brain.

                                                      (1825)

Thomas Moore
(1779–1852)

Thomas Moore's *Irish Melodies* (1807–1834) were hugely popular, as was his
Oriental romance *Lalla Rookh* (1817), which brought him financial success.
In 1830, he published a valuable biography of his close friend Lord Byron.
Earlier, with several others, he had been responsible for burning Byron's
memoirs in the drawing-room fireplace of the publisher John Murray.

369. No—Leave My Heart to Rest

No—Leave my heart to rest, if rest it may,
When youth, and love, and hope, have passed away.
Could'st thou, when summer hours are fled,
To some poor leaf that's fall'n and dead,
Bring back the hue it wore, the scent it shed?
No—leave this heart to rest, if rest it may,
When youth, and love, and hope, have passed away.

Oh, had I met thee then, when life was bright,
Thy smile might still have fed its tranquil light;
But now thou com'st like sunny skies,
Too late to cheer the seaman's eyes,
When wrecked and lost his bark before him lies!
No—leave this heart to rest, if rest it may,
Since youth, and love, and hope, have passed away.

                                                      (1825)

370. Fancy

The more I've viewed this world, the more I've found,
    That, filled as 'tis with scenes and creatures rare,
Fancy commands, within her own bright round,
    A world of scenes and creatures far more fair.
Nor is it that her power can call up there

A single charm, that's not from Nature won,—
No more than rainbows, in their pride, can wear
  A single tint unborrowed from the sun;
But 'tis the mental medium it shines through,
That lends to beauty all its charm and hue;
As the same light, that o'er the level lake
  One dull monotony of luster flings,
Will, entering in the rounded rain-drop, make
  Colors as gay as those on angels' wings!

                                                   (c. 1827)

William Ewart Gladstone
(1809–98)

One of the great statesmen of the nineteenth century, William Ewart Glad-
stone was a distinguished orator, classical scholar, political writer, and leader
of the Liberal Party. He served four terms as Prime Minister (1868–74,
1880–5, 1886, 1892–4), frequently clashing with his conservative rival Ben-
jamin Disraeli (1804–81). As a student at Eton, he edited the *Eton Miscellany*,
where this sonnet appeared.

371. To a Rejected Sonnet

Poor child of Sorrow! who did'st boldly spring,
  Like sapient Pallas, from thy parent's brain,
  All arm'd in mail of proof! and thou would'st fain
Leap further yet and, on exulting wing,
Rise to the summit of the printer's press!
  But cruel hand hath nipped thy buds amain,
  Hath fixed on thee the darkling inky stain,
Hath soiled thy splendor, and defiled thy dress!
Where are thy "full-orbed moon" and "sky serene?"
  And where thy "waving foam" and "foaming wave?"
All, all are blotted by the murderous pen,
  And lie unhonored in their papery grave!
Weep, gentle Sonnets! Sonneteers, deplore!
And vow—and keep the vow—you'll write no more!

                                                   (1827)

Mary Russell Mitford
(1787–1855)

Mary Russell Mitford was a respected dramatist and poet. She published
several accomplished volumes of poetry, including *Poems* (1810), *Christina,
or the Maid of the South Seas* (1811), and *Poems on the Female Character* (1813);
and her tragedy *Julian* was performed at Covent Garden to much acclaim
in 1823. However, it was *Our Village* (1824), with its amusing, affectionate,

and down-to-earth prose sketches of Berkshire life, that became an English classic. She had further success with *Foscari* (1826) and *Rienzi* (1828). Mitford's long friendship with Elizabeth Barrett was later immortalized by Virginia Woolf in her novel *Flush*.

372. The Forget-Me-Not

Blossom that lov'st on shadowy banks to lie,
  Gemming the deep rank grass with flowers so blue,
  That the pure turquoise matched with their rich hue
Pales, fades, and dims; so exquisite a dye,
That scarce the brightness of the autumn sky,
  Which sleeps upon the bosom of the stream,
  On whose fringed margent thy star-flowerets gleam
In its clear azure with thy tints may vie;
  Shade-loving flower, I love thee! not alone
That thou dost haunt the greenest coolest spot,
  For ever, by the tufted alder thrown,
Or arching hazel, or vine mantled cot,
  But that thy very name hath a sweet tone
Of parting tenderness—Forget me not!

                                   (1827)

373. On a Beautiful Woman

Look where she sits in languid loveliness,
  Her feet upgathered, and her turbaned brow
  Bent o'er her hand, her robe in ample flow
Disparted! Look in attitude and dress
She sits and seems an eastern sultaness!
  And music is about her, and the glow
  Of young fair faces, and sweet voices go
Forth at her call, and all about her press.
  But no sultana she! As in a book
In that fine form and lovely brow we trace
  Divinest purity, and the bright look
Of genius. Much is she in mind and face
Like the fair blossom of some woodland nook
  The wind-flower,——delicate and full of grace.

                                   (1827)

Barry Cornwall (Bryan Waller Procter)
(1787–1874)

Bryan Waller Procter, a London lawyer, used the pseudonym "Barry Cornwall," an anagram of his name. Though Percy Bysshe Shelley called him "filthy and dull," his lyrics and songs were extremely popular. His volume

Dramatic Scenes, and Other Poems (1819) was well received by critics; *English Songs* (1832) was his most popular work. In 1832, Procter became Metropolitan Commissioner of Lunacy, a sinecure post he held until 1861.

374. To My Child

Child of my heart! My sweet, beloved first-born!
Thou dove, who tidings bring'st of calmer hours!
Thou rainbow, who dost come when all the showers
Are past,—or passing! Rose which hath no thorn,—
No pain, no blemish,—pure and unforlorn,
Untouched—untainted—O, my flower of flowers!
More welcome than to bees are summer bowers,—
To seamen stranded life-assuring morn.
Welcome! a thousand welcomes! Care, who clings
Round all, seems loosening now her snake-like fold!
New hope springs upwards, and the bright world seems
Cast back into her youth of endless springs!—
—Sweet mother, *is* it so?—or grow I old,
Bewildered in divine Elysian dreams?

(1828)

Joseph Blanco White
(1775–1841)

Joseph Blanco White came to England from Spain in 1810, after quitting the Catholic priesthood. He studied at Oxford, became an Anglican clergyman, and wrote religious and theological tracts. "Night and Death," later published as "To Night," became one of the most enduring sonnets of the nineteenth century. Samuel Taylor Coleridge called it one of the best sonnets in English, and William Sharp praised it decades later in his anthology, *Sonnets of this Century* (1886).

375. Night and Death

Dedicated to S. T. Coleridge, Esq. by his sincere friend,
Joseph Blanco White

Mysterious night, when the first man but knew
Thee by report, unseen, and heard thy name,
Did he not tremble for this lovely frame,
This glorious canopy of light and blue?
Yet 'neath a curtain of translucent dew
Bathed in the rays of the great setting flame,
Hesperus, with the host of heaven, came,
And lo! creation widened on his view.

Who could have thought what darkness lay concealed
Within thy beams, oh Sun? Or who could find,
    Whilst fly, and leaf, and insect stood revealed,
That to such endless orbs thou mad'st us blind?
Weak man! Why to shun death, this anxious strife?
If *light* can thus deceive, wherefore not *life?*

(1828)

Thomas Hood
(1799–1845)

A gifted punster and professional man of letters, Thomas Hood was popular
for his comic and satirical verse as well as for serious, socially conscious
poems such as "The Song of the Shirt" (1843). After serving as assistant
editor of the *London Magazine,* he went on to edit many other periodicals,
including the *Gem,* the *Comic Annual,* and the *New Monthly Magazine.*

376. Written in the Workhouse

Oh, blessed ease! no more of heaven I ask:
    The overseer is gone—that vandal elf—
    And hemp, unpicked, may go and hang itself,
While I, untasked, except with Cowper's Task,
In blessed literary leisure bask,
    And lose the workhouse, saving in the works
    Of Goldsmiths, Johnsons, Sheridans, and Burkes;
Eat prose and drink of the Castalian flask;
The themes of Locke, the anecdotes of Spence,
    The humorous of Gay, the Grave of Blair—
Unlearned toil, unlettered labors hence!
    But, hark! I hear the master on the stair—
And Thomson's Castle, that of Indolence,
    Must be to me a castle in the air.

(1830)

377. To the Ocean

Shall I rebuke thee, Ocean, my old love,
That once, in rage with the wild winds at strife,
Thou darest menace my unit of a life,
Sending my clay below, my soul above,
Whilst roared thy waves, like lions when they rove
By night, and bound upon their prey by stealth?
Yet did'st thou ne'er restore my fainting health?—
Did'st thou ne'er murmur gently like the dove?
Nay, did'st thou not against my own dear shore
Full break, last link between my land and me?—

My absent friends talk in thy very roar,
In thy waves' beat their kindly pulse I see,
And, if I must not see my England more,
Next to her soil, my grave be found in thee!

(1846)

378. False Poets and True

Look how the lark soars upward and is gone,
Turning a spirit as he nears the sky!
His voice is heard, but body there is none
To fix the vague excursions of the eye.
So, poets' songs are with us, though they die
Obscured, and hid by death's oblivious shroud,
And Earth inherits the rich melody,
Like raining music from the morning cloud.
Yet, few there be who pipe so sweet and loud,
Their voices reach us through the lapse of space:
The noisy day is deafened by a crowd
Of undistinguished birds, a twittering race;
But only lark and nightingale forlorn
Fill up the silences of night and morn.

(1846)

379. Sonnet to a Sonnet

Rare composition of a poet-knight,
Most chivalrous among chivalric men,
Distinguished for a polished lance and pen
In tuneful contest and in tourney-fight;
Lustrous in scholarship, in honor bright,
Accomplished in all graces current then,
Humane as any in historic ken,
Brave, handsome, noble, affable, polite;
Most courteous to that race become of late
So fiercely scornful of all kind advance,
Rude, bitter, coarse, implacable in hate
To Albion, plotting ever her mischance,—
Alas, fair verse! how false and out of date
Thy phrase "sweet enemy" applied to France!

(1846)

Edward Moxon
(1801–58)

Edward Moxon was one of the most distinguished British publishers and
booksellers of the nineteenth century. His own poetry was never as widely
read as that of the impressive roster of poets he published, including William

Wordsworth, S. T. Coleridge, Robert Southey, Percy Bysshe Shelley, John
Keats, Robert Browning, Alfred Tennyson, and Henry Wadsworth Long-
fellow.

380. 'Loud midnight-soothing melancholy bird'

Loud midnight-soothing melancholy bird,
That send'st such music to my sleepless soul,
Binding her powers in thy fast control,
Few listen to thy song; yet I have heard,
When man and Nature slept, nor aspen stirred,
Thy mournful voice, sweet vigil of the sleeping—
And likened thee to some angelic mind,
That sits and grieves for erring mortals weeping.
The genius, not of groves, but of mankind,
Watch at this solemn hour o'er millions keeping.
In Eden's bowers, as mighty poets tell,
Didst thou repeat, as now, that plaintive call—
Those sorrowing notes might seem, sad Philomel,
Prophetic to have mourned of *man* the *fall*.

(1830)

William Stanley Roscoe
(1753–1831)

William Stanley Roscoe published on a variety of subjects, ranging from
jurisprudence to biography to botany. A frequent contributor to the annu-
als, he also wrote poetry for children, a distinguished biography of Lorenzo
de'Medici (1795), and edited Alexander Pope's poetry (1824). His innovative
children's poem *The Butterfly's Ball and the Grasshopper's Feast* (1807) empha-
sized the pleasure of imagination over moral instruction. He was also a book
collector, which adds to the poignancy of the sonnet in which he describes
having to part with his library.

381. The Camellia

As Venus wandered 'midst the Idalian bower,
    And marked the loves and graces round her play;
    She plucked a musk-rose from its dew-bent spray,
"And this," she cried, "shall be my favorite flower;
For o'er its crimson leaflets I will shower
    Dissolving sweets to steal the soul away;
    That Dian's self shall own their sovereign sway,
And feel the influence of my mightier power."
Then spoke fair Cynthia, as severe she smiled,—
"Be others by thy amorous arts beguiled,

Ne'er shall thy dangerous gifts these brows adorn:
To me more dear than all their rich perfume
The chaste camellia's pure and spotless bloom,
   That boasts no fragrance, and conceals no thorn."—

(1830)

382. To the Harvest Moon

Again thou reignest in thy golden hall,
Rejoicing in thy sway, fair queen of night!
The ruddy reapers hail thee with delight,
Theirs is the harvest, theirs the joyous call
For tasks well ended ere the season's fall.
Sweet orb, thou smilest from thy starry height,
But whilst on them thy beams are shedding bright,
To me thou com'st o'ershadowed with a pall:
To me alone the year hath fruitless flown,
Earth hath fulfilled her trust through all her lands,
The good man gathereth now where he had sown,
And the great master in his vineyard stands;
But I, as if my task were all unknown,
Come to his gates, alas, with empty hands.

(1834)

383. On Being Forced to Part with his Library for the Benefit of his Creditors

As one who destined from his friends to part,
   Regrets his loss, yet hopes again ere-while
   To share their converse and enjoy their smile,
And tempers, as he may, affliction's dart,—
Thus, loved associates! chiefs of elder art!
   Teachers of wisdom! who could once beguile
   My tedious hours, and lighten every toil,
I now resign you; nor with fainting heart—
For pass a few short years, or days, or hours,
   And happier seasons may their dawn unfold,
   And all your sacred fellowship restore;
When, freed from earth, unlimited its powers,
   Mind shall with mind direct communion hold,
   And kindred spirits meet to part no more.

(1841)

Charles Tennyson Turner
(1808–79)

Charles Tennyson Turner, with his brother Alfred, contributed to the volume
Poems by Two Brothers (1827) and went on to have a long literary career that

included the publication of hundreds of sonnets. His first book, *Sonnets and Fugitive Pieces,* published as "Charles Tennyson," established his reputation as an accomplished sonneteer. In 1835, he inherited from his great-uncle Samuel Turner his surname as well as a considerable fortune. Later volumes, including *Sonnets* (1864), *Small Tableux* (1868), and *Sonnets, Lyrics and Translations* (1873), bear the name "Charles Turner."

384. 'When lovers' lips from kissing disunite'

When lovers' lips from kissing disunite
With sound as soft as mellow fruitage breaking,
They loath to quit what was so sweet in taking,
So fraught with breathless magical delight:
The scent of flowers is long before it fade,
Long dwells upon the gale the vesper-tone,
Far floats the wake the lightest skiff has made,
The closest kiss when once impressed is gone;
What marvel then that youth so fondly kisses,
That deep and long he prints the ardent seal!
What marvel then with sorrow he dismisses
This thrilling pledge of trustful hearts and leal!
While eyes look into eyes and none represses
With meddling words, the passion they reveal!

(1830)

385. 'Hence with your jeerings, petulant and low'

Hence with your jeerings, petulant and low,
My love of home no circumstance can shake,
Too ductile for the change of place to break,
And far too passionate for most to know—
I and yon pollard-oak have grown together,
How on yon slope the shifting sunsets lie
None knew so well as I, and tending hither
Flows the strong current of my sympathy;
From this same flower-bed, dear to memory,
I learnt how marigolds do bloom and fade
And from the grove that skirts this garden glade
I had my earliest thoughts of love and spring:
Ye wot not how the heart of man is made,
I learn but now what change the world can bring!

(1830)

386. 'No trace is left upon the vulgar mind'

No trace is left upon the vulgar mind
By shapes which form upon the poet's thought

In instant symmetry: all eyes are blind
Save his, for ends of lowlier vision wrought;
Think'st thou, if Nature wore to every gaze
Her noble beauty and commanding power
Could harsh and ugly doubt withstand the blaze
Or front her Sinai Presence for an hour?
The seal of Truth is Beauty—When the eye
Sees not the token, can the mission move?
The brow is veiled that should attach the tie
And lend the magic to the voice of Love:
What wonder then that doubt is ever nigh
Urging such spirits to mock and to deny?

(1830)

387. 'O'erladen with sad musings'

This, and the following, are supposed to be written by one
on whom the death of an excellent woman has forced the conviction of a
future state.

O'erladen with sad musings, till the tear
Sprang to the pressure, I surveyed the tomb
All dressed in flowers, as though above thy bier
The breath yet hovering fed the gentle bloom:
I said, Maria! though I deemed too long
That souls would fade like music on the air—
Hast thou not brought me "confirmation strong,"
That they shall yet be beautiful elsewhere?
For thine was so immaculate and rare,
That but the thought of such deep purity
Linked with that other thought, I could not bear;
Range then bright soul, and take thy place on high,
I do confess thou wert so good and fair
That thou, if none beside, wert never born to die!

(1830)

388. 'The bliss of Heaven, Maria, shall be thine'

The bliss of Heaven, Maria, shall be thine,
Joy linked to joy by amaranthine bond,
And a fair harp of many strings divine
Shall meet thy touch with unimagined sound!
Divinity shall dwell within thine eye,
Fed by the presence of a loftier soul:
Thy brow shall beam with fairer dignity,
No more thy cheek shall blench with care's control,
Or yield its hues to changes of the heart,
That beats with plenitude of life and woe,

Taking all dyes that sorrow can impart,
Or ever-shifting circumstance bestow—
The prey of present pangs or after-smart,
For ever feeling pain or missing bliss below.

(1830)

389. 'His was a chamber in the topmost tower'

His was a chamber in the topmost tower,
A small unsightly cell with grated bars;
And wearily went on each irksome hour
Of dim Captivity and moody cares!
Against such visitants he was not strong,
But sate with laden heart and brow of woe,
And every morn he heard the stir and song
Of birds in royal gardens fair below,
Telling of bowers and dewy lawns unseen,
Drenched with the silver steam that night had left—
Part blossom-white, part exquisitely green,
And ringing all with thrushes on the left,
And finches on the right, to greet the sheen
Of the May-dawn; while he was thus bereft!

(1830)

Alfred Tennyson
(1809–92)

Alfred Tennyson succeeded William Wordsworth as poet laureate in 1850.
Early in his career, during a period of lyrical experimentation, he wrote son-
nets; most were published in his 1833 volume *Poems.* He would go on to
write the poems for which he is most admired, including the elegy *In
Memoriam* (1850), which expresses his grief over the early death of his friend
Arthur Henry Hallam (1811–33), and the Arthurian poems *Idylls of the King*
(1859–91).

390. 'Check every outflash, every ruder sally'

Check every outflash, every ruder sally
    Of thought and speech; speak low, and give up wholly
    Thy spirit to mild-minded melancholy;
This is the place. Through yonder poplar alley,
Below, the blue-green river windeth slowly;
    But in the middle of the somber valley,
    The crispèd waters whisper musically,
    And all the haunted place is dark and holy.
The nightingale, with long and low preamble,

Warbled from yonder knoll of solemn larches,
And in and out the woodbine's flowery arches
The summer midges wove their wanton gambol,
And all the white stemmed pinewood slept above—
When in this valley first I told my love.

(1831)

391. 'Mine be the strength of spirit fierce and free'

Mine be the strength of spirit fierce and free,
Like some broad river rushing down alone,
With the selfsame impulse wherewith he was thrown
From his loud fount upon the echoing lea:—
Which with increasing might doth forward flee
By town, and tower, and hill, and cape, and isle,
And in the middle of the green salt sea
Keeps his blue waters fresh for many a mile.
Mine be the power which ever to its sway
Will win the wise at once, and by degrees
May into uncongenial spirits flow;
Even as the great gulfstream of Florida
Floats far away into the Northern seas
The lavish growths of southern Mexico.

(1833)

392. 'As when with downcast eyes we muse and brood'

As when with downcast eyes we muse and brood,
And ebb into a former life, or seem
To lapse far back in a confusèd dream
To states of mystical similitude;
If one but speaks or hems or stirs his chair,
Ever the wonder waxeth more and more,
So that we say, "All this hath been before,
All this *hath* been, I know not when or where."
So, friend, when first I looked upon your face,
Our thought gave answer, each to each, so true,
Opposèd mirrors each reflecting each—
Although I knew not in what time or place,
Methought that I had often met with you,
And each had lived in the other's mind and speech.

(1833)

Agnes Strickland
(1796–1874)

After the death of their father in 1818, Agnes Strickland and her sister Eliz-
abeth published historical fiction for children. Thomas Campbell, editor of

the *New Monthly Magazine,* printed some of her translations of Petrarch's sonnets. She was a prolific contributor to the giftbooks and annuals, especially to the *Keepsake,* the *Forget-Me-Not,* and *Friendship's Offering.* She brought out a metrical romance *Worcester Field* in 1826 and *The Seven Ages of Woman* the following year. But she became most well known as a historian after publishing, from 1840 to 1848, with Elizabeth, the *Lives of the Queens of England;* this twelve-volume set was followed by several other major historical works, all of which showed strong Stuart partisanship.

393. The Self-Devoted

She hath forsaken courtly halls and bowers
   For his dear sake:—ay, cheerfully resigned
   Country and friends for him, and hath entwined
Her fate with his in dark and stormy hours,
As the fond ivy clings to ruined towers
   With generous love; and never hath inclined
   Round gilded domes and palaces to wind,
Or flung her wintry wreath midst summer flowers.
Her cheek is pale—it hath grown pale for him;
   Her all of earthly joy, her heaven below—
   He fades before her—fades in want and woe;
She sees his lamp of life wax faint and dim,
   Essays to act the Roman matron's part,
   And veils with patient smiles a breaking heart.

                      (1832)

394. The Forsaken

The bloom of youth had faded from her face,
And left her features tintless as the pale
New fallen blossoms, which the chilling gale
Of March has rudely scattered; every trace
Of joy had fled, and well, in touching grace,
Resembled she some lily of the vale,
Plucked and then left to perish—such the tale
Of her, in whose torn heart hope found no place.
The smiling luster of her eyes was flown
Or dimmed with weeping—but she wept not now—
The fount of tears had failed; her grief alone
Spoke in her sunken cheek and pensive brow,
And every sad expression that might well
A broken heart and early grave foretell.

                      (1850)

395. The Maniac

Sweet summer flowers were braided in her hair,
As if in mockery of the burning brow
Round which they drooped and withered—singing now
Strains of wild mirth, and now of vain despair,
Came the poor wreck of all that once was fair,
And rich in high endowments, ere deep woe
Like a dark cloud came o'er her, and laid low
Reason's proud fane, and left no brightness there.
Yet you might deem *that grief* was with the rest
Of all her cares forgotten, save when songs
And tales she heard of faithful love unblessed,
Of man's deceit, and trusting maiden's wrongs.
Then, and *then only,* in her lifted eyes,
Remembrance beamed, and tears would slowly rise.

(1850)

396. The Infant

I saw an infant—health, and joy, and light
Bloomed on its cheek and sparkled in its eye;
And its fond mother stood delighted by,
To see its morn of being dawn so bright.
Again I saw it, when the withering blight
Of pale disease had fallen, moaning lie
On that sad mother's breast—stern Death was nigh,
And Life's young wings were fluttering for their flight.
Last, I beheld it stretched upon the bier,
Like a fair flower untimely snatched away,
Calm and unconscious of its mother's tear,
Which on its placid cheek unheeded lay;
But on its lip the unearthly smile expressed,
"Oh! happy child! untried and early blessed!"

(1850)

Frederick Tennyson
(1807–98)

Frederick Tennyson assisted his brothers, Charles and Alfred, with the publication of their *Poems by Two Brothers* by silently contributing three or four poems. He wrote in both Greek and English, and his poetry reveals an interest in classical subjects. *Days and Hours* (1854) was well received by some, but others unfairly compared his work to that of his more famous brother. He had an interest in spiritualism and the paranormal and was a friend of Robert and Elizabeth Barrett Browning.

397. Poetical Happiness

There is a fountain, to whose flowery side
By diverse ways the children of the earth
Turn day and night athirst, to measure forth
Its sweet pure waters—health, and wealth, and pride,
Power clad in arms, and wisdom Argus-eyed.
But one apart from all is seen to stand,
And take up in the hollow of his hand
What to their golden vessels is denied;
Baffling their utmost reach. He, born and nursed
In the glad sound and freshness of that place,
Drinks momently its dews, and feels no thirst:
While from his bowered grot, or sunny space,
He sorrows for that troop, as it returns
Through the wide wilderness with empty urns!

(1832)

Hartley Coleridge
(1796–1849)

Hartley Coleridge had a strained relationship with his father, Samuel Taylor Coleridge, who named him after the associationist philosopher David Hartley (1705–57). As a child, he was precocious and imaginative, but William Wordsworth's poem "To H. C., Six Years Old" expresses an anxiety for him that proved all-too prophetic. As an adult poet, his favorite form was the sonnet, and his sonnets were greatly admired during his lifetime. Serious literary success, nonetheless, eluded him, primarily because of alcoholism and an insecurity derived in part from being his father's son.

398. 'Long time a child, and still a child'

Long time a child, and still a child, when years
Had painted manhood on my cheek, was I;
For yet I lived like one not born to die;
A thriftless prodigal of smiles and tears,
No hope I needed, and I knew no fears.
But sleep, though sweet, is only sleep, and waking,
I waked to sleep no more, at once o'ertaking
The vanguard of my age, with all arrears
Of duty on my back. Nor child, nor man,
Nor youth, nor sage, I find my head is gray,
For I have lost the race I never ran,
A rathe December blights my lagging May;
And still I am a child, though I be old,
Time is my debtor for my years untold.

(1833)

399. *Dedicatory Sonnet, To S. T. Coleridge*

Father, and Bard revered! to whom I owe,
Whate'er it be, my little art of numbers,
Thou, in thy night-watch o'er my cradled slumbers,
Didst meditate the verse that lives to show,
(And long shall live, when we alike are low)
Thy prayer how ardent, and thy hope how strong,
That I should learn of Nature's self the song,
The lore which none but Nature's pupils know.

The prayer was heard: I "wandered like a breeze,"
By mountain brooks and solitary meres,
And gathered there the shapes and fantasies
Which, mixed with passions of my sadder years,
Compose this book. If good therein there be,
That good, my sire, I dedicate to thee.

(1833)

400. *To a Friend*

When we were idlers with the loitering rills,
The need of human love we little noted:
Our love was nature; and the peace that floated
On the white mist, and dwelt upon the hills,
To sweet accord subdued our wayward wills:
One soul was ours, one mind, one heart devoted,
That, wisely doting, asked not why it doted,
And ours the unknown joy, which knowing kills.
But now I find, how dear thou wert to me;
That man is more than half of nature's treasure,
Of that fair beauty which no eye can see,
Of that sweet music which no ear can measure;
And now the streams may sing for others' pleasure,
The hills sleep on in their eternity.

(1833)

401. *'Is love a fancy, or a feeling?'*

Is love a fancy, or a feeling? No,
It is immortal as immaculate Truth.
'Tis not a blossom, shed as soon as youth
Drops from the stem of life—for it will grow
In barren regions, where no waters flow,
Nor ray of promise cheats the pensive gloom.
A darkling fire, faint hovering o'er a tomb,
That but itself and darkness nought doth show,
Is my love's being,—yet it cannot die,

Nor will it change, though all be changed beside;
Though fairest beauty be no longer fair,
Though vows be false, and faith itself deny,
Though sharp enjoyment be a suicide,
And hope a spectre in a ruin bare.

(1833)

402. November

The mellow year is hasting to its close;
The little birds have almost sung their last,
Their small notes twitter in the dreary blast—
That shrill-piped harbinger of early snows:
The patient beauty of the scentless rose,
Oft with the morn's hoar crystal quaintly glassed,
Hangs, a pale mourner for the summer past,
And makes a little summer where it grows:
In the chill sunbeam of the faint brief day
The dusky waters shudder as they shine,
The russet leaves obstruct the straggling way
Of oozy brooks, which no deep banks define,
And the gaunt woods, in ragged, scant array,
Wrap their old limbs with somber ivy twine.

(1833)

403. The First Birthday

The sun, sweet girl, hath run his year-long race
Through the vast nothing of the eternal sky—
Since the glad hearing of the first faint cry
Announced a stranger from the unknown place
Of unborn souls. How blank was then the face,
How uninformed the weak light-shunning eye,
That wept and saw not. Poor mortality
Begins to mourn before it knows its case,
Prophetic in its ignorance. But soon
The hospitalities of earth engage
The banished spirit in its new exile—
Pass some few changes of the fickle moon,
The merry babe has learned its mother's smile,
Its father's frown, its nurse's mimic rage.

(1833)

404. 'If I have sinned in act, I may repent'

If I have sinned in act, I may repent;
If I have erred in thought, I may disclaim

My silent error, and yet feel no shame—
But if my soul, big with an ill intent,
Guilty in will, by fate be innocent,
Or being bad, yet murmurs at the curse
And incapacity of being worse
That makes my hungry passion still keep Lent
In keen expectance of a carnival;
Where, in all worlds, that round the sun revolve
And shed their influence on this passive ball,
Abides a power that can my soul absolve?
Could any sin survive, and be forgiven—
One sinful wish would make a hell of heaven.

(1833)

405. 'All Nature ministers to Hope'

All Nature ministers to Hope. The snow
Of sluggard Winter, bedded on the hill,
And the small tinkle of the frozen rill—
The swol'n flood's sullen roar, the storms that go
With crash, and howl, and horrid voice of woe,
Making swift passage for their lawless will—
All prophecy of good. The hungry trill
Of the lone birdie, cowering close below
The dripping eaves—it hath a kindly feeling,
And cheers the life that lives for milder hours.
Why, then, since Nature still is busy healing,
And Time, the waster, his own work concealing,
Decks every grave with verdure and with flowers,—
Why should Despair oppress immortal powers?

(1833)

Letitia Elizabeth Landon
(1802–38)

Sarah Siddons helped Letitia Elizabeth Landon publish her first book, *The Fate of Adelaide; a Swiss Romantic Tale; and Other Poems* (1821). Beginning in the summer of 1821, under the initials "L.E.L.," she published a series of "Poetical Sketches" in the *Literary Gazette* that became the rage. These poems were collected in *The Improvisatrice and Other Poems* (1824), a smashing success that went through six editions in the first year. Several more poetry books followed. Landon also published two novels, *Romance and Reality* (1831) and *Ethel Churchill; or, The Two Brides* (1837), and a collection of prose tales for children, *Traits and Trials of Early Life.* In 1838 she married George Maclean, Governor of Cape Coast, Africa; within two months of her arrival in Africa, she was found dead under questionable circumstances.

406. The Dancing Girl

A light and joyous figure, one that seems
As if the air were her own element;
Begirt with cheerful thoughts, and bringing back
Old days, when nymphs upon Arcadian plains
Made musical the wind, and in the sun
Flashed their bright cymbals and their whitest hands.
These were the days of poetry—the woods
Were haunted with sweet shadows; and the caves,
Odorous with moss, and lit with shining spars,
Were homes where Naiads met some graceful youth
Beneath the moonlit heaven—all this is past;
Ours is a darker and a sadder age;
Heaven help us through it!—'tis a weary world
The dust and ashes of a happier time.

                                                        (1833)

407. The Castle of Chillon

Fair lake, thy lovely and thy haunted shore
    Hath only echoes for the poet's lute;
    None may tread there save with unsandalled foot,
Submissive to the great who went before,
Filled with the mighty memories of yore.
    And yet how mournful are the records there—
    Captivity, and exile, and despair,
Did they endure who now endure no more.
    The patriot, the woman, and the bard,
Whose names thy winds and waters bear along;
    What did the world bestow for their reward
But suffering, sorrow, bitterness, and wrong?—
    Genius!—a hard and weary lot is thine—
    The heart thy fuel—and the grave thy shrine.

                                                        (1837)

Jane Cross Simpson
(1811–86)

Jane Cross Simpson of Glasgow published poems in the mid-1830s in the
Edinburgh Literary Journal and literary annuals such as *Friendship's Offering* and
the *Juvenile Forget-Me-Not* using the pseudonym "Gertrude." A book of
poems, *April Hours,* came out in 1838, followed by *Woman's History* (1848)
and *Linda; or Beauty and Genius: a Metrical Romance* (1859). She was also the
author of a book of tales and sketches for children entitled *The Piety of Daily
Life* (1836) and of hymns, some of which were published in *Lyra Britannica*
(1867) and in the *Scottish Evangelical Hymnal* (1878). Her best-known hymn
is "Go, When the Morning Shineth."

408. 'Oh! if thou lov'st me, love me not so well!'

Oh! if thou lov'st me, love me not so well!
  For in this ceaseless mingling of the heart
I feel such power of mystery doth dwell,
  I sicken with the weight, and weeping start!
Are we of earth, and subject to decay—
  Walk we a world of sin, and change, and pain?
Yet dare we own that forms of mortal clay
  Our all of wealth and happiness contain?
Oh! surely souls for higher aims were made
  Than thus in love's fantastic realm to rove;
And ours might treasure find that ne'er shall fade,
  And soar from human to immortal love!
Then, if thou lov'st me, teach my hopes to rise,
And lead my heart with thine home—home into the skies!

(1833)

Felicia Hemans
(1793–1835)

Felicia Hemans was one of the most highly influential and widely read poets of the nineteenth century, both in Britain and America. Lord Byron considered Hemans's *Restoration of the Works of Art to Italy* (1816) "a good poem—very" even though he blasted her *Modern Greece* (1817) as the work of someone who had never been there. Hemans became a regular contributor to periodicals, and her work was ubiquitous in the literary annuals. *The Forest Sanctuary, and other Poems* (1825) did well, but *Records of Woman* (1828), a feminist rethinking of history and woman's artistic expression, was a best-seller. In a similar vein, Hemans's sonnets on female Biblical figures highlight the presence of women in the development of Western Culture.

409. The Vigil of Rizpah

And Rizpah, the daughter of Aiah, took sackcloth, and spread it
for her upon the rock, from the beginning of harvest until water
dropped upon them out of heaven; and suffered neither the birds
of the air to rest on them by day, nor the beasts of the field by night.
    —2 SAM. 21. 10.

Who watches on the mountain with the dead,
  Alone before the awfulness of night?—
  A seer awaiting the deep spirit's might?
A warrior guarding some dark pass of dread?
No, a lorn woman!—On her drooping head,
  Once proudly graceful, heavy beats the rain;
  She recks not—living for the unburied slain,
Only to scare the vulture from their bed.

So, night by night, her vigil hath she kept
With the pale stars, and with the dews hath wept;—
    Oh! surely some bright Presence from above
On those wild rocks the lonely one must aid!—
E'en so; a strengthener through all storm and shade,
    The unconquerable Angel, mightiest Love!

(1834)

410. Mary at the Feet of Christ

Oh! blest beyond all daughters of the earth!
    What were the Orient's thrones to that low seat,
Where thy hushed spirit drew celestial birth?
    Mary! meek listener at the Savior's feet!
    No feverish cares to that divine retreat
Thy woman's heart of silent worship brought,
    But a fresh childhood, heavenly truth to meet,
With love, and wonder, and submissive thought.
Oh! for the holy quiet of thy breast,
    Midst the world's eager tones and footsteps flying!
Thou, whose calm soul was like a wellspring, lying
So deep and still in its transparent rest,
That e'en when noontide burns upon the hills,
Some one bright solemn star all its lone mirror fills.

(1834)

411. The Memorial of Mary

Verily I say unto you, wheresoever this gospel shall be preached
in the whole world, there shall also this, that this woman hath
done, be told for a memorial of her.
                    ———MATTHEW, 26.13.—SEE ALSO JOHN, 12.3.

Thou hast thy record in the monarch's hall;
    And on the waters of the far mid sea;
And where the mighty mountain-shadows fall,
    The alpine hamlet keeps a thought of thee:
    Where'er, beneath some Oriental tree,
The Christian traveler rests—where'er the child
    Looks upward from the English mother's knee,
With earnest eyes in wondering reverence mild,
There art thou known—where'er the Book of Light
Bears hope and healing, there, beyond all blight,
    Is borne thy memory, and all praise above:
Oh! say what deed so lifted thy sweet name,
Mary! to that pure silent place of fame?
    One lowly offering of exceeding love.

(1834)

412. *Mountain Sanctuaries*

He went up to a mountain apart to pray.

A child midst ancient mountains I have stood,
　　Where the wild falcons make their lordly nest
On high. The spirit of the solitude
　　Fell solemnly upon my infant breast,
Though then I prayed not; but deep thoughts have pressed
　　Into my being since it breathed that air,
Nor could I *now* one moment live the guest
　　Of such dread scenes, without the springs of prayer
O'erflowing all my soul. No minsters rise
Like them in pure communion with the skies,
Vast, silent, open unto night and day;
　　So might the o'erburderned Son of man have felt,
　　When, turning where inviolate stillness dwelt,
He sought high mountains, there apart to pray.

(1834)

413. *The Olive Tree*

The Palm—the Vine—the Cedar—each hath power
To bid fair Oriental shapes glance by,
And each quick glistening of the Laurel bower
Wafts Grecian images o'er fancy's eye.
But thou, pale Olive!—in *thy* branches lie
Far deeper spells than prophet-grove of old
Might e'er enshrine:—I could not hear thee sigh
To the wind's faintest whisper, nor behold
One shiver of thy leaves' dim silvery green,
Without high thoughts and solemn, of that scene
When, in the garden, the Redeemer prayed—
When pale stars looked upon his fainting head,
And angels, ministering in silent dread,
Trembled, perchance, within *thy* trembling shade.

(1834)

414. *A Remembrance of Grasmere*

O vale and lake, within your mountain-urn
Smiling so tranquilly, and set so deep!
Oft doth your dreamy loveliness return,
Coloring the tender shadows of my sleep
With light Elysian:—for the hues that steep
Your shores in melting luster, seem to float
On golden clouds from spirit-lands remote,
Isles of the blest;—and in our memory keep

Their place with holiest harmonies:—Fair scene,
Most loved by evening and her dewy star!
Oh! ne'er may man, with touch unhallowed, jar
The perfect music of the charm serene!
Still, still unchanged, may *one* sweet region wear
Smiles that subdue the soul to love, and tears, and prayer!

(1836)

415. Foliage

Come forth, and let us through our hearts receive
The joy of verdure!—see, the honeyed lime
Showers cool green light o'er banks where wild-flowers weave
Thick tapestry; and woodbine tendrils climb
Up the brown oak from buds of moss and thyme.
The rich deep masses of the sycamore
Hang heavy with the fullness of their prime,
And the while poplar, from its foliage hoar,
Scatters forth gleams like moonlight, with each gale
That sweeps the boughs:—the chestnut flowers are past,
The crowning glories of the hawthorn fail,
But arches of sweet eglantine are cast
From every hedge:—Oh! never may we lose
Dear friend! our fresh delight in simplest nature's hues!

(1836)

Caroline Norton
(1808–77)

Best known today as a political reformer who played a crucial role in influ-
encing the passage through Parliament of the Infants' Custody Bill (1839)
and the Marriage and Divorce Act of 1857, Caroline Norton was also recog-
nized in her own time as a poet, a fiction writer, an essayist, an editor, and a
fashionable celebrity at the center of a major political scandal involving
the prime minister, Lord Melbourne. Her books of poetry included *The Sor-
rows of Rosalie: A Tale, with Other Poems,* published anonymously in 1829,
The Undying One (1830), *A Voice from the Factories* (1836), and *Child of the
Islands* (1845). In the early 1830s, she earned as much as 1400 pounds a year
publishing in the annuals and editing gift books.

416. 'In the cold change, which time hath wrought on love'

In the cold change, which time hath wrought on love
    (The snowy winter of his summer prime),
Should a chance sigh, or sudden tear-drop, move
    Thy heart to memory of the olden time;
Turn not to gaze on me with pitying eyes,

Nor mock me with a withered hope renewed;
But from the bower we both have loved, arise,
    And leave me to my barren solitude!
What boots it that a momentary flame
    Shoots from the ashes of a dying fire?
We gaze upon the hearth from whence it came,
    And know the exhausted embers *must* expire:
Therefore no pity, or my heart will break;
Be cold, be careless—for thy past love's sake!

                                                      (1836)

417. 'Like an enfranchised bird, who wildly springs'

Like an enfranchised bird, who wildly springs,
    With a keen sparkle in his glancing eye
And a strong effort in his quivering wings,
    Up to the blue vault of the happy sky,—
So my enamored heart, so long thine own,
    At length from Love's imprisonment set free,
Goes forth into the open world alone,
    Glad and exulting in its liberty:
But like that helpless bird, (confined so long,
    His weary wings have lost all power to soar,)
Who soon forgets to trill his joyous song,
    And, feebly fluttering, sinks to earth once more,—
So, from its former bonds released in vain,
My heart still feels the weight of that remembered chain.

                                                      (1840)

418. To My Books

Silent companions of the lonely hour,
    Friends, who can never alter or forsake,
Who for inconstant roving have no power,
    And all neglect, perforce, must calmly take,—
Let me return to you; this turmoil ending
    Which worldly cares have in my spirit wrought,
And, o'er your old familiar pages bending,
    Refresh my mind with many a tranquil thought:
Till, haply meeting there, from time to time,
    Fancies, the audible echo of my own,
'Twill be like hearing in a foreign clime
    My native language spoke in friendly tone,
And with a sort of welcome I shall dwell
On these, my unripe musings, told so well.

                                                      (1840)

Ebenezer Elliott
(1781–1849)
Ebenezer Elliott's *Corn Law Rhymes* (1830) urged the repeal of excessive taxes on bread and earned him the sobriquet "Corn Law Rhymer." Elliott was a crusader for social justice in many other poetic works. His sonnets show that he was fascinated with metrical experimentation.

419. Powers of the Sonnet

Why should the tiny harp be chained to themes
In fourteen lines with pedant rigor bound?
The sonnet's might is mightier than it seems:
Witness the bard of Eden lost and found,
Who gave this lute a clarion's battle sound.
And, lo! another Milton calmly turns
His eyes within on light that ever burns,
Waiting till Wordsworth's second peer be found!
Meantime, Fitzadam's mournful music shows
That the scorned sonnet's charm may yet endear
Some long deep strain, or lay of well-told woes;
Such as, in Byron's couplet, brings a tear
To manly cheeks, or o'er his stanza throws
Rapture and grief, solemnity and fear.

(1840)

420. Criticism

Yet art hath less of instinct than of thought,
All instinct though it seems; for as the flower
Which blooms in solitude, by noiseless power,
And skill divine, is wonderfully wrought,
So from deep study art's high charm is caught;
And as the sunny air, and dewy light,
Are spun in heavenly looms, till blossoms, bright
With honeyed wealth and sweetness, droop o'er-fraught,
And our eyes breathe of beauty; so the bard
Wrings from slow time inimitable grace;
So wins immortal music her reward,
E'en with a bee's industry; and we trace
The sculptor's home-thoughts through his labors hard,
Till beams, with deathless love, the chiseled face.

(1840)

Frederick William Faber
(1814–63)
Frederick William Faber studied at Oxford, where he helped to found the *Oxford University Magazine*. He became a disciple of John Henry Cardinal

Newman (1801–90), converted to Roman Catholicism, and became a priest in 1847. He became the superior of the Oratory of St. Philip Neri in London. His hymns have endured, often published in Protestant as well as Catholic hymnals.

421. The Confessional

Now thou hast seen my heart. Was it too near?
Didst thou recoil from the o'erpowering sight;
That vision of a scarred and seaméd soul?
Ah! yes: thy gentle eyes were filled with fear
When looks and thoughts broke out from my control,
Bursting themselves a road with fiercest might—
Wide-opening secret cells of foulest sin,
And all that lurks in that dark place within!
Well, be it so, dear friend! it was but right
That thou shouldst learn where blossoms yet may bless,
And where for ever now there must be blight.
Riven with burning passion's torrent course,
Shattered and splintered all with sin's mad force—
Thou saw'st my heart: and didst not love me less.

(1840)

422. The After-State

A Spirit came upon me in the night,
And led me gently down a rocky stair
Unto a peopled garden, green and fair,
Where all the day there was an evening light.
Trees out of every nation blended there.
The citron shrub its golden fruit did train
Against an English elm: 'twas like a dream
Because there was no wind; and things did seem
All near and big, like mountains before rain.
Far in those twilight bowers beside a stream
The soul of one who had but lately died
Hung listening, with a brother at his side;
And no one spoke in all that haunted place,
But looked quietly into each other's face.

(1840)

423. A Dream of Blue Eyes

I left thee when the midnight bell had tolled,
Full of fresh hopes and feelings: in thine eyes
All night perpetual meanings did unfold
Quick turns of thought and kindling sympathies.

Still those blue eyes looked at me through my sleep,
Changed by the power of dreams to fearful things.
They bore me far away, where evening flings
Her gorgeous blue on Atlas: they did sweep
Into the bluer sky, where comets blaze
And golden creatures live in starry rays.
Onward they went where filmy mist-wreaths creep
About the rolling moon; and fell with me
Into the sunless caverns of the sea,
Where spirits all of blue into my soul did gaze!

                                                        (1840)

424. Sonnet-writing. To F. W. F.

Young men should not write sonnets, if they dream
Some day to reach the bright bare seats of fame:
To such, sweet thoughts and mighty feelings seem
As though, like foreign things, they rarely came.
Eager as men, when haply they have heard
Of some new songster, some gay-feathered bird,
That hath o'er blue seas strayed in hope to find
In our thin foliage here a summer home—
Fain would they catch the bright things in their mind,
And cage them into sonnets as they come.
No; they should serve their wants most sparingly,
Till the ripe time of song, when young thoughts fail,
Then their sad sonnets, like old bards, might be
Merry as youth, and yet gray-haired and hale.

                                                        (1840)

Frances Anne Kemble
(1809–93)

Frances Anne Kemble published a verse melodrama, *Frances I*, in 1827. Two years later, she made her debut as an actress at Covent Garden, playing the role of Juliet. As a stage star, she toured the United States, where she met Pierce Butler, a Georgia plantation owner whom she married in 1834. She left him in 1845 and returned to England, shortly after publishing *Poems* (1844). She returned to the stage and gave Shakespearean readings for two decades, often returning to America. Her *Journal of a Residence on a Georgia Plantation* (1863) details the everyday workings of slavery, an institution she abhorred. At the age of eighty, Kemble published her first novel, *Far Away and Long Ago*.

425. 'Whene'er I recollect the happy time'

Whene'er I recollect the happy time
When you and I held converse dear together,

There come a thousand thoughts of sunny weather,
Of early blossoms, and the fresh year's prime;
Your memory lives for ever in my mind
With all the fragrant beauties of the spring,
With od'rous lime and silver hawthorn twined,
And many a noonday woodland wandering.
There's not a thought of you, but brings along
Some sunny dream of river, field, and sky;
'Tis wafted on the blackbird's sunset song,
Or some wild snatch of ancient melody.
And as I date it still, our love arose
'Twixt the last violet and the earliest rose.

(1844)

426. 'Cover me with your everlasting arms'

Cover me with your everlasting arms,
  Ye guardian giants of this solitude!
  From the ill-sight of men, and from the rude,
Tumultuous din of yon wild world's alarms!
Oh, knit your mighty limbs around, above,
  And close me in for ever! let me dwell
  With the wood spirits, in the darkest cell
That ever with your verdant locks ye wove.
  The air is full of countless voices, joined
  In one eternal hymn; the whispering wind,
  The shuddering leaves, the hidden water springs,
  The work-song of the bees, whose honeyed wings
  Hang in the golden tresses of the lime,
  Or buried lie in purple beds of thyme.

(1844)

Eliza Cook
(1818-89)

Eliza Cook published her first volume of poetry, *Lays of a Wild Harp,* in 1835.
Her verse appeared in various periodicals, and some compared it with that of
Robert Burns. From 1849–54, she edited the populist weekly *Eliza Cook's
Journal,* geared towards a middle-class readership.

427. Written at the Couch of a Dying Parent

  'Tis midnight! and pale Melancholy stands
    Beside me, wearing a funereal wreath
    Of yew and cypress; the faint dirge of death
  Moans in her breathing, while her withered hands
    Fling corse-bedecking rosemary around.
  She offers nightshade, spreads a winding-sheet,

Points to the clinging clay upon her feet,
  And whispers tidings of the charnel ground.
Oh! pray thee, Melancholy, do not bring
  These bitter emblems with thee; I can bear
With all but these,—'tis these, oh God! that wring
  And plunge my heart in maddening despair.
Hence, for awhile, pale Melancholy, go!
And let sweet slumber lull my weeping woe.

(1847)

Arthur Hugh Clough
(1819–61)

Arthur Hugh Clough was a pupil of Rugby headmaster Thomas Arnold
(1795–1842) and close friend of poet and essayist Matthew Arnold
(1822–88). He was an unconventional but accomplished poet much influ-
enced by classical prosody. Clough suffered a crisis of faith and emerged as a
skeptical and introspective thinker. His works include the poetic novel
Amours de Voyage (1858) and the Faustian psychodrama *Dipsychus,* published
posthumously in 1865. He is the subject of Matthew Arnold's pastoral elegy
"Thyrsis" (1866).

428. 'Here am I yet, another twelvemonth spent'

Here am I yet, another twelvemonth spent,
One-third departed of the mortal span,
Carrying on the child into the man,
Nothing into reality. Sails rent,
And rudder broken,—reason impotent,—
Affections all unfixed; so forth I fare
On the mid seas unheedingly, so dare
To do and to be done by, well content.
So was it from the first, so is it yet;
Yea, the first kiss that by these lips was set
On any human lips, methinks was sin—
Sin, cowardice, and falsehood; for the will
Into a deed e'en then advanced, wherein
God, unidentified, was thought-of still.

(1849)

429. 'Yes, I have lied, and so must walk my way'

Yes, I have lied, and so must walk my way,
Bearing the liar's curse upon my head;
Letting my weak and sickly heart be fed
On food which does the present craving stay,
But may be clean-denied me e'en today,

And though 'twere certain, yet were ought but bread;
Letting—for so they say, it seems, I said,
And I am all too weak to disobey!
Therefore for me sweet Nature's scenes reveal not
Their charm; sweet Music greets me and I feel not;
Sweet eyes pass off me uninspired; yea, more,
The golden tide of opportunity
Flows wafting-in friendships and better,—I
Unseeing, listless, pace along the shore.

(1849)

Calder Campbell
(1798–1857)

Born in Scotland, Major Calder Campbell served in India and was decorated
for his service in the Burmese war (1826–7). He had retired when the
sculptor Alexander Munro introduced him to Dante Gabriel and William
Michael Rossetti, with whom he became good friends. He published
sketches and poetry in various periodicals and assisted with the publication
of the *Germ* in 1850.

430. *'When midst the summer-roses'*

When midst the summer-roses the warm bees
    Are swarming in the sun, and thou—so full
    Of innocent glee—dost with thy white hands pull
Pink scented apples from the garden trees
To fling at me, I catch them, on my knees,
    Like those who gathered manna; and I cull
    Some hasty buds to pelt thee—white as wool
Lilies, or yellow jonquils, or heartsease;—
Then I can speak my love, even though thy smiles
    Gush out among thy blushes, like a flock
Of bright birds from rose-bowers; but when thou'rt gone
    I have no speech,—no magic that beguiles,
    The stream of utterance from the hardened rock:—
The dial cannot speak without the sun!

(1850)

William Bell Scott
(1811–90)

William Bell Scott was a poet, artist, and critic who was part of the Pre-
Raphaelite circle. His first published poem was a tribute to Percy Bysshe
Shelley. He contributed to the short-lived periodical the *Germ*, edited by
William Michael Rossetti, and published poetry throughout his life. He
achieved success as an engraver but gave up illustrating to become a painter.

431. Early Aspirations

How many a throb of the young poet-heart,
   Aspiring to the ideal bliss of fame,
   Deems that time soon may sanctify his claim
Among the sons of song to dwell apart.—
   Time passes—passes! The aspiring flame
Of hope shrinks down; the white flower poesy
Breaks on its stalk, and from its earth-turned eye
   Drop sleepy tears instead of that sweet dew
   Rich with inspiring odors, insect wings
Drew from its leaves with every changing sky,
   While its young innocent petals unsunned grew.
   No more in pride to other ears he sings,
But with a dying charm himself unto:—
   For a sad season: then, to active life he springs.

(1850)

William Michael Rossetti
(1829-1919)

As a poet, editor, art critic, and translator, William Michael Rossetti enjoyed a long career as a man of letters. A member of the Pre-Raphaelite Brotherhood, a revolutionary literary and artistic movement, Rossetti edited its journal, the *Germ* (1850), produced editions of Blake, Shelley, and Whitman, translated Dante, wrote a biography of Keats, and edited the poetry of his brother, Dante Gabriel Rossetti, and his sister, Christina Rossetti.

432. Jesus Wept

Mary rose up, as one in sleep might rise,
   And went to meet her brother's Friend: and they
   Who tarried with her said: "she goes to pray
And weep where her dead brother's body lies."
So, with their wringing of hands and with sighs,
   They stood before Him in the public way.
   "Had'st Thou been with him, Lord, upon that day,
He had not died," she said, drooping her eyes.
Mary and Martha with bowed faces kept
   Holding His garments, one on each side.—"Where
   Have ye laid him?" He asked. "Lord, come and see."—
   The sound of grieving voices heavily
   And universally was round Him there,
A sound that smote His spirit. Jesus wept.

(1850)

Dante Gabriel Rossetti
(1828–82)

Dante Gabriel Rossetti and his siblings, William Michael and Christina, were the children of an Italian patriot who came to England in 1824. A poet, highly influenced by Keats, and painter apprenticed to his mentor and life-long friend Ford Madox Brown (1821–93), and driven by his own aesthetic principles, Rossetti founded the Pre-Raphaelite Brotherhood in 1848 to re-form the styles and manners of Victorian art. His interests in poetry and painting are inextricably combined, as he demonstrates in his important early sequence *Sonnets for Pictures*. His later sonnet sequence, *The House of Life* (1870), in part a response to his wife's suicide, explores the metaphysics of erotic love, death, and spirituality. In 1871 Robert Buchanan (1841–1901) attacked it as pornography.

433–438. Sonnets for Pictures

433. I. A Virgin and Child, by Hans Memmeling; in the Academy of Bruges

Mystery: God, Man's Life, born into man
    Of woman. There abideth on her brow
    The ended pang of knowledge, the which now
Is calm assured. Since first her task began,
She hath known all. What more of anguish than
    Endurance oft hath lived through, the whole space
    Through night till night, passed weak upon her face
While like a heavy flood the darkness ran?
All hath been told her touching her dear Son,
    And all shall be accomplished. Where he sits
      Even now, a babe, he holds the symbol fruit
Perfect and chosen. Until God permits,
      His soul's elect still have the absolute
Harsh nether darkness, and make painful moan.

(1850)

434. II. A Marriage of St. Katharine, by the same; in the Hospital of St. John at Bruges

Mystery: Katharine, the bride of Christ.
    She kneels, and on her hand the holy Child
    Setteth the ring. Her life is sad and mild,
Laid in God's knowledge—ever unenticed
From Him, and in the end thus fitly priced.
    Awe, and the music that is near her, wrought
    Of Angels, hath possessed her eyes in thought:
Her utter joy is hers, and hath sufficed.
There is a pause while Mary Virgin turns

The leaf, and reads. With eyes on the spread book,
   That damsel at her knees reads after her.
   John whom He loved and John His harbinger
Listen and watch. Whereon soe'er thou look,
The light is starred in gems, and the gold burns.

                                 (1850)

435. III. A Dance of Nymphs, by Andrea Mantegna; in the Louvre

(* It is necessary to mention that this picture would appear to have
been in the artist's mind an allegory, which the modern spectator
may seek vainly to interpret.)

   Scarcely, I think; yet it indeed *may* be
      The meaning reached him, when this music rang
      Sharp through his brain, a distinct rapid pang,
   And he beheld these rocks and that ridged sea.
   But I believe he just leaned passively,
      And felt their hair carried across his face
      As each nymph passed him; nor gave ear to trace
   How many feet; nor bent assuredly
   His eyes from the blind fixedness of thought
      To see the dancers. It is bitter glad
      Even unto tears. Its meaning filleth it,
      A portion of most secret life: to wit:—
      Each human pulse shall keep the sense it had
With all, though the mind's labor run to nought.

                                 (1850)

436. IV. A Venetian Pastoral, by Giorgione; in the Louvre

(* In this picture, two cavaliers and an undraped woman are seated
in the grass, with musical instruments, while another woman dips a
vase into a well hard by, for water.)

   Water, for anguish of the solstice,—yea,
      Over the vessel's mouth still widening
      Listlessly dipped to let the water in
   With slow vague gurgle. Blue, and deep away,
   The heat lies silent at the brink of day.
      Now the hand trails upon the viol-string
      That sobs; and the brown faces cease to sing,
   Mournful with complete pleasure. Her eyes stray
In distance; through her lips the pipe doth creep
      And leaves them pouting; the green shadowed grass
      Is cool against her naked flesh. Let be:
Do not now speak unto her lest she weep,—
      Nor name this ever. Be it as it was:—
      Silence of heat, and solemn poetry.

                                 (1850)

437. V. Angelica Rescued from the Sea-Monster, by Ingres; in the Luxembourg

A remote sky, prolonged to the sea's brim:
  One rock-point standing buffeted alone,
  Vexed at its base with a foul beast unknown,
Hell-spurge of geomaunt and teraphim:
A knight, and a winged creature bearing him,
  Reared at the rock: a woman fettered there,
  Leaning into the hollow with loose hair
And throat let back and heartsick trail of limb.
The sky is harsh, and the sea shrewd and salt.
  Under his lord, the griffin-horse ramps blind
    With rigid wings and tail. The spear's lithe stem
  Thrills in the roaring of those jaws: behind,
The evil length of body chafes at fault.
    She doth not hear nor see—she knows of them.

(1850)

438. VI. The same

Clench thine eyes now,—'tis the last instant, girl:
  Draw in thy senses, set thy knees, and take
  One breath for all: thy life is keen awake,—
Thou may'st not swoon. Was that the scattered whirl
Of its foam drenched thee?—or the waves that curl
  And split, bleak spray wherein thy temples ache?—
  Or was it his the champion's blood to flake
Thy flesh?—Or thine own blood's anointing, girl? . . .
. . . Now, silence; for the sea's is such a sound
  As irks not silence; and except the sea,
    All is now still. Now the dead thing doth cease
  To writhe, and drifts. He turns to her: and she
Cast from the jaws of Death, remains there, bound,
    Again a woman in her nakedness.

(1850)

Elizabeth Barrett Browning
(1806–61)

Elizabeth Barrett lived most of her life as an invalid in the home of a tyrannical father until she began a correspondence with Robert Browning (1812–89), who was a relatively obscure poet during her lifetime. He fell in love with her through her poetry. The two secretly married and eloped to Italy, where they lived happily until her death in 1861. Barrett Browning describes her love for her husband in her enduring *Sonnets from the Portuguese*. The title seems to suggest that the sequence is a translation from the Portuguese language, but it is really a private reference to her poem "Catarina to

Camöens," about the love of a Portuguese woman for the Spanish poet. Her verse novel *Aurora Leigh* (1857) is a substantial literary achievement.

439–481. Sonnets from the Portuguese

439. I

I thought once how Theocritus had sung
Of the sweet years, the dear and wished-for years,
Who each one in a gracious hand appears
To bear a gift for mortals, old or young:
And, as I mused it in his antique tongue,
I saw, in gradual vision through my tears,
The sweet, sad years, the melancholy years, . .
Those of my own life, who by turns had flung
A shadow across me. Straightway I was 'ware,
So weeping, how a mystic Shape did move
Behind me, and drew me backward by the hair;
And a voice said in mastery, while I strove, . .
"Guess now who holds thee?"—"Death!" I said. But, there,
The silver answer rang . . "Not Death, but Love."

(1850)

440. II

But only three in all God's universe
Have heard this word thou hast said; Himself, beside
Thee speaking and me listening! and replied
One of us . . *that* was God! . . and laid the curse
So darkly on my eyelids as to amerce
My sight from seeing thee,—that if I had died,
The deathweights, placed there, would have signified
Less absolute exclusion. "Nay" is worse
From God than from all others, O my friend!
Men could not part us with their worldly jars,
Nor the seas change us, nor the tempests bend:
Our hands would touch, for all the mountain-bars;—
And, heaven being rolled between us at the end,
We should but vow the faster for the stars.

(1850)

441. III

Unlike are we, unlike, O princely Heart!
Unlike our uses, and our destinies.
Our ministering two angels look surprise
On one another, as they strike athwart

Their wings in passing. Thou, bethink thee, art
A quest for queens to social pageantries,
With gages from a hundred brighter eyes
Than tears, even, can make mine, to play thy part
Of chief musician. What hast *thou* to do
With looking from the lattice-lights at me,
A poor, tired, wandering singer? . . singing through
The dark, and leaning up a cypress tree?
The chrism is on thine head,—on mine, the dew,—
And Death must dig the level where these agree.

(1850)

442. IV

Thou hast thy calling to some palace floor,
Most gracious singer of high poems! where
The dancers will break footing from the care
Of watching up thy pregnant lips for more.
And dost thou lift this house's latch too poor
For hand of thine? and canst thou think and bear
To let thy music drop here unaware
In folds of golden fullness at my door?
Look up and see the casement broken in,
The bats and owlets builders in the roof!
My cricket chirps against thy mandolin.
Hush! call no echo up in further proof
Of desolation! there's a voice within
That weeps . . as thou must sing . . alone, aloof.

(1850)

443. V

I lift my heavy heart up solemnly,
As once Electra her sepulchral urn,
And, looking in thine eyes, I overturn
The ashes at thy feet. Behold and see
What a great heap of grief lay hid in me,
And how the red wild sparkles dimly burn
Through the ashen grayness. If thy foot in scorn
Could tread them out to darkness utterly,
It might be well perhaps. But if instead
Thou wait beside me for the wind to blow
The gray dust up, . . . those laurels on thine head,
O my beloved, will not shield thee so,
That none of all the fires shall scorch and shred
The hair beneath. Stand further off then! Go.

(1850)

444. VI

Go from me. Yet I feel that I shall stand
Henceforward in thy shadow. Nevermore
Alone upon the threshold of my door
Of individual life, I shall command
The uses of my soul, nor lift my hand
Serenely in the sunshine as before,
Without the sense of that which I forbore, . .
Thy touch upon the palm. The widest land
Doom takes to part us, leaves thy heart in mine
With pulses that beat double. What I do
And what I dream include thee, as the wine
Must taste of its own grapes. And when I sue
God for myself, He hears that name of thine,
And sees within my eyes, the tears of two.

                                                                (1850)

445. VII

The face of all the world is changed, I think,
Since first I heard the footsteps of thy soul
Move still, oh, still, beside me; as they stole
Betwixt me and the dreadful outer brink
Of obvious death, where I who thought to sink
Was caught up into love, and taught the whole
Of life in a new rhythm. The cup of dole
God gave for baptism, I am fain to drink,
And praise its sweetness, sweet, with thee anear.
The names of country, heaven, are changed away
For where thou art or shalt be, there or here;
And this . . this lute and song . . loved yesterday,
(The singing angels know) are only dear,
Because thy name moves right in what they say.

                                                                (1850)

446. VIII

What can I give thee back, O liberal
And princely giver, . . who hast brought the gold
And purple of thine heart, unstained, untold,
And laid them on the outside of the wall,
For such as I to take, or leave withal,
In unexpected largesse? Am I cold,
Ungrateful, that for these most manifold
High gifts, I render nothing back at all?
Not so. Not cold!—but very poor instead!
Ask God who knows! for frequent tears have run

The colors from my life, and left so dead
And pale a stuff, it were not fitly done
To give the same as pillow to thy head.
Go farther! Let it serve to trample on.

(1850)

447. IX

Can it be right to give what I can give?
To let thee sit beneath the fall of tears
As salt as mine, and hear the sighing years
Re-sighing on my lips renunciative
Through those infrequent smiles, which fail to live
For all thy adjurations? O my fears,
That this can scarce be right! We are not peers,
So to be lovers; and I own and grieve
That givers of such gifts as mine are, must
Be counted with the ungenerous. Out, alas!
I will not soil thy purple with my dust,
Nor breathe my poison on thy Venice-glass,
Nor give thee any love . . . which were unjust.
Beloved, I only love thee! let it pass.

(1850)

448. X

Yet, love, mere love, is beautiful indeed
And worthy of acceptation. Fire is bright,
Let temple burn, or flax! An equal light
Leaps in the flame from cedar-plank or weed.
And love is fire: and when I say at need
I love thee . . mark! . . I love thee! . . in thy sight
I stand transfigured, glorified aright,
With conscience of the new rays that proceed
Out of my face toward thine. There's nothing low
In love, when love the lowest: meanest creatures
Who love God, God accepts while loving so.
And what I *feel,* across the inferior features
Of what I *am,* doth flash itself, and show
How that great work of Love enhances Nature's.

(1850)

449. XI

And therefore if to love can be desert,
I am not all unworthy. Cheeks as pale
As these you see, and trembling knees that fail
To bear the burden of a heavy heart,

This weary minstrel-life that once was girt
To climb Aornus, and can scarce avail
To pipe now 'gainst the woodland nightingale
A melancholy music! . . why advert
To these things? O Beloved, it is plain
I am not of thy worth nor for thy place:
And yet because I love thee, I obtain
From that same love this vindicating grace,
To live on still in love and yet in vain, . .
To bless thee yet renounce thee to thy face.

                                                        (1850)

450. XII

Indeed this very love which is my boast,
And which, when rising up from breast to brow,
Doth crown me with a ruby large enow
To draw men's eyes and prove the inner cost, . .
This love even, all my worth, to the uttermost,
I should not love withal, unless that thou
Hadst set me an example, shown me how,
When first thine earnest eyes with mine were crossed,
And love called love. And thus, I cannot speak
Of love even, as a good thing of my own.
Thy soul hath snatched up mine all faint and weak,
And placed it by thee on a golden throne,—
And that I love, (O soul, I must be meek!)
Is by thee only, whom I love alone.

                                                        (1850)

451. XIII

And wilt thou have me fashion into speech
The love I bear thee, finding words enough,
And hold the torch out, while the winds are rough,
Between our faces, to cast light on each?—
I drop it at they feet. I cannot teach
My hand to hold my spirit so far off
From myself . . me . . that I should bring thee proof
In words, of love hid in me out of reach.
Nay, let the silence of my womanhood
Commend my woman-love to thy belief,—
Seeing that I stand unwon, however wooed,
And rend the garment of my life, in brief,
By a most dauntless, voiceless fortitude,
Lest one touch of this heart, convey its grief.

                                                        (1850)

452. XIV

If thou must love me, let it be for naught
Except for love's sake only. Do not say
"I love her for her smile . . her look . . her way
Of speaking gently, . . for a trick of thought
That falls in well with mine, and certes brought
A sense of pleasant ease on such a day"—
For these things in themselves, Beloved, may
Be changed, or change for thee,—and love so wrought,
May be unwrought so. Neither love me for
Thine own dear pity's wiping my cheeks dry,
Since one might well forget to weep who bore
Thy comfort long, and lose thy love thereby.
But love me for love's sake, that evermore
Thou may'st love on through love's eternity.

(1850)

453. XV

Accuse me not, beseech thee, that I wear
Too calm and sad a face in front of thine;
For we two look two ways, and cannot shine
With the same sunlight on our brow and hair.
On me thou lookest, with no doubting care,
As on a bee shut in a crystalline,—
For sorrow hath shut me safe in love's divine,
And to spread wing and fly in the outer air
Were most impossible failure, if I strove
To fail so. But I look on thee . . on thee . .
Beholding, besides love, the end of love,
Hearing oblivion beyond memory. . .
As one who sits and gazes, from above,
Over the rivers to the bitter sea.

(1850)

454. XVI

And yet, because thou overcomest so,
Because thou art more noble and like a king,
Thou canst prevail against my fears and fling
Thy purple round me, till my heart shall grow
Too close against thine heart, henceforth to know
How it shook when alone. Why, conquering
May prove as lordly and complete a thing
In lifting upward as in crushing low:
And, as a soldier struck down by a sword
May cry, "My strife ends here," and sink to earth,

Even so, Beloved, I at last record,
Here ends my doubt! If *thou* invite me forth,
I rise above abasement at the word.
Make thy love larger to enlarge my worth.

(1850)

455. XVII

My poet, thou canst touch on all the notes
God set between His After and Before,
And strike up and strike off the general roar
Of the rushing worlds, a melody that floats
In a serene air purely. Antidotes
Of medicated music, answering for
Mankind's forlornest uses, thou canst pour
From thence into their ears. God's will devotes
Thine to such ends, and mine to wait on thine!
How, Dearest, wilt thou have me for most use?
A hope, to sing by gladly? . . or a fine
Sad memory, with thy songs to interfuse? . .
A shade, in which to sing . . . of palm or pine?
A grave, on which to rest from singing? . . Choose.

(1850)

456. XVIII

I never gave a lock of hair away
To a man, Dearest, except this to thee,
Which now upon my fingers thoughtfully,
I ring out to the full brown length and say
"Take it." My day of youth went yesterday;
My hair no longer bounds to my foot's glee,
Nor plant I it from rose or myrtle-tree,
As girls do, any more. It only may
Now shade on two pale cheeks, the mark of tears,
Taught drooping from the head that hangs aside
Through sorrow's trick. I thought the funeral-shears
Would take this first; but Love is justified:
Take it thou, . . finding pure, from all those years,
The kiss my mother left here when she died.

(1850)

457. XIX

The soul's Rialto hath its merchandise;
I barter curl for curl upon that mart;
And from my poet's forehead to my heart,
Receive this lock which outweighs argosies,—

As purply black, as erst to Pindar's eyes
The dim purpureal tresses gloomed athwart
The nine white Muse-brows. For this counterpart, . .
The bay-crown's shade, Beloved, I surmise,
Still lingers on thy curl, it is so black!
Thus, with a fillet of smooth-kissing breath,
I tie the shadow safe from gliding back,
And lay the gift where nothing hindereth,
Here on my heart as on thy brow, to lack
No natural heat till mine grows cold in death.

(1850)

458. XX

Beloved, my Beloved, when I think
That thou wast in the world a year ago,
What time I sate alone here in the snow
And saw no footprint, heard the silence sink
No moment at thy voice, . . but link by link
Went counting all my chains as if that so
They never could fall off at any blow
Struck by thy possible hand. . . . . why, thus I drink
Of life's great cup of wonder. Wonderful,
Never to feel thee thrill the day or night
With personal act or speech,—nor ever cull
Some prescience of thee with the blossoms white
Thou sawest growing! Atheists are as dull,
Who cannot guess God's presence out of sight.

(1850)

459. XXI

Say over again, and yet once over again,
That thou dost love me. Though the word repeated
Should seem "a cuckoo-song," as thou dost treat it,
Remember never to the hill or plain,
Valley and wood, without her cuckoo-strain,
Comes the fresh Spring in all her green completed!
Beloved, I, amid the darkness greeted
By a doubtful spirit-voice, in that doubt's pain
Cry . . speak once more . . thou lovest! Who can fear
Too many stars, though each in heaven shall roll—
Too many flowers, though each shall crown the year?
Say thou dost love me, love me, love me—toll
The silver iterance!—only minding, Dear,
To love me also in silence, with thy soul.

(1850)

460. XXII

When our two souls stand up erect and strong,
Face to face, silent, drawing nigh and nigher,
Until the lengthening wings break into fire
At either curvèd point,—what bitter wrong
Can the earth do to us, that we should not long
Be here contented? Think. In mounting higher,
The angels would press on us, and aspire
To drop some golden orb of perfect song
Into our deep, dear silence. Let us stay
Rather on earth, Beloved,—where the unfit
Contrarious moods of men recoil away
And isolate pure spirits, and permit
A place to stand and love in for a day,
With darkness and the death-hour rounding it.

(1850)

461. XXIII

Is it indeed so? If I lay here dead,
Would'st thou miss any life in losing mine,
And would the sun for thee more coldly shine,
Because of grave-damps falling round my head?
I marveled, my Beloved, when I read
Thy thought so in the letter. I am thine—
But . . *so* much to thee? Can I pour thy wine
While my hands tremble? Then my soul, instead
Of dreams of death, resumes life's lower range!
Then, love me, Love! look on me . . breathe on me!
As brighter ladies do not count it strange,
For love, to give up acres and degree,
I yield the grave for thy sake, and exchange
My near sweet view of Heaven, for earth with thee!

(1850)

462. XXIV

Let the world's sharpness like a clasping knife,
Shut in upon itself and do no harm
In this close hand of Love, now soft and warm;
And let us hear no sound of human strife,
After the click of the shutting. Life to life—
I lean upon thee, Dear, without alarm,
And feel as safe as guarded by a charm,
Against the stab of worldlings who if rife
Are weak to injure. Very whitely still
The lilies of our lives may reassure

Their blossoms from their roots! accessible
Alone to heavenly dews that drop not fewer;
Growing straight, out of man's reach, on the hill.
God only, who made us rich, can make us poor.

(1850)

463. XXV

A heavy heart, Beloved, have I borne
From year to year until I saw thy face,
And sorrow after sorrow took the place
Of all those natural joys as lightly worn
As the stringed pearls . . each lifted in its turn
By a beating heart at dance-time. Hopes apace
Were changed to long despairs, . . till God's own grace
Could scarcely lift above the world forlorn
My heavy heart. Then *thou* didst bid me bring
And let it drop adown thy calmly great
Deep being! Fast it sinketh, as a thing
Which its own nature doth precipitate,
While thine doth close above it, mediating
Betwixt the starts and the unaccomplished fate.

(1850)

464. XXVI

I lived with visions for my company
Instead of men and women, years ago,
And found them gentle mates, nor thought to know
A sweeter music than they played to me.
But soon their trailing purple was not free
Of this world's dust,—their lutes did silent grow,
And I myself grew faint and blind below
Their vanishing eyes. Then *thou* didst come . . to *be,*
Beloved, what they *seemed.* Their shining fronts,
Their songs, their splendors . . (better, yet the same, . .
As river-water hallowed into fonts . .)
Met in thee, and from out thee overcame
My soul with satisfaction of all wants—
Because God's gifts put man's best dreams to shame.

(1850)

465. XXVII

My own Beloved, who hast lifted me
From this drear flat of earth where I was thrown,
And in betwixt the languid ringlets, blown
A life-breath, till the forehead hopefully

Shines out again, as all the angels see,
Before thy saving kiss! My own, my own,
Who camest to me when the world was gone,
And I who looked for only God, found *thee!*
I find thee: I am safe, and strong, and glad.
As one who stands in dewless asphodel
Looks backward on the tedious time he had
In the upper life . . so I, with bosom-swell,
Make witness here between the good and bad,
That Love, as strong as Death, retrieves as well.

(1850)

466. XXVIII

My letters! all dead paper, . . mute and white!—
And yet they seem alive and quivering
Against my tremulous hands, which loose the string
And let them drop down on my knee to-night.
This said, . . he wished to have me in his sight
Once, as a friend: this fixed a day in spring
To come and touch my hand . . . a simple thing,
Yet I wept for it!—this, . . the paper's light . .
Said, *Dear, I love thee:* and I sank and quailed
As if God's future thundered on my past:
This said, *I am thine*—and so its ink has paled
With lying at my heart that beat too fast:
And this . . . O Love, thy words have ill availed,
If, what this said, I dared repeat at last!

(1850)

467. XXIX

I think of thee!—my thoughts do twine and bud
About thee, as wild vines about a tree,—
Put out broad leaves, and soon there's nought to see
Except the straggling green which hides the wood.
Yet, O my palm-tree, be it understood
I will not have my thoughts instead of thee
Who art dearer, better! Rather instantly
Renew thy presence! As a strong tree should,
Rustle thy boughs, and set thy trunk all bare,
And let these bands of greenery which insphere thee,
Drop heavily down, . . burst, shattered, everywhere!
Because, in this deep joy to see and hear thee,
And breathe within thy shadow a new air,
I do not think of thee—I am too near thee.

(1850)

468. XXX

I see thine image through my tears tonight,
And yet to-day I saw thee smiling. How
Refer the cause?—Beloved, is it thou
Or I? Who makes me sad? The acolyte
Amid the chanted joy and thankful rite,
May so fall flat, with pale insensate brow,
On the altar-stair. I hear thy voice and vow
Perplexed, uncertain, since thou'rt out of sight,
As he, in his swooning ears, the choir's amen!
Beloved, dost thou love? or did I see all
The glory as I dreamed, and fainted when
Too vehement light dilated my ideal,
For my soul's eyes? Will that light come again,
As now these tears come . . . falling hot and real?

(1850)

469. XXXI

Thou comest! all is said without a word.
I sit beneath thy looks, as children do
In the noon-sun, with souls that tremble through
Their happy eyelids from an unaverred
Yet prodigal inward joy. Behold, I erred
In that last doubt! and yet I cannot rue
The sin most, but the occasion . . . that we two
Should for a moment stand unministered
By a mutual presence. Ah, keep near and close,
Thou dovelike help! and, when my fears would rise,
With thy broad heart serenely interpose!
Brood down with thy divine sufficiencies
These thoughts which tremble when bereft of those,
Like callow birds left desert to the skies.

(1850)

470. XXXII

The first time that the sun rose on thine oath
To love me, I looked forward to the moon
To slacken all those bonds which seemed too soon
And quickly tied to make a lasting troth.
Quick-loving hearts, I thought, may quickly loathe;
And, looking on myself, I seemed not one
For such man's love!—more like an out of tune
Worn viol, a good singer would be wroth
To spoil his song with, and which, snatched in haste,
Is laid down at the first ill-sounding note.

I did not wrong myself so, but I placed
A wrong on *thee*. For perfect strains may float
'Neath master-hands, from instruments defaced,—
And great souls, at one stroke, may do and dote.

(1850)

471. XXXIII

Yes, call me by my pet-name! let me hear
The name I used to run at, when a child,
From innocent play, and leave the cowslips piled,
To glance up in some face that proved me dear
With the look of its eyes. I miss the clear
Fond voices, which, being drawn and reconciled
Into the music of Heaven's undefiled,
Call me no longer. Silence on the bier,
While *I* call God . . call God!—So let thy mouth
Be heir to those who are now exanimate:
Gather the north flowers to complete the south,
And catch the early love up in the late!
Yes, call me by that name,—and I, in truth,
With the same heart, will answer, and not wait.

(1850)

472. XXXIV

With the same heart, I said, I'll answer thee
As those, when thou shalt call me by my name—
Lo, the vain promise! Is the same, the same,
Perplexed and ruffled by life's strategy?
When called before, I told how hastily
I dropped my flowers, or brake off from a game,
To run and answer with the smile that came
At play last moment, and went on with me
Through my obedience. When I answer now,
I drop a grave thought;—break from solitude:—
Yet still my heart goes to thee . . . ponder how . .
Not as to a single good but all my good!
Lay thy hand on it, best one, and allow
That no child's foot could run fast as this blood.

(1850)

473. XXXV

If I leave all for thee, wilt thou exchange
And *be* all to me? Shall I never miss
Home-talk and blessing, and the common kiss
That comes to each in turn, nor count it strange,

When I look up, to drop on a new range
Of walls and floors . . another home than this?
Nay, wilt thou fill that place by me which is
Filled by dead eyes, too tender to know change?
That's hardest! If to conquer love, has tried,
To conquer grief tries more . . . as all things prove:
For grief indeed is love, and grief beside.
Alas, I have grieved so I am hard to love—
Yet love me—wilt thou? Open thine heart wide,
And fold within, the wet wings of thy dove.

(1850)

474. XXXVI

When we met first and loved, I did not build
Upon the event with marble. Could it mean
To last, a love set pendulous between
Sorrow and sorrow? Nay, I rather thrilled,
Distrusting every light that seemed to gild
The onward path, and feared to overlean
A finger even. And, though I have grown serene
And strong since then, I think that God has willed
A still renewable fear . . O love, O troth . .
Lest these enclasped hands should never hold,
This mutual kiss drop down between us both
As an unowned thing, once the lips being cold.
And Love be false! if *he,* to keep one oath,
Must lose one joy by his life's star foretold.

(1850)

475. XXXVII

Pardon, oh, pardon, that my soul should make
Of all that strong divineness which I know
For thine and thee, an image only so
Formed of the sand, and fit to shift and break.
It is that distant years which did not take
Thy sovereignty, recoiling with a blow,
Have forced my swimming brain to undergo
Their doubt and dread, and blindly to forsake
Thy purity of likeness, and distort
Thy worthiest love to worthless counterfeit.
As if a shipwrecked Pagan, safe in port,
His guardian sea-god to commemorate,
Should set a sculptured porpoise, gills a-snort,
And vibrant tail, within the temple-gate.

(1850)

476. XXXVIII

First time he kissed me, he but only kissed
The fingers of this hand wherewith I write,
And ever since it grew more clean and white, . .
Slow to world-greetings . . quick with its "Oh, list,"
When the angels speak. A ring of amethyst
I could not wear here plainer to my sight,
Than that first kiss. The second passed in height
The first, and sought the forehead, and half missed,
Half falling on the hair. O beyond mead!
That was the chrism of love, which love's own crown,
With sanctifying sweetness, did precede.
The third, upon my lips, was folded down
In perfect, purple state! since when, indeed,
I have been proud and said, "My Love, my own."

                                                        (1850)

477. XXXIX

Because thou hast the power and own'st the grace
To look through and behind this mask of me,
(Against which, years have beat thus blenchingly
With their rains!) and behold my soul's true face,
The dim and weary witness of life's race:—
Because thou hast the faith and love to see,
Through that same soul's distracting lethargy,
The patient angel waiting for a place
In the new Heavens: because nor sin nor woe,
Nor God's infliction, nor death's neighborhood,
Nor all, which others viewing, turn to go, . .
Nor all which makes me tired of all, self-viewed, . .
Nothing repels thee, . . Dearest, teach me so
To pour out gratitude, as thou dost, good!

                                                        (1850)

478. XL

Oh, yes! they love through all this world of ours!
I will not gainsay love, called love forsooth.
I have heard love talked in my early youth,
And since, not so long back but that the flowers
Then gathered, smell still. Mussulmans and Giaours
Throw kerchiefs at a smile, and have no ruth
For any weeping. Polypheme's white tooth
Slips on the nut, if after frequent showers
The shell is over-smooth; and not so much
Will turn the thing called love, aside to hate,

Or else to oblivion. But thou art not such
A lover, my Beloved! thou canst wait
Through sorrow and sickness, to bring souls to touch,
And think it soon when others cry "Too late."

(1850)

479. XLI

I thank all who have loved me in their hearts,
With thanks and love from mine. Deep thanks to all
Who paused a little near the prison-wall,
To hear my music in its louder parts,
Ere they went onward, each one to the mart's
Or temple's occupation, beyond call.
But thou, who in my voice's sink and fall,
When the sob took it, thy divinest Art's
Own instrument, didst drop down at thy foot,
To hearken what I said between my tears, . .
Instruct me how to thank thee!—Oh, to shoot
My soul's full meaning into future years,
That *they* should lend it utterance, and salute
Love that endures, with Life that disappears!

(1850)

480. XLII

How do I love thee? Let me count the ways.
I love thee to the depth and breadth and height
My soul can reach, when feeling out of sight
For the ends of Being and Ideal Grace.
I love thee to the level of everyday's
Most quiet need, by sun and candlelight.
I love thee freely, as men strive for Right;
I love thee purely, as they turn from Praise;
I love thee with the passion put to use
In my old griefs, and with my childhood's faith;
I love thee with a love I seemed to lose
With my lost saints,—I love thee with the breath,
Smiles, tears, of all my life!—and, if God choose,
I shall but love thee better after death.

(1850)

481. XLIII

Beloved, thou hast brought me many flowers
Plucked in the garden, all the summer through
And winter, and it seemed as if they grew
In this close room, nor missed the sun and showers.

So, in the like name of that love of ours,
Take back these thoughts, which here unfolded too,
And which on warm and cold days I withdrew
From my heart's ground. Indeed, those beds and bowers
Be overgrown with bitter weeds and rue,
And wait thy weeding: yet here's eglantine,
Here's ivy!—take them, as I used to do
Thy flowers, and keep them where they shall not pine:
Instruct thine eyes to keep their colors true,
And tell thy soul, their roots are left in mine.

                                                                (1850)

Appendix

Mary Robinson's
Preface to *Sappho and Phaon*

I t must strike every admirer of poetical compositions, that the modern son-
net, concluding with two lines, winding up the sentiment of the whole,
confines the poet's fancy, and frequently occasions an abrupt termination of
a beautiful and interesting picture; and that the ancient, or what is generally
denominated, the *legitimate sonnet*, may be carried on in a series of sketches,
composing, in parts, one historical or imaginary subject, and forming in the
whole a complete and connected story.

With this idea, I have ventured to compose the following collection; not
presuming to offer them as imitations of *Petrarch*, but as specimens of that
species of sonnet writing, so seldom attempted in the English language;
though adopted by that sublime Bard, whose *Muse* produced the grand epic
of *Paradise Lost,* and the humbler effusion, which I produce as an example of
the measure to which I allude, and which is termed by the most classical
writers, the *legitimate sonnet.*

> O Nightingale, that on yon bloomy spray
>   Warblest at eve, when all the woods are still,
>   Thou with fresh hope the lover's heart dost fill,
> While the jolly hours lead on propitious May.
> Thy liquid notes that close the eye of day
>   First heard before the shallow cuckoo's bill,
>   Portend success in love; O if Jove's will
> Have link'd that amorous power to thy soft lay,
>   Now timely sing, ere the rude bird of hate
> Foretell my hopeless doom in some grove nigh,
>   As thou from year to year hast sung too late
> For my relief, yet hadst no reason why:

Whether the Muse, or Love call thee his mate,
Both them I serve, and of their train am I.

To enumerate the variety of authors who have written sonnets of all descriptions, would be endless; indeed few of them deserve notice: and where, among the heterogeneous mass of insipid and labored efforts, sometimes a bright gem sheds luster on the page of poesy, it scarcely excites attention, owing to the disrepute into which sonnets are fallen. So little is rule attended to by many, who profess the art of poetry, that I have seen a composition of more than thirty lines, ushered into the world under the name of Sonnet, and that, from the pen of a writer, whose classical taste ought to have avoided such a misnomer.

Doctor Johnson describes a Sonnet, as "a short poem, consisting of fourteen lines, of which the rhymes are adjusted by a particular rule." He further adds, "It has not been used by any man of eminence since *Milton*."[1]

Sensible of the extreme difficulty I shall have to encounter, in offering to the world a little wreath, gathered in that path, which, even the best poets have thought it dangerous to tread; and knowing that the English language is, of all others, the least congenial to such an undertaking, (for, I believe, that the construction of this kind of sonnet was originally in the Italian, where the vowels are used almost every other letter,) I only point out the track where more able pens may follow with success; and where the most classical beauties may be adopted, and drawn forth with peculiar advantage.

Sophisticated sonnets are so common, for every rhapsody of rhyme, from six lines to sixty comes under that denomination, that the eye frequently turns from this species of poem with disgust. Every school-boy, every romantic scribbler, thinks a sonnet a task of little difficulty. From this ignorance in some, and vanity in others, we see the monthly and diurnal publications abounding with ballads, odes, elegies, epitaphs, and allegories, the nondescript ephemera from the heated brains of self-important poetasters, all ushered into notice under the appellation of *sonnet*!

I confess myself such an enthusiastic votary of the Muse, that any innovation which seems to threaten even the least of her established rights, makes me tremble, lest that chaos of dissipated pursuits which has too long been growing like an overwhelming shadow, and menacing the luster of intellectual light, should, aided by the idleness of some, and the profligacy of others, at last obscure the finer mental powers, and reduce the dignity of talents to the lowest degradation.

As poetry has the power to raise, so has it also the magic to refine. The ancients considered the art of such importance, that before they led forth their heroes to the most glorious enterprises, they animated them by the recital of grand and harmonious compositions. The wisest scrupled not to reverence the invocations of minds, graced with the charm of numbers: so mystically fraught are powers said to be, which look beyond the surface of events, that an admired and classical writer,[2] describing the inspirations of the *muse,* thus expresses his opinion:

So when remote futurity is brought
Before the keen inquiry of her thought,
A terrible sagacity informs
The Poet's heart, he looks to distant storms,
He hears the thunder ere the tempest low'rs,
And, arm'd with strength surpassing human pow'rs,
Seizes events as yet unknown to man,
And darts his soul into the dawning plan.
Hence in a Roman mouth the graceful name
Of Prophet and of Poet was the same,
Hence British poets too the priesthood shar'd,
And ev'ry hallow'd druid—was a bard.

That poetry ought to be cherished as a national ornament, cannot be more strongly exemplified than in the simple fact, that, in those centuries when the poets' laurels have been most generously fostered in Britain, the minds and manners of the natives have been most polished and enlightened. Even the language of a country refines into purity by the elegance of numbers: the strains of *Waller* have done more to effect that, than all the labors of monkish pedantry, since the days of druidical mystery and superstition.

Though different minds are variously affected by the infinite diversity of harmonious effusions, there are, I believe, very few that are wholly insensible to the powers of poetic compositions. Cold must that bosom be, which can resist the magical versification of *Eloisa to Abelard;* and torpid to all the more exalted sensations of the soul is that being, whose ear is not delighted by the grand and sublime effusions of the divine Milton! The romantic chivalry of Spenser vivifies the imagination; while the plaintive sweetness of Collins soothes and penetrates the heart. How much would Britain have been deficient in a comparison with other countries on the scale of intellectual grace, had these poets never existed! Yet it is a melancholy truth, that here, where the attributes of genius have been diffused by the liberal hand of nature, almost to prodigality, there has not been, during a long series of years, the smallest mark of public distinction bestowed on literary talents. Many individuals, whose works are held in the highest estimation, now that their ashes sleep in the sepulchre, were, when living, suffered to languish, and even to perish, in obscure poverty: as if it were the peculiar fate of genius, to be neglected while existing, and only honored when the consciousness of inspiration is vanished for ever.

The ingenious mechanic has the gratification of seeing his labors patronized, and is rewarded for his invention while he has the powers of enjoying its produce. But the Poet's life is one perpetual scene of warfare: he is assailed by envy, stung by malice, and wounded by the fastidious comments of concealed assassins. The more eminently beautiful his compositions are, the larger is the phalanx he has to encounter; for the enemies of genius are multitudinous.

It is the interest of the ignorant and powerful, to suppress the effusions of enlightened minds: when only monks could write, and nobles read, authority rose triumphant over right; and the slave, spell-bound in ignorance, hugged his fetters without repining. It was then that the best powers of reason lay buried like the gem in the dark mine; by a slow and tedious progress they have been drawn forth, and must, ere long, diffuse an universal luster: for that era is rapidly advancing, when talents will tower like an unperishable column, while the globe will be strewed with the wrecks of superstition.

As it was the opinion of the ancients, that poets possessed the powers of prophecy, the name was consequently held in the most unbounded veneration. In less remote periods the bard has been publicly distinguished; princes and priests have bowed before the majesty of genius: Petrarch was crowned with laurels, the noblest diadem, in the Capitol of Rome: his admirers were liberal; his contemporaries were just; and his name will stand upon record, with the united and honorable testimony of his own talents, and the generosity of his country.

It is at once a melancholy truth, and a national disgrace, that this Island, so profusely favored by nature, should be marked, of all enlightened countries, as the most neglectful of literary merit! and I will venture to believe, that there are both *Poets* and *Philosophers,* now living in Britain, who, had they been born in any *other* clime, would have been honored with the proudest distinctions, and immortalized to the latest posterity.

I cannot conclude these opinions without paying tribute to the talents of my illustrious country-women; who, unpatronized by courts, and unprotected by the powerful, persevere in the paths of literature, and ennoble themselves by the unperishable luster of *mental pre-eminence*!

To The Reader

The story of the *Lesbian Muse*, though not new to the classical reader, presented to my imagination such a lively example of the human mind, enlightened by the most exquisite talents, yet yielding to the destructive control of ungovernable passions, that I felt an irresistible impulse to attempt the delineation of their progress; mingling with the glowing picture of her soul, such moral reflections, as may serve to excite that pity, which, while it proves the susceptibility of the heart, arms it against the danger of indulging a too luxuriant fancy.

The unfortunate lovers, Heloise and Abélard; and, the supposed platonic, Petrarch and Laura, have found panegyrists in many distinguished authors. *Ovid* and *Pope* have celebrated the passion of Sappho for Phaon; but their portraits, however beautifully finished, are replete with shades, tending rather to depreciate than to adorn the Grecian Poetess.

I have endeavored to collect, in the succeeding pages, the most liberal accounts of that illustrious woman, whose fame has transmitted to us some fragments of her works, through many dark ages, and for the space of more than two thousand years. The merit of her compositions must have been indisputable, to have left all contemporary female writers in obscurity; for it is known, that poetry was, at the period in which she lived, held in the most sacred veneration; and that those who were gifted with that divine inspiration, were ranked as the first class of human beings.

Among the many Grecian writers, Sappho was the unrivaled poetess of her time: the envy she excited, the public honors she received, and the fatal passion which terminated her existence, will, I trust, create that sympathy in the mind of the susceptible reader, which may render the following poetical trifles not wholly uninteresting.

—MARY ROBINSON
ST. JAMES'S PLACE, 1796

Account of Sappho

Sappho, whom the ancients distinguished by the title of the *tenth muse,* was born at Mytilene in the island of Lesbos, six hundred years before the Christian era. As no particulars have been transmitted to posterity, respecting the origin of her family, it is most likely she derived but little consequence from birth or connections. At an early period of her life she was wedded to Cercolus, a native of the isle of Andros; he was possessed of considerable wealth, and though the Lesbian Muse is said to have been sparingly gifted with beauty, he became enamored of her, more perhaps on account of mental, than personal charms. By this union she is said to have given birth to a daughter; but Cercolus leaving her, while young, in a state of widowhood, she never after could be prevailed on to marry.

The Fame which her genius spread even to the remotest parts of the earth, excited the envy of some writers who endeavored to throw over her private character, a shade, which shrunk before the brilliancy of her poetical talents. Her soul was replete with harmony; that harmony which neither art nor study can acquire; she felt the intuitive superiority, and to the Muses she paid unbounded adoration.

The Mytilenians held her poetry in such high veneration, and were so sensible of the honor conferred on the country which gave her birth, that they coined money with the impression of her head; and at the time of her death, paid tribute to her memory, such as was offered to sovereigns only.

The story of Antiochus has been related as an unequivocal proof of Sappho's skill in discovering, and powers of describing the passions of the human mind. That prince is said to have entertained a fatal affection for his mother-in-law Stratonice; which, though he endeavored to subdue its influence, preyed upon his frame, and after many ineffectual struggles, at length reduced him to extreme danger. His physicians marked the symptoms attending his malady, and found them so exactly correspond with Sappho's delineation of the tender passion, that they did not hesitate to form a decisive opinion on the cause, which had produced so perilous an effect.

That Sappho was not insensible to the feelings she so well described, is evident in her writings: but it was scarcely possible, that a mind so exquisitely tender, so sublimely gifted, should escape those fascinations which even apathy itself has been awakened to acknowledge.

The scarce specimens now extant, from the pen of the Grecian Muse, have by the most competent judges been esteemed as the standard for the pathetic, the glowing, and the amatory. The ode, which has been so highly estimated, is written in a measure distinguished by the title of the Sapphic. *Pope* made it his model in his juvenile production, beginning—

"Happy the man—whose wish and care"—

Addison was of opinion, that the writings of Sappho were replete with such fascinating beauties, and adorned with such a vivid glow of sensibility, that, probably, had they been preserved entire, it would have been dangerous to have perused them. They possessed none of the artificial decorations of a feigned passion; they were the genuine effusions of a supremely enlightened soul, laboring to subdue a fatal enchantment; and vainly opposing the conscious pride of illustrious fame, against the warm susceptibility of a generous bosom.

Though few stanzas from the pen of the Lesbian poetess have darted through the shades of oblivion: yet, those that remain are so exquisitely touching and beautiful, that they prove beyond dispute the taste, feeling, and inspiration of the mind which produced them. In examining the curiosities of antiquity, we look to the perfections, and not the magnitude of those relics, which have been preserved amidst the wrecks of time: as the smallest gem that bears the fine touches of a master, surpasses the loftiest fabric reared by the labors of false taste, so the precious fragments of the immortal Sappho, will be admired, when the voluminous productions of inferior poets are moldered into dust.

When it is considered, that the few specimens we have of the poems of the Grecian Muse, have passed through three and twenty centuries, and consequently through the hands of innumerable translators: and when it is known that envy frequently delights in the base occupation of depreciating merit which it cannot aspire to emulate; it may be conjectured, that some passages are erroneously given to posterity, either by ignorance or design. Sappho, whose fame beamed round her with the superior effulgence which her works had created, knew that she was writing for future ages: it is not therefore natural that she should produce any composition which might tend to tarnish her reputation, or to lessen that celebrity which it was the labor of her life to consecrate. The delicacy of her sentiments cannot find a more eloquent advocate than in her own effusions; she is said to have commended in the most animated panegyric, the virtues of her brother Lanychus; and with the most pointed and severe censure, to have contemned the passion which her brother Charaxus entertained for the beautiful Rhodope. If her writings were, in some instances, too glowing for the fastidious refinement of modern times, let it be her excuse, and the honor of her country, that the liberal education of the Greeks was such, as inspired them with an unprejudiced enthusiasm for the works of genius: and that when they paid adoration to Sappho, they idolized the *muse,* and not the *woman.*

I shall conclude this account with an extract from the works of the learned and enlightened *Abbé Barthelemi,* at once the vindication and eulogy of the Grecian Poetess.

> Sappho undertook to inspire the Lesbian women with a taste for literature; many of them received instructions from her, and foreign women increased the number of her disciples. She loved them to excess, because it was impossible for her to love otherwise; and she expressed her tenderness in all the violence of passion: your surprise at this will cease, when you are acquainted with the extreme sensibility of the Greeks; and discover, that amongst them the most innocent connections often borrow the impassioned language of love.
>
> A certain facility of manners, she possessed; and the warmth of her expressions were but too well calculated to expose her to the hatred of some women of distinction, humbled by her superiority; and the jealousy of some of her disciples, who happened not to be the objects of her preference. To this hatred she replied by truths and irony, which completely exasperated her enemies. She repaired to Sicily, where a statue was erected to her; it was sculptured by *Silanion,* one of the most celebrated staturists of his time. The sensibility of *Sappho* was extreme! she loved *Phaon,* who forsook her; after various efforts to bring him back, she took the leap of Leucata,[3] and perished in the waves!
>
> Death has not obliterated the stain imprinted on her character; for *Envy,* which fastens on *illustrious names,* does not expire; but bequeaths her aspersions to that calumny which *never dies.*
>
> Several Grecian women have cultivated *Poetry,* with success, but none have hitherto attained to the excellence of *Sappho.* And among other poets, there are few, indeed, who have surpassed her.

Notes

1. Since the death of Doctor Johnson a few ingenious and elegant writers have composed sonnets, according to the rules described by him: of their merits the public will judge, and the *literati* decide. The following quotations are given as the opinions of living authors, respecting the legitimate sonnet.

> The little poems which are here called Sonnets, have, I believe, no very just claim to that title: but they consist of fourteen lines, and appear to me no improper vehicle for a single sentiment. I am told, and I read it as the opinion of very good judges, that the legitimate sonnet is ill calculated for our language. The specimens Mr. Hayley has given, though they form a strong exception, prove no more, than that the difficulties of the attempt vanish before uncommon powers.
> —*Mrs. C. Smith's Preface to her Elegiac Sonnets*

Likewise in the preface to a volume of very charming poems, (among which are many *legitimate sonnets*) by Mr. William Kendall, of Exeter, the following opinion is given of the Italian rhythm, which constitutes the legitimate sonnet: he describes it as—

> A chaste and elegant model, which the most enlightened poet of our country disdained not to contemplate. Amidst the degeneracy of modern taste, if the studies

of a Milton have lost their attraction, legitimate sonnets, enriched by varying pauses, and an elaborate recurrence of rhyme, still assert their superiority over those tasteless and inartificial productions, which assume the name, without evincing a single characteristic of distinguishing modulation.   [Robinson's note]

2. Cowper. [Robinson's note]

3. Leucata was a promontory of Epirus, on the top of which stood a temple dedicated to Apollo. From this promontory despairing lovers threw themselves into the sea, with an idea, that, if they survived, they should be cured of their hopeless passions. The Abbé Barthelemi says, that, "many escaped, but others having perished, the custom fell into disrepute; and at length was wholly abolished."—*Vide Travels of Anasharsis the Younger.*

[Robinson's note]

Notes to the Poems and Sources

Thomas Edwards (1–2). From *The Canons of Criticism, and Glossary; The Trial of the Letter [Y], alias Y, and Sonnets.* 7th ed. (London, 1765).

1. Edwards's sonnets, including this one, first appeared in the second volume of *A Collection of Poems by Several Hands,* popularly known as "Dodsley's Miscellany" (1748).

2. See also Ebenezer Elliott's sonnet "Criticism" (420).

Thomas Gray (3). From *The Poems of Mr. Gray. To which are Prefixed Memoirs of his Life and Writings by W. Mason, M.A.* (York, 1775).

3. line 2, Phoebus: the sun in classical mythology.

Thomas Warton (4–5). From *The Poetical Works of the Late Thomas Warton, B.D. Fellow of Trinity College, Oxford; and Poet Laureate,* ed. Richard Mant. 5th ed., 2 vols. (Oxford, 1802). Warton's sonnets were first published in 1777.

4. line 2, Surrey: a county in southeast England, near London.

line 2, Epsom: a town in southeast England, near London.

5. title, the River Lodon: now called the River Chet, it flows through Norfolk, England.

John Codrington Bampfylde (6–9). From *Sixteen Sonnets* (London, 1778).

6. line 8, gins: machines worked by horses.

7. line 2, The myrtle never-sear: Myrtle is the common name for several evergreen plants used since ancient times for wreaths, decorations, and perfume and symbolizing love, marriage, and happiness.

line 2, gadding: wandering.

line 5, pied: multi-colored.

line 6, woodbine: Virginia Creeper, a high-climbing, woody vine.

line 7, eglantine: common name for *rosa eglanteria* or sweetbrier, a rose noted for its fragrant foliage and pink flowers.

8. line 9 would make more sense beginning "And prayer, essayed to mar . . ."

9. line 1, yclad: clothed.

line 7, ruddy prattlers dear: the shepherd's children.

Charlotte Smith (10–35). 10–30. From *Elegiac Sonnets, and Other Poems.* 9th ed. (London, 1800). Smith continued to add sonnets to each edition of *Elegiac Sonnets* through the 9th edition. We have indicated the dates for the editions in which the sonnets first appeared. Stuart Curran's edition of *The Poems of Charlotte Smith* (New York, 1993) was a source for some of the references below.

10. line 14: "The well-sung woes shall soothe my pensive ghost; / He best can paint them who shall feel them most." *Pope's "Eloisa to Abelard,"* 366th *line* [Smith's note].

11. line 3, Anemonies: Anemony Nemeroso. The wood Anemony [Smith's note].

12. The idea from the 43[r]d Sonnet of Petrarch. Secondo parte. "Quel rosigniuol, che si soave piagne" [Smith's note].

13. line 1, Queen of the silver bow: Diana, in classical mythology, the goddess of the moon.

14. line 2, "your turf, your flowers among": "Whose turf, whose shades, whose flowers among." Gray [Smith's note]. From Thomas Gray's "Ode on a Distant Prospect of Eton College" (1747), line 8.

line 9, Aruna: The river Arun [Smith's note]. A river in West Sussex, England.

line 11, Lethean cup: The river Lethe, according to classical mythology, ran through Hades, and drinking its waters brought forgetfulness.

15. line 3, Morpheus: In Greek mythology, the guardian of dreams and son of Hypnos, god of sleep.

line 4: "Float in light vision round the poet's head." *Mason* [Smith's note]. From William Mason's "Elegy V. On the Death of a Lady" (1760), line 12.

line 7: "Wilt thou upon the high and giddy mast / Seal up the ship boy's eyes, and rock his brains / In cradle of the rude impetuous surge?" &c. *Shakespeare's Henry IV* [Smith's note]. From *2 Henry IV* 3.1.18-20.

16. In this and the following two sonnets, Smith adopts the persona of Werther, the protagonist of Goethe's popular novel of sensibility *The Sorrows of Young Werther* (1774). In the novel, Werther's hopeless love for Lotte, or Charlotte, and his excessive, passionate nature compel him to take his own life.

line 5, the poor maniac: See the "Story of the Lunatic." "Is this the destiny of man? Is he only happy before he possesses his reason, or after he has lost it?—Full of hope you go to gather flowers in Winter, and are grieved not to find any—and do not know why they cannot be found." *Sorrows of Werter. Volume Second* [Smith's note].

line 8, "And drink delicious poison from her eyes!" Alexander Pope [Smith's note]. From Pope's "Eloisa to Abelard," line 122.

17. See also John Keats's sonnet "To Solitude" (301).

line 1: "I climb steep rocks, I break my way through copses, among thorns and briars which tear me to pieces, and I feel a little relief." *Sorrows of Werter. Volume First* [Smith's note].

18. line 1: "At the corner of the churchyard which looks towards the fields, there are two lime trees—it is there I wish to rest." *Sorrows of Werter. Volume Second* [Smith's note].

19. line 1: *"Erano i capei d'oro all aura sparsi." Sonnetto 69. Parte primo* [Smith's note]. Actually, Sonnet 90 ("Erano i capei d'oro a l'aura sparsi") in Petrarch's *Canzoniere.* The Italian features Petrarch's famous pun on Laura's name, "l'aura" or "the breeze."

line 2, Zephyr: the west wind.

20. line 10: "And hard Unkindness' altered eye, / That mocks the tear it forced to flow." *Gray* [Smith's note]. From Thomas Gray's "Ode on a Distant Prospect of Eton College" (1747), lines 76–7.

21. line 8: Young [Smith's note]. See the opening lines of Edward Young's tragedy *The Revenge* (1721), 1.1.5–7.

22. line 5: Otway was born at Trotten, a village in Sussex. Of Woolbeding, another village on the banks of the Arun (which runs through them both), his father was rector.

Here it was, therefore, that he probably passed many of his early years. The Arun is here an inconsiderable stream, winding in a channel deeply worn, among meadow, heath, and wood [Smith's note]. Thomas Otway (1652-85), actor and playwright, died in poverty in his early thirties.

24. title, Naiad: river nymph.

line 9, thy natives: Otway, Collins, Hayley [Smith's note]. In addition to Otway, the poet William Collins (1721–59) and Smith's patron William Hayley (1745–1820) were, like Smith herself, natives of Sussex, through which the Arun flows.

26. This sonnet first appeared in Smith's novel, *Emmeline: The Orphan of the Castle* (1788).

27. line 7: Middleton is a village on the margin of the sea, in Sussex, containing only two or three houses. There were formerly several acres of ground between its small church and the sea, which now, by its continual encroachments, approaches within a few feet of this half-ruined and humble edifice. The wall, which once surrounded the church-yard is entirely swept away, many of the graves broken up, and the remains of bodies interred washed into the sea; whence human bones are found among the sand and shingles on the shore [Smith's note].

28. Henrietta O'Neill (1758-93) was a close friend and patron of Smith's. Her poem "Ode to the Poppy" (1793) became well known.

29. line 7, "the shepherd's clock": *Shakespeare* [Smith's note]. "When shepherds pipe on oaten straws, / And merry larks are ploughmen's clocks," *Love's Labour's Lost* 5.2.892–93.

line 14, the Mountain Nymph: The mountain goddess, Liberty. *Milton* [Smith's note]. See John Milton's *L'Allegro,* line 36.

31–35. From *Elegiac Sonnets, and Other Poems.* Vol. 2., 2nd ed. (London, 1800).

31. line 11: "'Tis delicate felicity that shrinks / When rocking winds are loud." *Walpole* [Smith's note]. As Stuart Curran notes, the lines Smith cites are not in the standard edition of Horace Walpole's works.

32. line 2, darkling: in darkness.

35. line 2, tremulous Aspens: poplar trees whose leaves seem to tremble in the wind.

Samuel Egerton Brydges (36–37). From *Poems.* 4th ed. (London, 1807).

36. First appeared in Brydges's *Sonnets and Other Poems; with a Versification of the Six Bards of Ossian* (1785).

lines 7–8: refer to an aeolian harp, a stringed instrument that makes pleasant sounds when the wind blows upon it.

William Hayley (38). From *Poems and Plays.* Vol. 1 (London, 1785).

Mary Hays (39). From *Letters and Essays, Moral, and Miscellaneous* (London, 1793).

line 6, lethean waves: the classical river of forgetfulness.

Helen Maria Williams (40–46).

40. From *Poems.* Vol. 1. (London, 1786).

41–42. From *Julia, A Novel* (London, 1790).

41. "To Hope" is the first sonnet to appear in Williams's novel *Julia* and is also one of the first sonnets to appear in any novel of the time. In her collection *Poems on Various Subjects* (1823), she says she begins her series of sonnets with this one because of "a predilection in its favor, for which I have proud reason; it is that of Mr. Wordsworth . . . having repeated it to me from memory, after a lapse of many years." "To the Moon" also first appeared in *Julia.*

43–46. From Bernardin Saint-Pierre, *Paul and Virginia.* Trans. Helen Maria Williams (n.p., 1795). Williams incorporated these original sonnets into her 1795 translation of Bernardin Saint-Pierre's romance *Paul et Virginie* (1790), which she completed while a prisoner in France during the Reign of Terror.

45. The Torrid Zone is the geographical area between the tropics of Cancer and Capricorn.

line 5, amadavid-bird: also called avadavat, or waxbill, a bird native to southeast Asia.

line 6, his gay plumes: The male avadavat has brilliant red feathers with white spots.

46. line 2, pinions: wings.

William Lisle Bowles (47–55). From *Sonnets, Written Chiefly on Picturesque Spots, During a Tour*, 2nd ed. (Bath, 1789). Bowles's sonnets first appeared anonymously as *Fourteen Sonnets, Elegiac and Descriptive. Written During a Tour* (1789), which included an advertisement: "The following Sonnets, (or whatever they may be called) were found in a Traveler's Memorandum-Book. They were selected from amongst many others, chiefly of the same kind. The Editor has ventured to lay a few of them before the Public, as he hopes there may be some Readers to whom they may not be entirely unacceptable." A subsequent expanded edition appeared soon after that named Bowles as the author; and since the poet notes in the advertisement to the second edition that the previous sonnets "were before committed too hastily to the Press," we reprint the revised texts.

50. "Bamborough Castle in Northumberland, where there is the most liberal provision established for mariners shipwrecked on the coast" [Bowles's note to the first edition].

52. The Tweed flows through southern Scotland and along the northeast border of England.

53. The Itchen runs through Hampshire, England.

55. The Cherwell flows through Oxford and into the Thames.

Thomas Russell (56–60). From Thomas Russell. *Sonnets and Miscellaneous Poems* (Oxford, 1789).

57. Francesco Patrarca (1304–1374), known in English as Petrarch, Italian poet and humanist, spent much of his later life wandering throughout northern Italy; Valclusa, or Vaucluse, is where much of his poetry takes place, particularly the love sonnets to Laura, whose death is a source of great grief in Petrarch's sonnets. The sonnet became identified with Petrarch (see introduction).

line 1, Bard: Petrarch.

line 2, Fair: Laura.

Mary Locke (61). From the *Gentleman's Magazine* (1791).

line 1, parti-colored: multi-colored.

Ann Radcliffe (62–67).

62–64. From Radcliffe's novel *The Romance of the Forest: Interspersed with Some Pieces of Poetry*, 3 vols. (London, 1791). In these as well as "Storied Sonnet" below, Radcliffe experiments with extending the traditional length of the sonnet, while maintaining its characteristic rhyme patterns and compactness. See note to Mary Bryan's "The Maniac" (294) below.

65–67. From Radcliffe's Gothic novel *The Mysteries of Udolpho, a Romance* (London, 1794).

Anna Maria Jones (68–69). From *The Poems of Anna Maria Jones* (Calcutta, 1793).

68. According to classical mythology, Echo was a mountain nymph who loved Narcissus, pining for him until nothing was left of her but her voice.

Samuel Taylor Coleridge (70–93).

70. From the *Morning Chronicle* (1 Dec. 1794). Thomas Erskine (1750–1823), states-man and attorney, lost his office as attorney-general for defending Thomas Paine (1737-1809), author of the *Rights of Man* (1790) and sympathizer of the French Revolution. In 1793–4, Erskine arranged acquittals for many who were charged with treason and con-spiracy for supporting radical political causes.

71. From the *Morning Chronicle* (9 Dec. 1794). To Edmund Burke (1729-97), states-man and author of *Reflections on the Revolution in France* (1790). Burke supported the American Revolution but opposed the French Revolution. He retired from political life in 1794 and received a lucrative and somewhat controversial pension. Sonnets 71–75 and 77 feature the titles given to them in subsequent editions.

72. From the *Morning Chronicle* (11 Dec. 1794). To Joseph Priestley (1733-1804), sci-entist and political radical, best known today for his discovery of oxygen. He was forced to emigrate to America after a mob burned his home because of his outspoken support of the French Revolution.

73. From the *Morning Chronicle* (15 Dec. 1794). The Marquis de Lafayette (1757–1834) served as a general under George Washington during the American Revo-lution. A political moderate, he fled for his life to Austria in 1792, after his failed coup d'état against the more radical revolutionary government in Paris.

74. From the *Morning Chronicle* (16 Dec. 1794). To Thaddeus Kosciusko (1746–1817), Polish patriot and general in the American Revolutionary army. See also Keats's sonnet to Kosciusko (313).

75. From the *Morning Chronicle* (23 Dec. 1794). To William Pitt the Younger (1759–1806), Prime Minister from 1783 to 1801 and from 1804 to 1806 and son of the Earl of Chatham, a Whig politician. Coleridge here attacks the younger Pitt's pro-war policies but withdrew this sonnet from his poems after 1803 because of his changing political views.

line 7, Iscariot: surname of Judas, who betrays Jesus in Mark 3.19, 14.10–11.

line 8, a godlike father's name: Earl of Chatham [Coleridge's note].

line 12, thy stern-browed sister: Justice [Coleridge's note].

76. From the *Morning Chronicle* (26 Dec. 1794). Coleridge greatly admired the son-nets of William Lisle Bowles and writes at some length of their influence on him in his *Biographia Literaria* and elsewhere. His long note for this sonnet praises Bowles's sonnets for their "exquisite delicacy of painting," their "tender simplicity," and for their "manly Pathos," calling them "compositions of, perhaps, unrivaled merit." He adds, "Yet, while I am selecting these [qualities], I almost accuse myself of causeless partiality; for surely never was a Writer so equal in excellence!" Coleridge revised this sonnet substantially several times; most editions of Coleridge's works provide the later, revised text.

77. From the *Morning Chronicle* (29 Dec. 1794). To Sarah Siddons (1755–1831), Eng-land's most celebrated actress from 1782 until her retirement in 1812, famous for her tragic roles, including particularly her portrayal of Shakespeare's Lady Macbeth. This son-net was attributed to Charles Lamb in *Poems, by S. T. Coleridge, Second Edition. To which are now added Poems by Charles Lamb, and Charles Lloyd* (1797).

78. From the *Morning Chronicle* (10 Jan. 1795). William Godwin (1756–1836), polit-ical philosopher whose *Enquiry concerning Political Justice* (1793) argued that human reason could bring about social progress, harmony and benevolence.

line 3, the mimic morn: Aurora Borealis [Coleridge's note].

79. From the *Morning Chronicle* (14 Jan. 1795). Robert Southey (1774–1843), a close friend of Coleridge's at this time and fellow poet. In 1813, he became poet laureate of England.

80. From the *Morning Chronicle* (29 Jan. 1795). Richard Brinsley Sheridan (1751–1816), proprietor of Drury Lane Theater, author of the well-known play *The*

School for Scandal (1777), political ally of Whig statesman Charles James Fox, and esteemed orator in the House of Commons.

line 4, Hymettian flowers: Hymettus, a mountain of Attica, famous for Honey [Coleridge's note]. Located just east of Athens, Greece, its flora, described by Ovid, fell victim to erosion in modern times. This passage is an allusion to Sheridan's classicism and the sweetness of his verse.

lines 5 and 6, Laura's bier and Vauclusa's glade: references to Petrarch's grief over the death of his beloved Laura, whom he saw in Avignon and Vaucluse.

line 14, Michael's Sword: The biblical archangel Michael often appears with a sword. See Daniel 10.13.

81. From *Poems on Various Subjects* (London, 1796).

82. From S. T. Coleridge, ed., *Sonnets from Various Authors* (n.p., 1796).

83–84. From *Poems, by S. T. Coleridge, Second Edition. To which are now added Poems by Charles Lamb, and Charles Lloyd* (Bristol, 1797).

83. This sonnet clearly shows William Lisle Bowles's influence on Coleridge as a sonneteer: see Bowles's "River Itchin" sonnet (53). The Otter is a river in Devon near Coleridge's birthplace.

line 8, straight: in copytext, "strait".

84. title: The friend is Charles Lloyd; the infant is Hartley Coleridge, born in 1796.

85–87. From the *Monthly Magazine* 4.24 (Nov. 1797). In these three sonnets, Coleridge pokes fun at the poetic practices of Charles Lloyd, Charles Lamb, and himself. He signed them "Nehemiah Higginbottom." The first is intended "to excite a good-natured laugh at the spirit of doleful egotism, and at the recurrence of favorite phrases, with the double effect of being at once trite, and licentious." In "To Simplicity," he satirizes "low, creeping language and thoughts, under the pretense of simplicity." Coleridge notes that "On a Ruined House in a Romantic Country" uses phrases from his own poems to point out "the indiscriminate use of elaborate and swelling language and imagery" *(Biographia Literaria,* eds. James Engell and W. Jackson Bate [Princeton, 1983], Vol. 1, p. 27).

87. line 5, In the copytext, this line ends with an exclamation point.

88. From the *Annual Anthology,* Vol. 2. (Bristol, 1800). To William Linley (1771–1835), English composer and author.

89. From the *Poetical Works of S. T. Coleridge,* Vol. 1. (London, 1835). First published in *Felix Farley's Bristol Journal* in 1818.

title, Nubibus: as in "nubilous," meaning cloudy or foggy, vague or obscure.

line 11, blind bard: Homer, believed to be the author of the *Iliad* and the *Odyssey.* The island Chios, or "Chian," is one of seven sites claimed as his birthplace.

90. From *The Bijou; or Annual of Literature and the Arts* (London, 1828). For later versions of this sonnet, Coleridge modified the subtitle to specify the date: "Lines Composed 21st February 1825."

91. From *Blackwood's Edinburgh Magazine* 31 (June 1832). This sonnet is derived from a longer poem, "Youth and Age," which Coleridge published in 1828. He published it as a sonnet to accompany a brief essay "What is an English Sonnet?" as a satirical example of the requirements for a sonnet. Coleridge sarcastically points out that this sonnet stands "the test of counting the lines, twice seven exactly."

92. From *The Poetical Works of S. T. Coleridge,* Vol. 1 (London, 1835). "Life" is one of Coleridge's earliest sonnets, written in 1789. It was not published, however, until 1834 when it appeared among a selection of "Juvenile Poems" in Coleridge's *Poetical Works.*

93. From *The Life and Correspondence of Robert Southey,* ed. Charles Cuthbert Southey, Vol. 1, 2nd ed. (London, 1849). "Pantisocracy" is the name Coleridge gave to a projected but never-realized Utopian community that he and Robert Southey planned to build on the Susquehanna River in Pennsylvania. Coleridge sent the poem in a letter to Southey dated 18 September 1794, but it was not published until 1849, when it appeared in Charles Cuthbert Southey's memoir of his father.

Amelia Opie (94–95).
    94. From *The Cabinet,* Vol. 2. (Norwich, 1795).
    95. From the *Annual Anthology,* Vol. 1. (Bristol, 1799).

John Thelwall (96–99). From the *Poetical Recreations of the Champion, and his Literary Correspondents; with a Selection of Essays, Literary and Critical, which have appeared in The Champion Newspaper* (London, 1822). Thelwall composed sonnets 96, 97, and 98 in mid–July 1794.
    96–98. For more information on Thelwall's politics and his relationship with Wordsworth and Coleridge, see Nicholas Roe's *Wordsworth and Coleridge: The Radical Years* (Oxford, 1988).
    99. Lord Holland: Henry Richard Vassall Fox, third Baron Holland (1773–1840), champion of liberal causes such as abolition of the slave trade and abolition of capital punishment.
    line 12, Phoebus', or with Dian's softer light: the sun's or the moon's light.

Mary Julia Young (100–105).
    100. From *Genius and Fancy; or Dramatic Sketches; with other Poems on Various Subjects* (London, 1795).
    101–105. From *Poems* (London, 1798).
    101. line 12, halcyon: mythical bird that had the power to calm the ocean.

Charles Lamb (106–110).
    106. From S. T. Coleridge, *Poems on Various Subjects* (London, 1796). Coleridge included a number of Lamb's sonnets, including this one, in his *Poems on Various Subjects.* This sonnet also appeared in Coleridge's pamphlet *Sonnets from Various Authors* (1796).
    107. From *Sonnets from Various Authors,* ed. Samuel Taylor Coleridge (1796). The sonnet also appeared in the July 1796 issue of the *Monthly Magazine.*
    line 1, the youngest she: Mary Ann Lamb (1764–1847), Charles Lamb's sister.
    line 11, awful: Innocence, which while we possess it, is playful, as a babe, becomes *awful* when it has departed from us.—This is the sentiment of the line, a fine sentiment and nobly expressed [Coleridge's note].
    108. From *Sonnets from Various Authors,* ed. Samuel Taylor Coleridge (1796).
    109. From S. T. Coleridge, *Poems, To which are now added Poems by Charles Lamb, and Charles Lloyd,* 2nd ed. (Bristol, 1797). Lamb prefaces his poems in this volume with a dedication to Mary Lamb, "the author's best friend and sister."
    110. From the *Works of Charles Lamb,* Vol. 1 (London, 1818).
    line 5, Lincolnian plains: Lincolnshire, a mainly agricultural county in east central England.
    line 9, Salem: Jerusalem.
    line 11, Saracens: Muslims, during the Crusades.

Mary Robinson (111–155).
    111–154. From *Sappho and Phaon. In a Series of Legitimate Sonnets, with Thoughts on Poetical Subjects, and Anecdotes of the Grecian Poetess* (London, 1796). See Appendix for Robinson's prose preface to this sequence of sonnets. Sappho (b. 612 BC), the lyric poet, lived most of her life in Lesbos. Most of her nine books of poetry are now lost. She loved several women but also married and bore a daughter. The legend that she committed suicide by throwing herself into the ocean after being rejected by Phaon is not supported by evidence. Titles to these sonnets originally appeared only in the table of contents of the copytext.
    epigraph, "Love taught my tears in sadder notes to flow, / And tuned my heart to elegies of woe": lines 7–8 from Alexander Pope's *Sappho to Phaon* (1712), translated from the

fifteenth epistle of Ovid's *Heroides,* a sequence of 21 verse epistles from legendary women figures to their lovers. These lines from Pope are a translation of the first epigraph from Ovid. Robinson obviously knew Pope's poem, and her sonnet sequence contains many verbal echoes of Pope's translation.

111. line 5, tuneful numbers: poetic meter.

line 13, Elysian bowers: Elysium, land of the blessed dead in classical mythology; heaven.

112. line 1, coeval: as old as.

line 13, vestals: virgins associated with Vesta, the Roman goddess of the hearth.

113. line 8, panoply: covering.

115. title, Contemns: scorns, despises.

118. line 5, Lesbian Vales: on the ancient island of Lesbos.

121. line 7, wreath of fame: the laurel, symbol of poetic accomplishment.

122. line 1, tessellated: mosaic.

line 2, saffron: *crocus sativa,* a member of the iris family long cultivated in the Mediterranean to color and flavor foods.

123. line 4, chrysolite: formerly referring to several green gems such as zircon but after 1790 meaning olivine, a precious stone found in lava rock (*Oxford English Dictionary*).

line 6, pinions: wings.

124. line 1, Eolian harp: stringed instrument placed in a casement window to make pleasant sounds when the wind blows through it.

line 7, Philomel: the nightingale.

125. line 5, timbrel: instrument similar to a tambourine.

line 6, cassia: mezereon, a fragrant shrub-like plant mentioned by Virgil and Ovid.

line 9, porphyry: a hard, purplish stone which takes a high polish and is quarried in Egypt.

line 10, Phœnicia: beautiful, ancient kingdom on the coast of Syria, northwest of Palestine.

129. line 3, Nereides: sea nymphs.

130. line 4, Scythia: ancient land in southeast Europe and Asia.

line 12, snowdrop: herb that blooms in spring with white flowers, *Galanthus nivalis.*

line 14, sue: pursue.

131. Below and following, Robinson acknowledges her paraphrases from Ovid's account of Sappho and Phaon or from Alexander Pope's translation. We include all of her notes. Our references to Pope's translation are from *Alexander Pope,* ed. Pat Rogers (Oxford, 1993).

line 9:

> *Sex mihi nateles ierant, cum lecta parentis*
> *Ante diem lacrymas ossa bibere meas.*
> *Arsit inops frater, victus meretricis amore;*
> *Mistaque cum turpi damna pudore tulit.*
> ————Ovid

[Robinson's note].

See Pope's *Sappho to Phaon,* lines 72–80.

133. line 1: Arva Phaon celebrat diversa Typhoïdos Ætnæ. Ovid [Robinson's note]. See Pope's *Sappho to Phaon,* line 11: "Phaon to Etna's scorching fields retires."

line 1, Etna: volcano in Sicily.

line 7, Idalian: Idalium, ancient village in Cyprus associated with Aphrodite, the Greek goddess of erotic love, known in Roman mythology as Venus.

line 10: Me calor Ætæo non minor igne coquit. Ovid [Robinson's note]. See Pope's *Sappho to Phaon,* line 12: "While I consume with more than Etna's fires."

137. line 1, ebon: ebony.

139. line 8, Hybla: Sicilian town, known for producing honey.

140. line 7, Siren band: According to classical mythology, sirens were sea nymphs, part woman and part bird, who lured sailors to their deaths with their singing.

142. line 1: Vide Sappho's Ode [in Longinus, "Essay on the Sublime"; Robinson's note].

143. line 3, halcyon: mythical bird that made its nest on the sea and had the power to calm the waters.

144. line 2, Mytilenian: Mytile was a city on the island of Lesbos.

line 3, Echo: in classical mythology, the nymph who loved Narcissus until nothing was left of her but her voice.

line 14, Nine: There were nine Muses.

145. line 6, Erebus: darkness personified.

lines 9 and 11: Pope.

> Si tam certus eras hinc ire, modestius isses,
> Et modo dixisses Lesbi puella, vale.
> ————OVID

[Robinson's note].

Lines 9 and 11 are nearly identical to lines 113-14 of Pope's *Sappho to Phaon*.

148. line 12, Lethe: river of forgetfulness.

149. line 1, Aonian maids: the Muses.

line 4, Erato: muse of lyric and erotic poetry; parian marble: white marble from the island of Paros.

150. line 5, Leucadian deep: According to legend, Sappho leapt from the rock of Leucadia into the ocean and drowned.

line 6, empyrean: fiery.

line 12, phalanx: the crowd of visions she sees.

152. line 14: Pope.

> Grata lyram posui tibi Phœbe, poëtria Sappho:
> Convenit illa mihi, convenit illa tibi.
> ————OVID

[Robinson's note].

Line 14 is a direct quotation from line 216 of Pope's *Sappho to Phaon;* see lines 212–16 for Pope's translation of the passage from Ovid which Robinson cites.

155. From *The Poetical Works of the Late Mrs. Mary Robinson: Including Many Pieces Never Before Published,* 3 vols. (London, 1806). See also Elizabeth Cobbold's *Sonnets of Laura* (361–363).

Ann Yearsley (156). From *The Rurual Lyre* (London, 1796).

William Beckford (157). From *Azemia: A Descriptive and Sentimental Novel. Interspersed with Pieces of Poetry,* 2 vols. (London, 1797). In *Azemia,* Beckford also satirizes the contemporary critical debates over the "illegitimacy" of the English sonnet compared with the "legitimate" Italian sonnet. One of the novel's heroines, Iphanissa, for instance,

> loved a sonnet if it was *legitimate,* joining issue with the Reverend Solomon Sheeppen in asserting, that fourteen lines rhyming unlawfully together, in quatrains or alternate rhymes, was a *nullius filius* in poetry, begotten and born between licentiousness and incapacity, had no claim to the support and countenance of the orthodox and chaste poets and poetesses of the present day, and of course should be banished from all decent society, such as from that of Milton (Shakespeare was a dreadful encourager of illegitimacy), Miss Seward and Miss Mary Robinson . . . (1.118-19).

Both Anna Seward and Mary Robinson followed the Italian model with full confidence that it was the more challenging and prestigious sonnet form. See Seward's "To Mr. Henry Cary, On the Publication of his Sonnets" (185) and Robinson's Preface to *Sappho and Phaon* (Appendix).

Charles Lloyd (158–164).

158–162. From *Poems, by S.T. Coleridge, Second Edition. To which are now added Poems by Charles Lamb, and Charles Lloyd* (Bristol, 1797). These sonnets come from "Poems, on The Death of Priscilla Farmer, By her Grandson Charles Lloyd," a group of poems published in S.T. Coleridge's 1797 volume, that includes also a prefatory sonnet by Coleridge, "Dedicatory Lines to the Author's Brother," and "Lines Written on a Friday, the Day in each Week formerly devoted by the Author and his Brothers and Sisters to the Society of their Grandmother."

163–164. From *Nugæ Canoræ*, 3rd ed. (London, 1819). Lloyd notes that 163 was written in 1807, 164 in 1794.

Robert Southey (165–172).

165–170. From *Poems*, 2nd ed. (Bristol, 1797). Southey's 1797 edition of *Poems* includes the following preface to the sonnets:

When first the Abolition of the *Slave-Trade* was agitated in England, the friends of humanity endeavored by two means to accomplish it—To destroy the Trade immediately by the interference of Government; or by the disuse of West-Indian productions: *a slow but certain method.* For a while Government held the language of justice, and individuals with enthusiasm banished sugar from their tables. This enthusiasm soon cooled; the majority of those who had made this *sacrifice,* (I prostitute the word, but such they thought it,) persuaded themselves that Parliament would do all, and that individual efforts were no longer necessary. Thus ended the one attempt; it is not difficult to say why the Minister has once found himself in the minority, and on the side of justice. Would to God that the interests of those who dispose of us as they please, had been as closely connected with the preservation of Peace and Liberty, as with the continuance of this traffic in human flesh!

There are yet two other methods remaining, by which this traffic will probably be abolished. By the introduction of East-Indian or Maple Sugar, or by the just and general rebellion of the Negroes.

To these past and present prospects the following Poems occasionally allude: to the English custom of exciting wars upon the Slave Coast that they may purchase prisoners, and to the punishment sometimes inflicted upon a Negro for murder, of which Hector St. John was an eye-witness.

above, Hector St. John: Michel-Guillaume Jean de Crèvecoeur (1735–1813), French essayist who emigrated to Canada and for many years traveled in America. He wrote *Letters from an American Farmer* (1782) under the pseudonym J. Hector de St. John. He became French consul in New York and was the friend of Washington, Jefferson, and Franklin.

167. line 10, the blood-sweetened beverage: West-Indian slaves cultivated sugar cane for Europeans.

171–172. From the *Poetical Works of Robert Southey, Collected by Himself,* Vol. 2 (London, 1838).

171. First published in the *Morning Post* (10 January 1799); also published in the *Annual Anthology* (Bristol, 1800).

Edward Gardner (173–174). From *Miscellanies, in Prose and Verse.* Vol. 2 (Bristol, 1798).

173. title, Tintern Abbey: a ruined medieval abbey near the River Wye in Wales.

Joseph Hucks (175). From *Poems* (Cambridge, 1798).
line 1, Gallia: France

Anna Seward (176–190). From *Original Sonnets on Various Subjects; and Odes Paraphrased from Horace,* 2nd ed. (London, 1799). These sonnets were published in Seward's *Original Sonnets* (1799), though some were composed as early as 1770.
177. line 2, indurate: hard or unfeeling.
178. line 1, Derwent: a river that flows through central England, near Lichfield, the town in which Seward lived.
line 4, umbrageous: shady.
179. line 1, Lesbia: Lesbos was the home of the poet Sappho.
line 14, Narcissus: mythological youth who fell in love with his own reflection.
180. title, Honora Sneyd: Seward's beloved adopted sister and later stepmother of Maria Edgeworth (1767-1849). Seward dated this sonnet April 1773.
181. Seward dated this sonnet July 1773.
183. This sonnet was written in an apartment of the west front of the Bishop's Palace at Lichfield, inhabited by the author from her thirteenth year. It looks upon the cathedral area, a green lawn encircled by prebendal houses, which are white from being rough-cast [Seward's note]. Seward dated this sonnet 19 December 1782.
185. An earlier, slightly different version of this sonnet appeared as a preface to Henry Francis Cary's book *Sonnets and Odes* (1788) and again in S. T. Coleridge's *Sonnets from Various Authors* (1796).
line 6, From him derived: Petrarch.
186. line 9: *"Rusticus exspectat dum defluit amnis: at ille / Labitur, et labetur in omne volubilis ævum."* Horace [Seward's note].
190. line 8, Aonian clime: region of the Muses.

Jane West (191). From *A Tale of the Times,* Vol. 2 (London, 1799).
line 4, Pomona: Roman goddess of fruit trees.

Ann Home Hunter (192). From *Poems* (London, 1802).

Eliza Kirkham Mathews (193). From *Poems* (Doncaster, 1802).

William Cowper (194–195). From William Hayley's *Life, and Posthumous Writings, of William Cowper, Esq.,* Vol. 2, 2nd ed. (Chichester, 1803).
194. Mary Unwin, mother of Cowper's friend William Cawthorne Unwin, suffered a stroke in 1792 and never fully recovered. Cowper composed this sonnet in 1793 and it appeared in print in 1803.
195. Cowper sent this sonnet in a 1792 letter to William Hayley, seeking encouragement to send it in tribute to the painter George Romney (1734–1802). He writes, "I must premise, however, that I intended nothing less than a sonnet when I began. I know not why, but I said to myself, it shall not be a sonnet; accordingly I attempted it in one sort of measure, then in a second, then in a third, till I had made the trial in half a dozen different kinds of shorter verse, and behold it is a sonnet at last. The Fates would have it so."

Henry Kirke White (196–197). From the *Remains of Henry Kirke White, of Nottingham, Late of St. John's College, Cambridge; With an Account of his Life,* by Robert Southey, Vol. 2 (London, 1807). These sonnets first appeared in White's 1803 volume *Clifton Grove.* In his preface, White writes, "The Sonnets are chiefly irregular; they have, perhaps, no other claim to that *specific* denomination, than that they consist only of fourteen lines."
196. line 1, Cambrian wild: Wales.
197. line 11, thee: In the copytext a comma follows this word.

Mrs. B. Finch (198–199). From *Sonnets, and Other Poems: To Which are Added Tales in Prose* (London, 1805).

199. line 4, panoply: covering

line 6, the Christmas rose: Helleborus Niger. This plant, in mild winters and a proper soil, sometimes blows in December [Finch's note].

line 14, vespers: evening prayers

Anna Maria Smallpiece (200–201). From *Original Sonnets, and Other Small Poems* (London, 1805).

William Wordsworth (202–257).

202. From *European Magazine* 12 (1787). Wordsworth published this sonnet—his first published poem—when he was seventeen years old, under the pseudonym "Axiologus," which literally means "Wordsworth," in the *European Magazine* in 1787. He would not actually meet Helen Maria Williams for many years, though he did attempt to see her when he visited France in 1791, armed with a letter of introduction by Charlotte Smith. An English expatriate, Williams was well known for her radical sympathies and for her vivid published descriptions of events in France. Here, Wordsworth appears to be responding to a moment in her long poem *Peru* (1784).

203–218. From *Poems, In Two Volumes* (London, 1807).

203. Wordsworth published this sonnet in the *Morning Post* in 1802, shortly after his sister, Dorothy, read Milton's sonnets to him. He later recalled, "I took fire, if I may be allowed to say so, and produced three Sonnets the same afternoon." It reflects his growing disillusionment at the progress of the French Revolution in having cast off one tyrant, Louis XVI, only to embrace another. Napoleon, at this time, had served as executive general of the French army from 1796–99 and was named First Consul of the Republic in 1799 and Consul for life in 1802. He would proclaim himself Emperor in 1804. Meanwhile, England's war with France was becoming increasingly costly and unpopular.

204. This sonnet, published in *Poems, In Two Volumes,* appears in the sequence of poems entitled "Poems Composed During a Tour, Chiefly on Foot." Although the sonnet here has 15 lines, Wordsworth later revised it as a conventional 14-line sonnet.

lines 1–2: From a sonnet of Sir Philip Sydney [Wordsworth's note]. These lines come from the thirty-first sonnet of Sir Philip Sidney's 1591 sequence *Astrophel and Stella* and are an unusual instance of Wordsworth nodding to the sonnet explosion of the 1590s.

line 14, Cynthia: the moon.

205. This poem was called "Prefatory Sonnet," heading a series of sonnets, in Wordsworth's 1807 volume *Poems, In Two Volumes.*

line 6, Furness Fells: hills in England's Lake District.

line 7, foxglove bells: large showy bell-shaped flowers growing in a spiked cluster; of the family *digitalis.*

206. line 7, mountebanks: wandering quack doctors.

208. The correct name of the town in Yorkshire is "Hambleton." In October 1802, on the eve of his marriage, Wordsworth made this journey with his new bride, Mary Hutchinson, and his sister, Dorothy, in order to share a famous vista. Dorothy Wordsworth records in her Grasmere journal that it was dark when they arrived:

> . . . far off from us, in the western sky we saw shapes of Castles, Ruins among groves, a great, spreading wood, rocks, & single trees, a minster with its tower unusually distinct, minarets in another quarter, & a round Grecian Temple also—the colours of the sky of a bright grey & the forms of a sober grey, with a dome. As we descended the hill there was no distinct view, but of a great space, only near us, we saw the wild & (as the people say) bottomless Tarn in the hollow at the side of the

hill. It seemed to be made visible to us only by its own light, for all the hill about us was dark. (Dorothy Wordsworth. *Grasmere Journals,* ed. Pamela Woof [Oxford, 1993], p. 128.)

209. This sonnet revises the conclusion of sonnet 208.

210. line 8, Her tackling rich, and of apparel high: From a passage in Skelton, which I cannot here insert, not having the Book at hand [Wordsworth's note].

213. line 13, Proteus: sea god with the power to assume any shape.

line 14, Triton: son of Poseidon; half man, half fish, often pictured with a conch shell.

214. line 12, Abraham's bosom: a place where the dead go before meeting God; see Luke 16.22: "And it came to pass, that the beggar died, and was carried by the angels into Abraham's bosom."

215. This and the following three sonnets are part of a sequence entitled "Sonnets Dedicated to Liberty" published in *Poems, In Two Volumes.*

title: Calais, France is directly opposite Dover, England across the English Channel.

216. title, Pierre François Dominique Toussaint (c.1749-1803), Haitian political leader who successfully fought the British and the French but died in prison, after being arrested by Napoleon in 1802. He became a symbol for the struggle for black emancipation from colonial Europe.

219. From the *Poetical Works of William Wordsworth,* Vol. 2 (London, 1827). Wordsworth later remarked that this sonnet was inspired by the death of his three year old daughter Catherine in 1812. He first published this sonnet in his 1815 *Poems.*

220–252. From *The River Duddon, A Series of Sonnets: Vaudracour and Julia: and Other Poems. To Which is Annexed, A Topographical Description of the Country of the Lakes, In the North of England* (London, 1820).

220. line 3, Bandusia: Italian fountain that appears in Horace's *Odes;* scholars believe that it was located near Horace's Sabine farm or that it was a spring near Venusia, Horace's birthplace. Wordsworth, celebrating his native stream, thus connects himself with Horace's poetry.

221. line 11: The deer alluded to is the Leigh, a gigantic species long since extinct [Wordsworth's note].

223. line 3, A Protean change: In mythology Proteus had the power to assume any shape.

line 13, dastard: coward.

224. line 6, alders: moisture-loving shrubs and trees that grow in cooler climates, belonging to the genus *Alnus* in the birch family.

226. line 2, stripling: young man.

230. line 14, autumnal gossamer: thin, delicate cobwebs that cling to bushes and grass in autumn.

231. line 5, Niagaras: cataracts, waterfalls.

line 6, Naiads: river nymphs.

233. This sonnet first appeared in Wordsworth's 1807 *Poems, In Two Volumes.*

line 3, anchorite: Christian hermit.

234. line 5, dire affray: a serious quarrel or brawl.

235. line 3, Oroonoko: a river in South America.

line 14: See Humboldt's Personal Narrative [Wordsworth's note]. Alexander von Humboldt (1769-1859), a German scientist and explorer, whose accounts of his expeditions to Mexico and South America were translated into English by Helen Maria Williams (1814–21).

236. line 11, Jove: Jupiter.

237. line 12, Such priest as Chaucer sang: Chaucer's virtuous Parson, whose tale concludes the *Canterbury Tales* (ca. 1387).

line 13, Herbert: George Herbert (1593–1633), English devotional poet.

line 14, Goldsmith: *The Deserted Village* (1770), by Oliver Goldsmith (1730–74), contains a description of a virtuous rural preacher (lines 139–194).

239. line 13, Bacchanal: a drunken revel.

243. line 14, idless: female idler.

249. line 1, Kirk: Scots term for church.

251. In later versions of *The River Duddon,* this sonnet is entitled "Conclusion" and the following sonnet "After-Thought," suggesting a correction to the finality expressed here and a resistance to its closure.

253. From *Ecclesiastical Sketches* (London, 1822). This sonnet comes from Wordsworth's sonnet sequence *Ecclesiastical Sketches,* his poetic history and defense of the Church of England.

254. From *The Poetical Works of William Wordsworth,* Vol. 2 (London, 1827).

line 5, Tasso: Torquato Tasso (1544–95), a prolific Italian poet.

line 6, Camöens: Luis Vaz de Camöens (1524–80), Portugal's most famous poet, wrote sonnets, elegies, and other lyric forms; he was banished because of an impolitic love affair.

255–256. From *Yarrow Revisited, and Other Poems* (London, 1835). From the sequence "Sonnets Composed or Suggested During a Tour in Scotland, in the Summer of 1833."

256. This sonnet concludes "Sonnets Composed or Suggested During a Tour in Scotland, in the Summer of 1833."

257. From the *Poetical Works of William Wordsworth, D.C.L., Poet Laureate, Honorary Member of the Royal Society of Edinburgh, and of the Royal Irish Academy,* Vol. 6 (London, 1846).

line 2, rash assault: The degree and kind of attachment which many of the yeomanry feel to their small inheritances can scarcely be over-rated. Near the house of one of them stands a magnificent tree, which a neighbor of the owner advised him to fell for profit's sake. "Fell it!" exclaimed the yeoman, "I had rather fall on my knees and worship it." It happens, I believe, that the intended railway would pass through this little property, and I hope that an apology for the answer will not be thought necessary by one who enters into the strength of the feeling [Wordsworth's note]. Wordsworth dated this sonnet 12 October 1844.

line 9, Orrest-head: a peak near Windermere in the English Lake District.

Mathilda Betham (258–259). From *Poems* (London, 1808).

259. Sarah Ponsonby (1735–1831) lived with Eleanor Butler (1739–1829) in Llangollen Vale in Wales. The two, popularly known as "The Ladies of Llangollen," established a model of female friendship that attracted the curiosity of such visitors as Anna Seward, William Wordsworth, and Edmund Burke. Betham dated this sonnet 22 July 1799.

Susan Evance (260–265). From *Poems,* ed. James Clarke (London, 1808).

Martha Hanson (266–269). From *Sonnets and Other Poems,* 2 vols. (London, 1809).

269. Hanson greatly admired Smith and wrote two other sonnets in tribute to Smith, "Occasioned by the Death of Lieut. G.A. Smith, at Surinam, Five Days after that of his mother, the celebrated Charlotte Smith, in England" and "To Mrs Charlotte Smith. Occasioned by Reading her very Pathetick and Beautiful Sonnets, 'Written in the churchyard at Middleton' and 'To Night.'" Most remarkable, however, is her thirteen-page "Stanzas Occasioned by the Death of Mrs. Charlotte Smith."

line 8, vermeil: brilliant red.

Mary F. Johnson (270–275). From *Original Sonnets, and Other Poems* (London, 1810).
271. line 3, vermeil: brilliant red.
273. line 8, mansioned park: Appuldurcomb Park [Johnson's note].

Mary Tighe (276–286). 276–284. From *Psyche, with Other Poems*, ed. William Tighe, 3rd ed. (London, 1811).
276. title, Scarborough: a seaport in northeast England.
278. line 1, Phoebus: the sun.
281. title, Rossana: near Wicklow, Ireland.
282. title, Killarney: a town in southwest Ireland.
line 1, meridian blaze: noon.
line 3, Zephyrs: winds.
285–286. From *Mary, A Series of Reflections During Twenty Years*, ed. William Tighe (1811).

Leigh Hunt (287–293).
287. From the *Examiner* 296 (29 Aug. 1813). This and the following two sonnets were first published in the newspaper Hunt cofounded and coedited with his brother John. The first two of these are part of a series of sonnets to Hampstead that Hunt wrote while he and his brother served a two-year prison sentence for libeling the Prince Regent. During this time, Hunt was allowed to have visitors and to continue his work on the *Examiner*. Hunt dated this sonnet Surrey Jail, 27 August 1813.
288. From the *Examiner* 364 (18 Dec. 1814). Hunt dated this sonnet Surrey Jail, November 1814.
289. From the *Examiner* 508 (21 Sept. 1817). John Keats and Leigh Hunt challenged each other to a sonnet-writing contest on the subject of "the Grasshopper and Cricket." Both poets met the challenge, writing their sonnets in fifteen minutes. The results appeared together in the *Examiner* on 21 September 1817. Hunt dated this sonnet 30 December 1816, the date of the contest. See Keats's contribution, sonnet 312.
290–293. From *Foliage; or Poems Original and Translated* (London, 1818).
292. line 12, Charles's: Charles C. C., a mutual friend [Hunt's note]. Charles Cowden-Clarke (1787-1877) was a close friend of both Keats and Hunt as well as of Charles and Mary Lamb and, later, of Charles Dickens.
293. Hunt, Percy Bysshe Shelley, and John Keats wrote competitive sonnets on this subject at a party in February of 1817.
line 7, Sesostris: (1971-1928 BC) also known as Senusert I, ancient king of Egypt during the twelfth dynasty and son of Amenemhet I. He sponsored literary propaganda and many building projects.

Mary Bryan (294–298). From *Sonnets and Metrical Tales* (Bristol, 1815).
294. In this Sonnet I was aware that I had passed the legal bounds—and as Innovators are considered presumptuous in proportion as they are weak, I am very happy to hear that an eminent Poet has anticipated the irregularity. Under the wings of this mighty Eagle I hope a poor little melancholy Monotone will escape the terrible hawk-eyed Critics.—I believe that in no instance I had adopted an *unprecedented* measure or arrangement of the stanzas of the legitimate sonnet [Bryan's note]. The "eminent Poet" may well be Ann Radcliffe, whose sonnets frequently extend the bounds of the sonnet in a similar way.
297. line 8, And as my trembling fingers touched the spell: Superstitious relics, witchcrafts, spells, &c. have already appeared in so many notes of various writers, that I fear I am scarcely justified in adding to the number: and, as in the present instance, I can produce no positive testimony, either recorded or verbal, whether it be ancient or modern,

local or general, (for, whether practiced only in the dear little vale of C. or if its influence extend over the United Kingdoms I am wholly uncertain) it shrinks into comparative insignificance. Yet I think some explanation necessary, and this I can with certainty communicate:—In C. and its neighborhood when fowls make part of a repast, it is very common for some of the company to challenge others to break with them a bone, called, I suppose from this custom, the merry-thought. The possessor of the longer piece will, it is said, in the country phrase, be married first.—Lest my spell should be despised for its simplicity, I beg to assure my readers, that seeing it once tried by two lovers, who were soon after united; the bone in question, which is forked, snapped off, in equal parts on each side the root that joins it, to the extreme astonishment, and no little amusement of all present. Alas! I once saw a trembling hand try this spell, and when similarly successful saw a blushing cheek, a sweet but fearful smile that anticipated a broken heart.—I fear I have in these pieces introduced sentiments too connected with circumstances unknown to the reader to produce a separate interest [Bryan's note].

George Gordon, Lord Byron (299–300). From *The Prisoner of Chillon, and Other Poems* (London, 1816).

299. line 13, Bonnivard: Byron's long poem *The Prisoner of Chillon* describes the long imprisonment of Swiss patriot François de Bonnivard (1496–1570). Byron provides a long note in French detailing Bonnivard's life. The castle of Chillon, site of Bonnivard's imprisonment, is on Lake Geneva. When Byron visited it, he inscribed his name in a pillar in the dungeon, where it can still be seen.

300. line 1: Jean Jacques Rousseau (1712–78), Swiss-French philosopher; Voltaire, pen name of François Marie Arouet (1694–1778), French philosopher and satirist; Edward Gibbon (1737–94), English historian; Anne Louise Germaine Necker de Staël (1766–1817), Swiss-French novelist and essayist.

line 2, Leman: Lake Geneva.

John Keats (301–329).

301. From *The Examiner* 436 (5 May 1816). This is Keats's first published poem.

line 8, fox-glove bell: large showy bell-shaped flower growing in a spiked cluster; of the family *digitalis* (an echo of line 7 of Wordsworth's "'Nuns fret not'" [205]).

302–314. From *Poems* (London, 1817).

302. This famous sonnet first appeared in the *Examiner* (1 Dec. 1816). The editors, Leigh and John Hunt, included it along with a consideration of promising new poets: Keats, they write,

> has not yet published any thing except in a newspaper; but a set of manuscripts was handed us the other day, and fairly surprised us with the truth of their ambition, and ardent grappling with Nature. In the following Sonnet there is one incorrect rhyme, which might easily be altered, but which shall serve in the mean time as a peace-offering to the rhyming critics. The rest of the composition, with the exception of a little vagueness in calling the regions of poetry "the realms of gold," we do not hesitate to pronounce excellent, especially the last six lines. The word *swims* is complete; and the whole conclusion is equally powerful and quiet. (761)

We have chosen the text from Keats's 1817 *Poems* because of several improvements, among them the line "Yet did I never breathe its pure serene" replacing "Yet could I never judge what men could mean" in the original published version.

title, Chapman: George Chapman (1559–1634), English poet, playwright, and scholar, best known for his fine translations of Homer—the first in English. Keats was unable to read Homer in the original and thus knew his work only through translation, first Alexander Pope's and then later Chapman's.

line 11, Cortez: Keats mistakes Cortez for Vasco de Núñez de Balboa (1475–1519), Spanish explorer who discovered the Pacific Ocean in 1513.

line 14, Darien: a mountain range in Central America.

303. line 6, cuirass: breastplate armor.

line 10, Hybla: a Sicilian town, known for producing honey.

304. title: Hunt and his brother John had been imprisoned for libeling the Prince Regent in 1811. Hunt was allowed to have his books while serving his term.

306. line 8, Titania: queen of the fairies in Shakespeare's *A Midsummer Night's Dream.*

line 11, "O Wells!": Keats's friend Charles Jeremiah Wells (1800–79), also a poet, sent the roses either as a tribute or as an apology or both. Keats replied with this sonnet on 29 June 1816 (Walter Jackson Bate, *John Keats* [Cambridge: Harvard University Press, 1963], p. 64).

307. lines 11–12: Milton's *Lycidas* (1637) is a pastoral elegy on the death of Edward King (1612-37).

308. line 1: See Milton's *Paradise Lost,* Book 9, line 445: "As one who long in populous city pent."

line 10, Philomel: the nightingale.

310. This and the following sonnet are addressed to the painter Benjamin Robert Haydon (1786–1846), a close friend of Keats's.

311. The three "great spirits" Keats praises in this sonnet are William Wordsworth, Leigh Hunt, and Benjamin Robert Haydon.

line 3, Helvellyn's summit: Helvellyn is a mountain not far from Wordsworth's home in Grasmere.

312. See sonnet 289 above and note to Leigh Hunt, "On the Grasshopper and Cricket." Keats dated this sonnet 30 December 1816.

313. Published also in the *Examiner* 477 (16 Feb. 1817). See note to Coleridge's sonnet to Kosciusko above (sonnet 74).

line 11, Alfred's: Alfred the Great (849-99), king of the West Saxons.

315. From the *Examiner* 478 (21 February 1817).

316–317. From the *Examiner* 480 (9 March 1817). These sonnets were inspired by a visit Keats made with Benjamin Robert Haydon in March of 1817 to an exhibit of ancient Greek sculpture at the British Museum. The Elgin marbles, recently taken from the Parthenon, had been brought to England by Thomas Bruce, seventh earl of Elgin (1761-1841).

316. line 7, Heliconian springs: In Greek mythology, Helicon is the mountain home of the Muses, symbolic of poetic inspiration.

line 13, Hesperean: western.

318. From Richard Monckton Milnes, ed., *Life, Letters, and Literary Remains of John Keats,* Vol. 1 (London, 1848). This sonnet first appeared in Leigh Hunt's *Literary Pocket-Book* for 1818. It was reprinted in Richard Monckton Milnes's *Life, Letters, and Literary Remains,* prefaced by the following note:

> Returning from Ireland, the travelers [Keats and his friend Charles Brown] proceeded northwards by the coast, Ailsa Rock constantly in their view. That fine object first appeared to them, in the full sunlight, like a transparent tortoise asleep upon the calm water, then, as they advanced, displaying its lofty shoulders, and, as they still went on, losing its distinctness in the mountains of Arran and the extent of Cantire that rose behind. At the inn at Girvan Keats wrote this. (Vol. 1, p.167)

319. From the *Comic Annual,* ed. Thomas Hood (London, 1830). Later editions of Keats's poetry identify this sonnet as "To Mrs. Reynolds's Cat." It originally appeared as "Sonnet to a Cat" in Thomas Hood's *Comic Annual.*

line 1, climacteric: period of time; lifespan.

320–329. From Richard Monckton Milnes, ed., *Life, Letters, and Literary Remains, of John Keats*, 2 vols. (London, 1848).

320. In May 1818, Keats sent this sonnet letter to George and Georgiana Keats prefaced by the following remarks: "I have been endeavouring to discover a better sonnet stanza than we have. The legitimate [the Italian sonnet] does not suit the language overwell from the pouncing rhymes—the other kind [the English sonnet] appears too elegiac—and the couplet at the end of it has seldom a pleasing effect—I do not pretend to have succeeded—It will explain itself . . . " *(Letters of John Keats*, ed. Robert Gittings. 1970. [Oxford, 1990], p. 255). It was first published in the *Plymouth, Devonport, and Stonehouse News* (15 October 1836) and, like the following sonnets, was collected for Milnes's edition.

line 2, Andromeda: In Greek mythology, Andromeda was chained to a rock to be devoured by a sea-monster but was rescued by Perseus, who freed her, killed the monster, and married her.

line 11, Midas: king of Phrygia; everything he touched turned to gold.

321. Keats wrote this sonnet in 1819, and it was first published in the *Ladies Companion* for August of 1837.

line 9, Nilus: the Nile.

line 10, Potiphar: an Egyptian officer whose wife tried to seduce Joseph in Genesis 39.

322. For his collection, Milnes entitled this sonnet "Keats's Last Sonnet." Keats wrote it in 1819, and it was first published in the *Plymouth and Devonport Weekly Journal* for 27 September 1838.

line 4, eremite: religious hermit.

323. Keats wrote this sonnet in 1819, and it was first published in the *Plymouth and Devonport Weekly Journal* for 4 October 1838.

324. Keats wrote this sonnet in 1819, and it was first published in the *Plymouth and Devonport Weekly Journal* for 11 October 1838.

325. Keats wrote this sonnet in 1815, and, like the following sonnets (322–325), it was first published in *Life, Letters, and Literary Remains*. The young poet Thomas Chatterton (1752–70), unable to support himself by writing poetry, committed suicide in abject poverty. His early tragic death brought him fame.

326. Keats wrote this sonnet in 1818, and it first appeared in *Life, Letters, and Literary Remains*. Keats wrote in a letter to John Hamilton Reynolds that he was inspired "by beauty of the morning operating on a sense of idleness. I have not read any books—the morning said I was right—I had no idea but of the morning, and the thrush said I was right—seeming to say, [the sonnet follows as the voice of the bird]" (Vol. 1, p. 90).

327. Keats wrote this sonnet in 1818.

328. Keats wrote this sonnet in 1819.

329. Keats wrote this sonnet in 1819.

Percy Bysshe Shelley (330–336).

330–331. From *Alastor; or, The Spirit of Solitude: and Other Poems* (London, 1816).

331. After escaping from his exile in Elba, Napoleon lost to British and Prussian troops at Waterloo on 18 June 1815.

332. From the *Poetical Works of Percy Bysshe Shelley*, ed. Mary Shelley, 2 vols. (London, 1839). Shelley signed this sonnet "Glirastes." Horace Smith and Shelley wrote their "Ozymandias" sonnets in competition with one another, after several visits to the British Museum where Egyptian artifacts were on display. See note to Horace Smith's "Ozymandias" (342) below. First published in the *Examiner* 524 (11 Jan. 1818).

333. From *Prometheus Unbound: A Lyrical Drama in Four Acts, with Other Poems* (London, 1820). "Ode to the West Wind" is first and foremost an ode; however, Shelley's

five-part structure suggests a short sonnet sequence. The parts themselves consist of four *terza rima* units followed by a couplet, making fourteen lines.

line 21, Mænad: a female servant of Dionysus, the Greek god of wine and fertility; the term suggests a mad or frenzied woman.

line 32, Baiæ's bay: an ancient Roman resort near Naples.

334. From *Posthumous Poems of Percy Bysshe Shelley,* ed. Mary W. Shelley (London, 1824). Mary Shelley gave the sonnet its title for her 1824 and 1839 editions of Shelley. Later editions entitle it "Sonnet: To the Republic of Benevento," because it was inspired by the town of Benevento claiming its independence of Naples in 1820. Benevento's freedom, however, was short-lived.

335. From *Posthumous Poems of Percy Bysshe Shelley,* ed. Mary W. Shelley (London, 1824).

line 14, the Preacher: a reference to the Teacher in Ecclesiastes who claims, "All is vanity" (1.2) and preaches the futility of wisdom (1.18).

336. From *The Poetical Works of Percy Bysshe Shelley,* ed. Mary Shelley, 2 vols. (London, 1839).

line 1: George III (1738–1820) was declared insane in 1811 and died the year after Shelley wrote this sonnet.

Jane Alice Sargant (337–338). From *Sonnets and Other Poems* (London, 1817).

Thomas Doubleday (339-341). From *Sixty-Five Sonnets* (London, 1818).

339. lines 4-5: The poppy is the source of opium.

Horace Smith (342). From the *Examiner* 527 (1 Feb. 1818). See note to Shelley's "Ozymandias" (332) above. Smith's appeared in the *The Examiner* a few weeks after Shelley's.

line 8, Babylon: ancient city in Mesopotamia located about 55 miles south of modern Baghdad. After the fall of the Babylonian Empire, the city was rebuilt and reached magnificence under Nebuchadnezzar II.

John Clare (343–356). Clare's sonnets pose a difficult problem for an editor: should we use the highly regularized and edited versions published during the poet's lifetime or Clare's own manuscripts which many scholars believe reflect better the poet's own intentions? The editions of Clare prepared by Eric Robinson and David Powell take the latter approach. Theirs are the versions of the poems most common in anthologies today. In keeping with our editorial principle, we have used the early published texts of the sonnets in order to demonstrate the way in which Clare's contemporaries read his sonnets. However, it is useful to compare these normalized texts with Clare's idiosyncratic manuscript versions, available in other editions.

343–344. From *Poems Descriptive of Rural Life and Scenery* (1820), 4th ed. (London, 1821).

343. title, Primrose: a herbaceous perennial plant of the genus *Primula* of which there are 500 species in many different colors, including the cowslip.

line 3, spinney: *sub.* a natural wood,—a hedge-row thicket,—a young coppice [from the glossary appended to *Poems Descriptive of Rural Life and Scenery*].

344. line 4, Boreas: the north wind.

line 10, proggling: *adj.* meddling, poking [from the glossary appended to *Poems Descriptive of Rural Life and Scenery*].

345–349. From the *Village Minstrel, and Other Poems* (London, 1821).

346. line 6, neatherd: cowherd.

348. line 8, dithering: shivering [from the glossary appended to the *Village Minstrel*].
line 9, croodling: crouching, shrinking [from the glossary appended to the *Village Minstrel*]
350–356. From the *Rural Muse* (London, 1835).

Samuel Rogers (357). From *Poems* (London, 1820).
line 11: In the gardens of the Vatican, where it was placed by Julius II, it was long the favorite study of those great men to whom we owe the revival of the arts, Michael Angelo, Raphael, and the Caracci [Rogers's note].
line 13, long-lost spell: Once in the possession of Praxiteles, if we may believe an ancient epigram on the Gnidian Venus [Rogers's note].

Thomas Lovell Beddoes (358). From *The Improvisatore, in Three Fyttes, with Other Poems* (Oxford, 1821).
line 12, eyrie: aerie, the nest of a large bird of prey.
line 14, maw: throat or mouth of a carnivorous animal.

Charles Johnston (359–360). From *A Collection of Poems, Chiefly Manuscript, and From Living Authors,* ed. Joanna Baillie (London, 1823).
360. line 14, incarnardined: made red with blood.

Elizabeth Cobbold (361–364). From *Poems,* ed. Laetitia Jermyn (Ipswich, 1825).
361–363. Petrarch claims to have fallen in love with Laura in the church of St. Claire at Avignon in 1327. Scholars formerly believed her to be Laure de Noves of Avignon; however, many modern scholars believe that she was not a real person. Cobbold's sonnets, too, are poetic fictions. See Mary Robinson's "Laura to Petrarch" (155).

John F. M. Dovaston (365–366). From *Poems, Legendary, Incidental, and Humorous* (Shrewsbury, 1825).

Sarah Hamilton (367–368). From *Sonnets, Tour to Matlock, Recollections of Scotland, and Other Poems* (London, 1825).
367. Mary Stuart (1542–87), queen of Scotland, returned to her native land in 1560 after spending most of her life in France. An uprising forced her to abdicate, and she fled to England, where she was later executed for conspiring to murder Queen Elizabeth.

Thomas Moore (369–370).
369. From the *Poetical Works of Thomas Moore, Collected by Himself,* Vol. 4 (London, 1841). Published in 1825 in the fifth issue of Moore's series of Irish songs, *National Airs,* which first were collected in 1841. While not technically a sonnet, this poem, with its couplets and alternating pentameters and tetrameters, shows an unorthodox treatment of the fourteen-line poem.
370. From the *Poetical Works of Thomas Moore, Collected by Himself,* Vol. 7 (London, 1841). Published at least as early as 1827.

William Ewert Gladstone (371). From the *Eton Miscellany,* Vol. 2 (Eton, 1827).
line 2, Pallas: Pallas Athena, Greek goddess of war and wisdom, was born fully armed for battle when Hephaestus split open the head of her father, Zeus, with an axe.

Mary Russell Mitford (372–373). From *Dramatic Scenes, Sonnets, and Other Poems* (London, 1827).

Barry Cornwall (374). From the *Bijou; or Annual of Literature and the Arts* (London, 1828).
line 14, Elysian: heavenly.

Joseph Blanco White (375). From the *Bijou; or Annual of Literature and the Arts* (London, 1828). William Sharp, in his anthology *Sonnets of this Century* (1886), emended "fly" in line 11 to "flow'r," believing the original to be aesthetically absurd.
line 7, Hesperus: the evening star, Venus.

Thomas Hood (376–379).
376. From the *Comic Annual* (London, 1830). This sonnet is part of a short group of poems entitled "Poems, by a Poor Gentleman."
line 3, hemp: coarse plant fiber used for making rope for sailing ships in the nineteenth century; *cannabis salvea,* an annual plant in the mulberry family.
line 4, Cowper's Task: William Cowper's popular blank-verse poem, *The Task* (1785), which, significantly, celebrates retirement.
line 7: Oliver Goldsmith (1730–74), English poet and playwright; Samuel Johnson (1709–84), English poet, essayist, moralist, best known for his *Dictionary of the English Language* (1755); Richard Brinsley Sheridan (1751–1816), English playwright, poet, and statesman; Edmund Burke (1729–97), Irish-English statesman and writer.
line 8, Castalian flask: Castalia, a fountain of the muses whose waters inspired poetry.
line 9: John Locke (1632–1704), English philosopher; Joseph Spence (1699–1768), English clergyman whose anecdotes were published posthumously in 1820.
line 10: John Gay (1685–1732), English playwright and poet, author of the *Beggar's Opera* (1728); Robert Blair (1699–1746), Scottish poet, author of the *Grave* (1743).
line 13, Thomson's Castle: the *Castle of Indolence* (1748), a poem in Spenserian stanzas on idleness written by James Thomson (1700–48), a Scottish poet.
377–379. From *Poems,* Vol. 2., 2nd ed. (London, 1846).
377. Hood dated this poem Coblentz, May 1835.
379. line 12, Albion: England.

Edward Moxon (380). From the *Keepsake,* ed. Frederic Mansel Reynolds (London, 1830).
line 5, aspen: poplar tree whose leaves appear to tremble in the wind.
line 13, Philomel: the nightingale.

William Stanley Roscoe (381–383).
381. From the *Keepsake,* ed. Frederic Mansel Reynolds (London, 1830).
line 1, Idalian: Idalium, an ancient village in Cyprus associated with Aphrodite, the Greek goddess of erotic love, or Venus, the Roman goddess of erotic love.
line 7, Dian: the moon, also called Cynthia (line 9).
382. From *Poems* (London, 1834).
383. From the *Remembrancer; or, Fragments for Leisure Hours* (Philadelphia, 1841).

Charles Tennyson Turner (384–389). From *Sonnets and Fugitive Pieces* (Cambridge, 1830).
386. line 8, Sinai: the mountain upon which Moses stood to receive the Ten Commandments and the Book of the Covenant *(Exodus* 19).

Alfred Tennyson (390–392).
390. From *Friendship's Offering; and Winter's Wreath: A Christmas and New Year's Pre-*

sent, for MDCCCXXXIII (London, 1833). This sonnet first appeared in the short-lived *Englishman's Magazine* for August 1831.
    391–392. From *Poems* (London, 1833).

Agnes Strickland (393–396).
    393. From *The Keepsake,* ed. Frederic Mansel Reynolds (London, 1832).
    394–396. From *Historic Scenes and Poetic Fancies* (London, 1850).

Frederick Tennyson (397). From the *Amulet. A Christian and Literary Remembrancer,* ed. S. C. Hall (London, 1832).
    line 5, Argus: in classical mythology, a giant with one hundred eyes.

Hartley Coleridge (398–405). From *Poems Songs and Sonnets* (Leeds, 1833).
    398. line 12, rathe: early.
    399. This sonnet prefaces Hartley Coleridge's 1833 volume, *Poems Songs and Sonnets,* which collected many previously published poems. It is a tribute to his father, Samuel Taylor Coleridge.
    lines 3-8: These lines refer to S. T. Coleridge's conversation poem "Frost at Midnight" (1798) in which the infant Hartley Coleridge is the object of the poet's meditation: e.g., "Dear Babe, that sleepest cradled by my side, / Whose gentle breathings, heard in this deep calm, / Fill up the interspersed vacancies / And momentary pauses of the thought!" (lines 44–47).
    line 9, "Thy prayer was heard: I wandered like a breeze": Here, he asserts that he has fulfilled his father's prophecy in "Frost at Midnight": "But thou, my babe! shalt wander like a breeze . . . " (line 54 and following).
    401. This sonnet is featured prominently in the 1995 film version of Jane Austen's *Sense and Sensibility,* scripted by Emma Thompson. The sonnet does not appear in the original novel since it was published some years after Austen's death.
    404. line 14: see Milton's *Paradise Lost,* Book 1, lines 254–55: "The mind is its own place, and in itself / Can make a Heaven of Hell, a Hell of Heaven."
    405. See Samuel Taylor Coleridge's sonnet "Work Without Hope" (90) above.

Letitia Elizabeth Landon (406–407).
    406. From *Fisher's Drawing Room Scrap-book, 1834* (London, 1833). L.E.L. wrote this and the following sonnet to accompany illustrations of their subjects.
    407. From *Fisher's Drawing Room Scrap-book, 1838* (London, 1837).
    title: The Castle of Chillon is on Lake Geneva. See Lord Byron's "On Chillon" (299).

Jane Cross Simpson (408). From *Friendship's Offering; and Winter's Wreath: A Christmas and New Year's Present, for MDCCCXXXIII* (London, 1833). Simpson used the pseudonym "Gertrude" when she published this sonnet, dated Edinburgh May 1832.

Felicia Hemans (409–415).
    409–413. From *Scenes and Hymns of Life, with Other Religious Poems* (Edinburgh, 1834).
    414–415. From *Poetical Remains of the Late Mrs Hemans* (Edinburgh, 1836).
    414. title, Grasmere: a lake and town in the English Lake District and home of William Wordsworth.

Caroline Norton (416–418).
    416. From the *Keepsake*, ed. Caroline Norton (London, 1836).
    417–418. From the *Dream, and Other Poems* (London, 1840).

Ebenezer Elliott (419–420). From the *Poetical Works of Ebenezer Elliott, the Corn-Law Rhymer* (Edinburgh, 1840).

419. line 9, Fitzadam's mournful music: Adam Fitzadam, pseudonym of Edward Moore (1712-57), editor of the *World* (1753-56), whose elegiac sonnets, Elliott writes in his preface to his *Rhymed Rambles,* "fully show that the measure of the sonnet, as he has managed it, is as proper for a long and serious poem as the Spenserian stanza itself."

Frederick William Faber (421–424). From *The Cherwell Water-Lily, and Other Poems* (London, 1840).

Frances Anne Kemble (425–426). From *Poems* (Philadelphia, 1844).

Eliza Cook (427). From *Poems* (London, 1847).

line 8, charnel ground: burial ground.

Arthur Hugh Clough (428–429). From *Ambarvalia* (London, 1849). This and the following sonnet are part of a group of poems (not all sonnets) entitled "Blank Misgivings of a Creature moving about in Worlds not realised" (taken from Wordsworth's "Intimations Ode") which appeared in Clough's first volume of poetry, *Ambarvalia,* published with his friend Thomas Burbidge in 1849. The two sonnets here are the first and fourth poems in the series.

Calder Campbell (430). From the *Germ: Thoughts towards Nature in Poetry, Literature, and Art* 2 (Feb. 1850).

line 6, manna: divine or miraculous food which the Israelites ate in the wilderness as they wandered for 40 days *(Exodus* 16.14–36).

line 8, heartsease: pansy.

William Bell Scott (431). From the *Germ: Thoughts towards Nature in Poetry, Literature, and Art* 3 (March 1850).

William Michael Rossetti (432). From the *Germ: Thoughts towards Nature in Poetry, Literature, and Art* 4 (May 1850). This sonnet is based upon the Gospel's account of the death of Mary and Martha's brother Lazarus, whom Jesus raised from the dead (John 11.1–44). "Jesus wept" is the shortest verse in the King James version of the Bible (John 11.35).

Dante Gabriel Rossetti (433–438). From the *Germ: Thoughts towards Nature in Poetry, Literature, and Art* 4 (May 1850).

433. title: Hans Memling (1430–94), German-Flemish painter famous for his madonnas.

435. title: Andrea Mantegna (1431–1506), Italian painter and engraver.

436. title: Il Giorgione (Giorgio Barbarelli da Castelfranco) (1478–1510), Venetian painter.

437. title: Jean Auguste Dominique Ingres (1780–1867), French painter.

Elizabeth Barrett Browning (439–481). From *Poems,* Vol. 2 (London, 1850). Browning's 1850 *Poems* was the first publication of her *Sonnets from the Portuguese.* Later editions of the sequence have forty-four sonnets because Browning inserted an additional sonnet between sonnets XLI (476) and XLII (477). We have preserved her idiosyncratic ellipses (. .) throughout.

439. line 1, Theocritus: Greek poet of the third century BC, known for his *Idylls* and for originating pastoral poetry. Browning translated some of his work.

441. line 13, chrism: consecrated balm.

443. line 2, Electra: Electra solemnly receives her brother's ashes from Orestes then learns that he is alive, in Sophocles's drama *Electra*.

449. line 6, Aornus: Browning's early editors, Charlotte Parker and Helen A. Clarke interpret this obscure reference not as the entrance to Hades but as "the Aornus of India . . . a lonely, lofty rock whither only the birds of strong pinion soared to" *(Complete Works of Elizabeth Barrett Browning.* eds. Parker and Clarke [New York, 1900], Vol. 3, p. 395).

457. line 1, Rialto: commercial center of Venice.

line 4, argosies: riches.

line 5, Pindar: (518?-438 BC); ancient Greeks regarded Pindar as their greatest lyric poet. He is known for his odes.

line 6, purpureal: purple.

459. line 3, a cuckoo-song: A cuckoo repeats its call.

465. line 10, asphodel: In classical mythology, Asphodel is a field where shadows of the dead wander.

475. line 11–14: According to Parker and Clarke, these lines refer "to the custom of giving to the god through whom came deliverance a statue in the temple, as a votive offering. Such a piece must be but a travesty of the power and majesty of the god himself" *(Complete Works of Elizabeth Barrett Browning,* eds. Parker and Clarke [New York, 1900], Vol. 3, p. 400).

476. line 10, chrism: consecrated balm.

478. line 5, Mussulmans and Giaours: Muslims and non-Muslims.

line 7, Polypheme's white tooth: A baffling allusion, interpreted by Parker and Clarke as follows: "Polyphemus, the Cyclops, one-eyed giant son of Neptune, who was in love with Galatea, the sea-nymph, in a crude and petulant way; but she, scoffing at his one eye and shaggy eyebrow, escaped him, hence the image of the white tooth of his appetite slipping on the coveted kernel" *(Complete Works of Elizabeth Barrett Browning,* eds. Parker and Clarke [New York, 1900], Vol. 3, p. 400). In Homer's *Odyssey,* Odysseus blinds Polyphemus before revealing his identity, a revelation that incurs the wrath of the cyclops's father, Poseidon, who then hinders Odysseus on his journey home to Ithaca and his wife, Penelope.

Appendix: Mary Robinson's Preface to *Sappho and Phaon*

From *Sappho and Phaon. In a Series of Legitimate Sonnets, with Thoughts on Poetical Subjects, and Anecdotes of the Grecian Poetess* (London, 1796).

Index of Titles, Authors, and First Lines

The following references are both to sonnet numbers (in parentheses) and to page numbers. Each poet (in boldface) is alphabetized by surname; each title (in italics) by first word, except when it begins with the definite or indefinite articles, which are ignored; and each first line by first word (including articles). Since we have supplied certain sonnets with titles derived from their first lines, we have avoided the repetition of indexing both; these poems may be found alphabetized according to the first word of the first line.